To Miss
from Peter York.

18. 5. 81.

NEW YORK!
10ᴛ 320 E 57th St
935-9815.

LONDON:
2 CHADWICK ST
LONDON S.W1.
office 01- 222 - 1923.
home 01 969 - 3852
or 373 - 1959.
or 726-6671

Style Wars

Style Wars

Peter York

SIDGWICK & JACKSON
LONDON

First published by Sidgwick and Jackson Limited
in Great Britain in 1980.

Picture research, other than *Harpers & Queen* illustrations,
by Anne Horton.

ISBN 0 283 98673 5

Printed in Great Britain by
R.J. Acford, Chichester, Sussex
for Sidgwick and Jackson Limited
1 Tavistock Chambers, Bloomsbury Way
London WC1A 2SG

Phototypesetting by Swiftpages Limited, Liverpool

Contents

Illustrations •

Introduction

The earliest of the pieces in this book – 'The Sloane Rangers' – appeared in *Harpers & Queen* in October 1975; it was the first of a sort of intermittent series about modern social types and styles.

Most of the published pieces are reproduced here substantially as they appeared, with the exception of one on Margaret Thatcher – 'New Model' – where I have restored the *Spectator's* cuts. I have written short postscripts to most of the pieces where the types and the styles and the people have moved on in interesting ways. Certain people kept on turning up.

Six of the pieces are 'new', in the sense of unpublished, though I have been writing them on and off since 1976 and just completed them in 1980. The last three are simply expanded from my diary.

Most of the published pieces originally appeared in *Harpers & Queen,* a remarkable magazine. I owe a lot to everyone on it, but especially Ann Barr and Willie Landels. Miles Chapman helped a great deal with 'Machomania' and 'Post Modern', though he didn't much like the results. I have had a lot of other help: 'The Mayfair Mercenaries' was co-written with Emma Soames, 'The German Connection' with Steven Lavers. I also owe a great many ideas to people I met in 1976/7, particularly Tony Parsons and Julie Burchill, Danny Baker, Vivien Goldman, Jon Savage and Simon Frith.

Diana Avebury, Jane Heller, Felicity Hatton, Pam Graham, Lendal Scott-Ellis and Kim Evans made everything else possible.

Peter York
London, April 1980

Style Wars

Early in 1980, a man I know in the go-go end of publishing (reprint illustrated books, printed in Roumania and such like) told me how a friend of his who ran a print works had another friend who knew they were bringing conscription back because he'd been printing the forms. My friend hadn't seen the conscription forms but his friend's friend had for sure. It seemed on the cards. At the beginning of 1980 one would have believed absolutely anything, particularly anything in the global war line. This was just after Afghanistan and while that extraordinary Olympics battle was going on with Governments saying one thing and the athletes another, they were going to fight their war their way.

Around this time, A.L. Rowse, the historian and cat lover, was on the *Parkinson Show* with little Shirley Williams, the Labour Party's centre-right soubrette. Rowse had just started to come out then as a media personality, he'd just done a promotional tour of America and he was going full tilt. What he was saying on Parkinson was that in the sixties – and here he was looking very hard at Shirley – the *soft* people ran things and now it was time for the *hard* men – and here he looked even harder at Shirley who demurred and gurgled and nodded as if she was listening politely to a Central African student talking about the chopping off of hands in a Sussex seminar on penal reform. The hard men, so Rowse said, lips pursed like the acid queen, were taking over. A few weeks later, in March, Mrs Thatcher – John Wayne Thatcher, Julie Burchill called her – had also gone full tilt, into a Churchillian number to the Conservative Council at Bournemouth. She was on about *hope*, in a way that made it sound like blood, sweat and tears.

In 1976, when the youth sub-culture world started on a new radical slide in London, a set of changes so fundamental that they're only just working through in 1980, the main thing that struck one about all these new names – The Clash, Sex Pistols and 999s – was that they were so military, it was all conflict stuff. Most people who read this language at all, read it *very* straight as the frustrations of the submerged 10th, etc. I kept harking back, however, to this little piece of early seventies Gonzo prophecy, namely the New York – London social journalist Anthony Haden-Guest's joke band, The Third World War. Of course, Haden-Guest and the early seventies were one thing and most commentaries either took punk seriously, as quite another, or not at all. But it seemed to me that punk actually fitted in very precisely with a lot of other odd Phoney War conflicts that were going on then, particularly the kind of leisure nightmares you had in New York, like *terrorist chic* window dressing on Fifth Avenue; the whole Fascinating Fascism, sado-masochistic theme that cropped up all over the place in fashion photography and, freakiest of all, the New York fist-fucking parlours the Anvil and Mineshaft, and the schlock horror movies. All of these, when you looked closer, seemed to link back to hippy in a number of curious ways.

There was a New York academic, Michael Selzar, who made quite a deal out of terrorist chic. He did a book on it and a college circuit tour with his show. He had some interesting little theories which came down to, basically, the notion that terrorist chic was the last option of people who'd run the gamut of late sixties experiences and aesthetics – and become quite 'affectless', meaning they needed bigger and bigger fixes to get them even moderately excited about anything. He found that most of these people had been heavily into *the* late sixties things, either on the Political front or the politics of personality (the Tibet route etc.), or both. The people who were involved in the terrorist chic stuff, according to Selzar, were quiet, artistic types who loved beauty and who'd got a big charge out of the terrorist things because they were such a *strong style,* had such very definite images, such an aesthetic that they appealed to the art director in them. One of the keys to the fascinating fascism was this interest the soft people started to have in the hard ones.

Fascism scares were a regular feature of the seventies. There was one every year – indeed there *was* a lot of freak-show fascism turning up in this country and America, all sorts of surreal things like the British Movement kids who started to turn up regularly at rock performances, and the new American leather men who marched through the Jewish areas of big cities; and there was, of course, quite a big industry in drawing parallels with the thirties. When you looked closer, however, it seemed that all that these loopy sets had in common was the absolute long term *ungovernability* of their members. The violence was, sometimes, real and parts of London *were* getting really heavy, but the 'fascism' – that was harder to grasp, particularly when fascist *parties* like the National Front were losing membership.

A point about seventies violence was that a lot of it had that participative leisure feel to it, certainly a lot was organized on a nice commercial basis. In the future there will be Rollerball, Death Race 2000 . . . There were a whole group of *heavy metal* movies about violence as a fantasy leisure option, like motor sport violence or roller skate violence – kung-fu ice skating movies seemed entirely possible. One of the most interesting seventies movies was something called *Westworld*, which was *holiday camp violence*, patterned after the style of a Participative Theme Park. In *Westworld*, like in any well-planned shopping mall, the tourist could take his choice – shoot-outs with robot cowboys, jousting with robot knights, etc. – and he always won . . . until the robot programmes went wrong. No doubt in the remake they will have Star Wars World.

Caroline Coon – and now there *is* a modern career – who was, at one point, punk spokesman and interpreter, said a lot of the violence in punk was because the boys hadn't had a war in so many years, it made them kind of bloodthirsty. She said a great many other things about it, that it was the hippies' revenge and so on, but this war point struck me as being really on the ball.

But in the Golden Age, that is the 1970s, the Phoney Wars

were . . . style wars. In the seventies, that cute Warhol line – he actually said it in the sixties – about being famous for fifteen minutes really started to come onstream. Style became a weapon to forge your own legend. Style started to be accessible in a quite unprecedented way in the seventies. The continuing prosperity of all the major Western countries meant that style – far more than just *fashion,* a pre-style sixties idea – came practically on the rates, everything was designed, styled-up. The most important point about this wasn't just that style became an expectation, *down-market* (a *marketing* word that started to come in in a major way in the late seventies – I once heard a priest use it to describe another's flock), but right up the age range, which was one of the things that helped scramble fashion off its head in the 1970s, into the Perversity Spiral. By the late 1970s the Presley generation was in its forties and still expected style as of right. You saw it in the way the jeans market moved, the way Levis spent real money on developing the cut to deal with . . . *the older buttock.*

The story of the seventies was the story of everyone getting in on what a minority within a minority got in the sixties because they were around at the right time. Of course, that sixties made-it generation had no intention of giving up. One gossip columnist doing his seventies end of decade round-up said it was all the *old faces* hanging on in there, meaning all the new faces of the sixties, still professionally young – the Rod and Britt, Mick and Bianca league. There would be absolutely no giving up style gracefully ever again.

All this produced crisis in the fashion industry and the record business which both, until fairly late on, had a one-look big-trend sixties view of the world. The fact was that style *fragmentation* followed mass youth fashion in a sophisticated economy as inexorably as the call for devolution followed total planning. The third great awakening wasn't just 'religious' – or rather that was only one way of expressing it – nor just about physical narcissism, but was about developing your own style and then *legitimizing* it. Sometimes you had to bust a few heads.

The second great business philosophy of the 1970s – the more important because it had never come out as an ideology – was *market segmentation*. Mass culture critics liked to think of marketing as totally conspiratorial, coercive and infinitely manipulative – it elevated their struggle. They hadn't realised how marketing responded to and compounded trends – trying to create them was old-fashioned – and how the whole participative, fragmented, self-expressive set of post-hippie movements in themselves created the greatest marketing opportunities ever.

The vogue word for it was *segmentation* – define your group (get under their skins) and their (style) aspirations and then gear up to service them. In America there is this service discreetly called environmental analysis which is a euphemism for homing in on the segments. Month by month, using psychological scales in mass surveys, these services chart the growth and decline of the 'attitude configurations' in the population or, in other words, what kinds of people are coming off the production line now (lifestyle trends). This way General Foods, say, gets a read-out on who's going to be in the market for organic, compost-grown health food, or C.B.S. about solaria or safaris, and of course new political directions. The ideology was *go with it,* whatever it is. New opportunities in Goods and Services.

If the great Lifestyle market opportunity of the 1970s was style for all, by the later seventies it had been upped in a big way to Creativity for all – or everything as Art. The Art idea had gone to such a point that you found an extraordinary range of people who had never been inside an advertising agency using words like 'creativity' without a trace of self-consciousness – creative cookery, creativity for tots (plasticine, fingerpainting), job-enrichment; you couldn't avoid it. Creativity – as you go – had lift-off, it helped deal with the problem of dying. The notion of everyone's innate right to creativity, to be an interesting person as they say in America, was the real Declaration of Rights.

As the definition of Art grew more blurred (Tom Wolfe had this wonderful figure, the Greatest Artist In The World who drew the greatest picture in the world for one moment with a water smear on an Automat table) the boundaries of self-expression became on the wide side. There was more Art around – Art business, Art therapy, Art fashion, Art planning – in the seventies than ever in the history of the world. This was a development which was out of line with what Marx had said or common sense had ever observed, which was simply this: that culture became pluralist (or shot to bits) even if the money and power didn't move an inch. The Marxist idea of 'cultural hegemony' or, broadly, the notion that the dominant style at a given time is that of the ruling class, had always been such a self-evident one that hopeful left-wingers had always taken the converse to be true. They thought a change of styles would show a different world, or (the Shirley Williams position) a *consensus* style, a classless/middle-class style, would show the world was going to rights. That wasn't how it worked; the new styles and the new tribes grew at the margins like one of those T.V. slides of cells dividing, and there was simply no way you could order them. The inequalities of money, power and life chances showed no sign of going away but the *expectations* frothed and bubbled quite uncontrollably.

Styles were constantly described as schizophrenic in the seventies, meaning it wasn't clear what they were saying about their owners. There were too many styles, *too many options . . . too much repertoire.* I knew one fashion editor who went right off her head. She started saying fashion was irrelevant, left her job and described herself as *anti-fashion.* She got involved, so she said, with *politics* in 1977, style as a *statement;* into this eclectic trip where she'd be expressing her creativity by juxtaposing those legwarmers, different colours, with the shoes (like the black kids wore in Harlem), with Vivienne Westwood's bondage suits, and the whole big thing became not just making herself an art object but one that meant something. In the 1970s, fashion became *very* intellectual, ironic, political and Artistic and fragmented. Quite ordinary fashion editors and buyers generally had a crisis of confidence. Where was it? How to cover it? Who was it for? Oh, for an A-line, a sack . . . Courrèges!

Along with this came the development of the human theme parks that started to blossom in the late seventies, particularly

the new Gossip World and Punk World, both of which had
essentially *middle-class* déraciné origins in the first place (the
real thing came later) and represented middle-class fantasy
ideas of what it was, on the one hand, to be rich and smart and,
on the other, to be a rough working-class person. They both
dramatized ironic ideas. Not the real class war – not yet – but
the Phoney One. In the first place, there weren't real
aristos – except commercial ones – in the gossip world of *Ritz;*
it was a Seventh Avenue idea of class, and there was little
enough Social Realism in punk, which started off as an Art
Idea.

Punk World and Gossip World were both dead risky because
they played with some *heavy* things, things which used to mean
something and were exciting precisely because they were so far
off to the *right* and the *left* of the post hippy mainstream consensus. *Try it.* I remember John Ingham, one of the first journalists to really work up the original rhetoric of punk, telling
me that the thing that really summed it all up for him was the
famous picture which went the rounds of Sid Vicious chain
whipping this hippy in the front row of the Nashville in 1976.
I'd seen the picture a few months earlier when Vivienne
Westwood had been telling me about that night when Sid had
stepped out of the performance to give this poor dork a going over.
That was a cause.

And there was all the playing about with the *Doc
Martens* – the big boots – which was the biggest race memory of
real heavy styles. In 1976 you didn't actually see skins around
that much, they were only just beginning to filter back. You'd
see more of the skinhead style in those macho gay magazines
('Sam, hot and heavy') where it was reckoned as one of the
traditional costumes. And, of course, there were the punk
Swastikas which faded out when punk bore left the following
year and people were shamed out of it. John Krevine, who had
the Boy shop on the King's Road, had skinhead and schlock
horror tableaux which was a funny mix. Part of it came from
the old New York Mutilation Art style, pushing the boat out;
some of it was more home-grown memories of ironists in their
late twenties, the kind of people who would have a complete set

of the Richard Allen books – *Skinhead, Suedehead, Terrace Terrors*. The big incentive then was *Liberal baiting* which by 1976 had become a major hobby, you only had to talk about a *social worker* or an *ethnic print dress* or any kind of Liberal stereotype figure to get a laugh. It was a lot of fun baiting the sixties Liberal consensus styles and it was dead easy. The main thing was to be a bit extreme. As for sex, drugs or rock and roll, *leave it out,* aggression was this year's model. That was when all the styles got really tight and aggressive, all the big floppy shambolic post-hippie styles started to disappear from 1975 on. *Tighten up.* At the same time, the Conservative radicals were sounding really sharp. On the right (or the hard-nut left right), that was where the action was. *Try it.* Margaret Thatcher, who liked to call people 'wet', was definitely in for the Liberal baiting. The Thatcher government – the British Experiment – was *definitely* an act of faith in the hard style. Might work, *try it.*

All this moving off to the 'right' and the 'left', this *polarizing,* made you wonder if you could carry anything through on the right style, like those experiments where the subjects had to administer successively higher doses of electric shocks to people who screamed and writhed. The thing that so excited the journalists who wrote the experiments up was just how far these mainstream mothers and fathers were prepared to go – hate to do it but . . .

They put on the cocktail kitsch cruelty wear, the Doc Martens, and the Swastika T-shirts in the name of irony. In the mid-seventies the signs didn't mean anything any more, so the party line went, rather like the uneasy old game – passé now – of joshing the black guys with a few race jokes to show you're relaxed about it all.

The coolest thing around was the *class* issue. The old class number had been an absolutely no-go territory in the media, with people drabbing off their accents or cleaning them up and *aiming for the middle,* the Parkinson territory, N.W.1, the *Time Out* Poly left. A touch of class was really the most exciting thing ever – given you couldn't get much going on the old sex, drugs or rock and roll. After ten years of official classlessness, it was

meaty and risky, but safe because, like all those other exhumations, it suggested the old conflicts were thoroughly dead at the
roots so you could muck around now and then, just like putting
on the leathers.

A piece I wrote for *Harpers & Queen* called 'Sloane Rangers'
provided a lot of funny responses that gave one a clue. I'd written it very much as a bit of fun, about what I thought was an
historical aside, a traditional style *tightening up* to cope with the
new world, pulling together for comfort and starting to look a
little uniform. But one was definitely keeping a light tone.
Some people took it very seriously though. First, I met one of
the famous Tangier Queens at a party – the kind whose houses
get written up in *House and Garden* magazines as 'in a house
belonging to', meaning these people have houses like you and I
have shoes – and he got really serious about Sloane Rangers.

He said it was *dangerous* sending up these poor upper middle-
class girls with their precious little totems, a nice scarf or one or
two Georgian bits. He'd been in Italy and he knew what could
happen. He thought it was stirring things up. A few months
later Thames did a T.V. documentary based on Sloane
Rangers and really pushed the boat out, laying on the accents
and the shooting parties and putting in a scene where one of the
girls goes into Hèrmes in Bond Street and looks at *£800* bags.
Of course, those girls – the real thing – wouldn't have done
that in a million years, they'd make a £40 job do five years.
After that people used to ask me, perfectly seriously, etiquette
questions – Mitford questions – as to whether a *true* Sloane
would do this or that and – here was the really heavy-breathing
part – was this girl or that a *true* Sloane or a Sub-Sloane. There
was a lot of harping on it. While people would keep the tone
light you could see they really wanted to know. It was after that
Gossip World really started to take off in a big way. They were
pretty vacant and they didn't care. Gossip World was
Ritz – absolutely anyone could be in *Ritz*. It was straight down
the line vanity publishing, and most of the names were just
people working in the trade. In the wings, however, there was a
raft of people who took it all dèad straight, the cocktail kitsch
swanning and the Doc Martens, without a touch of irony. You

had all these suburban middle-class Fleet Streeters getting *ab-solutely fixated* on the high society idea, the kind of girls who five years before would have been up to their necks in the Monsoon Indian print three-piece doing a little story on a play group were on to Roddy this and Di that and Mynah and Bryan and *Margaret Argyll* (never say die). One was asked to do pieces on *the Season* and where the Smart money was going and what it was really like at Annabel's or Tramp and the most amazing set of Rome's Burning ideas you ever heard.

A bit later the class war business began to show through in publishing with the new snob publishing, which was for the same market as the new snob accessories with the initials. It started off a bit tentatively with the little Debrett books, which were in a very fifties mould – keep the tone light and jokey little line drawings – but then it got going seriously with State secrets never before revealed. The Mitford line, hitherto somewhat private, developed into a big market with things like Jilly Cooper's *Class* book, which was a tourist guide with the same jokey line drawings, but also a piece of romantic *propaganda* for the old régime which would have been Breaking Faith ten years before.

You found people who had seemed to be tinkering about with this very stylized interest in luxury as kitsch – and were therefore O.K. – were playing it absolutely straight. The direction in 1975 was – *up-market*; so many people were going up-market you couldn't make out where all the business would be coming from. You saw all these old hippie retreads going full tilt for the Savoy Cocktail book and the patent shoes. *Try it.* Then in a little while you found they were turning really Right – like those progressive rock groups who said they were voting Tory in 1979.

The way the gays moved gave one a clue, from tentative camp to Lumberjack clone, so that was what it had been about all along (my body, your body, any body). With all the minorities out and running you felt safe to despise everybody. Everybody had had their break, 1967, 1971, etc., the blacks were out, the gays were out, so you didn't need to observe any of the little Liberal niceties. On the Punk World front come

1977 you started to see some extraordinary reactions around, particularly with the skinhead revival developing in a serious way – the hard-nut baldies. When the baldies came round again – any time from Manson to the Krishna Kids to the Deerhunter – you knew you were in for trouble.

Come Easter 1980 and the Seaside battles and you could see what had been going on in 1976 and how all the little kids who were ten and twelve then had taken it in. The mid-seventies Phoney War. The journalists who went down to cover the mods and rockers reruns got themselves tied in knots, because they found these battles, these Style wars, with four or five different armies pitching in – skins, rude boys and punks and teds and rockers and rockabillies – they couldn't sort them out. The *Mirror*'s centre spread, 'disturbing truth about the cults that breed on violence, see centre pages', came out of the Fleet Street Wax Museum since it was pretty much line for line Marjorie Proops talks to a mod girl (1964) save for a few smart 1980s touches like *class*. There was a nice little secondary piece on a disco in Manchester, however, where they almost caught the tone. The disco manager explained how they followed the same principle as tripling and quadrupling in cinemas – he had a room for the Bowie freaks and New Wavers, one for the soulies, one for the discos and another for the Two-Tones. 'The youngsters', he said, 'go into the rooms where their kind of music is being played and we have very little trouble.'

Boys Own

On Tuesday, 16 August 1977, down the Vortex in Wardour Street, which had been Crackers disco and in a time to come would be Vespas, London's leading Nouveau Mod night spot, most if not all the usual people are around – the January 1977 feeling is slacking off a bit – meaning some of the people who had been at the 100 Club the previous year and some of the punk chicsters and S.W.3 slummers who'd joined up at the Roxy and some of those American girls who told one they'd knocked around with the Pistols and been up Sid's mum's place and everything. Plus, there are some kids from nowhere – meaning no one knows them – and they tend to look a bit starey, like *real* psychopaths, prototype thug rockers/pinheads who've crawled out of the woodwork. It's like an old *Avengers* segment, spot the real nutters in the chainsaw massacre set (*Texas Chainsaw Massacre* had been *the* film in 1976), and it's a bit tense, though nothing much happens.

If you'd written the Vortex up straight then any intelligent editor would've told you to go a little easy on the humour schlock and get at the *disaffected Nihilist thing,* the social problems, tower block angle. The reality sounded like middle-aged satire that missed the point: chubby Adam Ant, in leathers, doing the Berlin obsessional routine with Jordan, the Art Object who worked in Malcolm McClaren's Seditionaries shop, coming in on the heavy notes. What I liked best was a little band that opened with things like 'here's a little song about London Transport' or 'here's a song about a psychopaf . . . for all the psychopafs in the audience', and the hippy film crew that panned their cameras over the garbage after a cheap little record company junket . . . looking for the Trash Aesthetic. Punks, being the bohemian type, were dead messy.

The place is *really run* though, because the Vortex people are pro's, unlike Andy Czezowski's place, the Roxy, where it'd been amateur hour. Vortex had these guys on the door who could've been Sweeney extras, John Binden lookalikes and they kept order – the kids are frisked before they go in which is something new. Punks, by then, did have this *reputation*.

16 August is the night the Clash's famous little prophecy 'No more Elvis, Beatles and Rolling Stones in 1977' seems to be coming onstream, because around midnight the D.J. tells them the King is dead, and this *almighty cheer* goes up.

Danny Baker just can't believe it, or rather he can because it confirms this line he's always maintained, that most humankind is dumb – *99 per cent is thick*. Up till then he's kept up this number about 'the kids' – which is a big word in punky reggae party circles, meaning the *vital/young/proletarian* element in the whole thing – being a cut above dismal mid-seventies youth, the *dummies* in the Take 6 three-pieces in tweed effect and the Ravel two tones – Holborn secretaries with Sunsilk pageboy dos on their arms (Up West, pathetic); the Status Quo headbangers – the zombies' revenge, pathetic; the discos and footballs, pathetic; the Bowie clones with that *wedge* cut from the Low cover and the Fioruccis and snob T-shirts, half their wages gone down South Molton Street. *Pathetic.*

Croydon, where's that? Bermondsey, that's very *exotic*. That was how they talked about the dummies in the squares up off the Fulham Road, like South London and the suburbs *didn't really exist,* like they were laid on as some sort of quaint entertainment. Those houses didn't look much from the outside but Jesus, once you were inside, when the girl had let you in, you could pretty soon clock sixty thousand on the furniture and knick-knacks and that was without the pictures. And these people had *always* had it. The dummies were no threat. Worst of all, probably, were the Fulham Road posers, the Kensington friends, these Art School freaks who went down those parties on the riverside wharves. Those people saw punk as a second chance for the Art Statements; they were the most pathetic of all, and a bit gruesome besides because they were getting on and they should know better. They thought they could patronize the kids, sleep with them, put them on as *cabaret*. They had it coming too. The kids are different, or to use the old hippie line, 'they won't be fooled again'.

Danny Baker means something in this milieu, having been half – the better half – of *the* fanzine *Sniffin' Glue* and he's doing some pieces for *Zig-Zag* which has gone punk in a big way, leaving the obscure West Coast stuff behind. He's also a dead ringer for the young David Bailey which gives him considerable Cockney Sparrer chic, and he never dresses really ridiculous. He's from Bermondsey, which for most of S.W.3, 7 or 10 is the same as Bailey (actually from Leyton), i.e. East End gamey. These people don't even know the difference between South London and the East End, let alone Leyton. By then Danny has already been on I.T.V. with Janet Street-Porter (who's put him in her Golden Notebook for later) and interviewed by the rock press who are mostly a bunch of old, middle-class, hippie retreads and jazzers – although Parsons and Burchill are different and he reckons they're sincere. He knows what, say, the *Daily Mail* or the *Evening News* wants out of you, like acting your number on cue. You tell them what it's really like, what's going to happen and they use about a quarter of it and they change the quotes about so you're saying things you never said, using words you never use.

When this almighty cheer goes up at the Vortex, he realizes this load of deadbeats are about as capable of independent thought, *discernment,* as a cartload of hippies are of reckoning disco, which, unlike most of the Vortex crowd, is something Danny knows from right back.

So he gets up on stage and harangues them. *But for Elvis* none of you would be here. If you've got no sense of the past you don't deserve, don't get *no future.* You must have standards, a code, or it's *just a little art show,* dead amateur. He gets the usual big hand on his opening, some gobbing which is the 1976 period word for spit but with these fruity overtones of congealing, greenish, marbled mucus dragged from the passages and flying.– slap, like a wet fish in the kisser. (Danny had helped originate a brisk little revival trade in this *apple and pears* way of talking which the lower middle-class boys on the rock

press were trying to get down pat without blushing as they
wrote – barnet for hair, boatrace/face – that kind of thing.)
And even the occasional flying beer can, which is the other
1976 thing – not that punks had invented the flying beer can
but they'd written this into the Situation, *participation* you see,
all these Peter Brook theatre jamrags of the sixties, come here
to roost.

Plus a lot of stuff to the effect that Elvis was a *cabaret artist* – Showbiz in fact. As bad as a hippie. Old. Fat.

It was *pathetic*. Here are the kids, this new breed, bright
working-class kids, like the only hope, not processing their accents (it never works, those people just snigger) and moving
out to Ilford and Croydon, pathetic. But these kids are doing
more than S.W.P., N.F., *Sunday Times, Time Out, Sun* and the
whole set-up, which is basically all out to sell tickets, keep the
dummies travelling hopefully and get their share of the action
on the hot prole scene, whatever it is – Bay City Rollers, punk
T-shirts – it's all the same to those people. Fashion/music/
money/politics. Which is why there was this 'no leaders/no
heros' number with punk, although you could see a lot of kids
just thought it was a fab little fashion thing and were really
impressed that you knew the Pistols and the Clash – just like they
was *rock stars*.

And now here was this Parlov reaction – *great, this bloke's
dead*. We'd been bluffing ourselves, they was thick as a plank.
It was enough to turn you into a disco. This was just before
Danny joined the *New Musical Express*.

In autumn 1979, in a 'personal view' in the *Daily Telegraph*
under the headline 'The New Young Literati', someone called
Roy Kerridge, thirty-five going on sixty, had picked up on it:
'In 1960 . . . the sign of a good *would-be* intellectual was a copy
of the *New Statesman* . . . nearly twenty years later the paper
carried by today's young thinkers is more likely to be the
Melody Maker, New Musical Express or *Sounds* – the *self-styled* rock
press.'

This type of *Telegraph* writing is always heavy on the 'would-
be', 'self-styled' and 'so-calleds' and you can see how he's setting up for this sub-sub-Kingsley Amis number, 'today's young

thinker' etc. Most of it's in this arch young fogey vein 'I can now reveal' etc. and most of the detail is hopelessly off-key. But the point is: better late than never. This is the first national newspaper piece I've seen – even three years later – which has a clue about.what's happened to the rock press or just how important it's been from 1976 to 1978. And some of the *morals* he's drawing, about the old bohemian petit-bourgeois habit of confusing the working and criminal classes and idealizing hooligans, dissolving moral values with hipness, a light editorial touch, is pretty accurate.

That piece aside, and its really *very* late, it's quite amazing the way the rock press seems to have this airlock around it which makes it *invisible* to Fleet Street and T.V. No one seems to have noticed it. What would you say if I told you there were three-quarters of a million pale boys buying these *hard core* papers, full of National Front, Socialist Workers Party and anarchy for tots, in W.H. Smith, and some of their writers can really write. Quite right, *call the cops.* If I was to say all this came from I.P.C. – which produces the *Daily Mirror* and *Woman's Own* – and Morgan Grampian, which is Victor Matthews of the *Express,* you'd say *conspiracy,* C.I.A. containment, like the police keeping all the villains in one place.

It's a secret world, the rock press. When you're twenty-five I'll count to ten and you'll forget everything you ever read. As for the writers, when they're twenty-nine they *retire.* In *Logan's Run,* a third-rate sci-fi feature with Michael York and Jenny Agutter about a culture of gerontophobes who live in an underground shopping mall, they have this sort of computer kaleidoscope that folk go into like Premium Bonds when they're thirty so that, so *they* say, they'd be re-assembled for another go. The York character finds out they're being *pulped,* so he makes for the open air before he's thirty. Rock writers get pulped at twenty-nine, they lose their feature names and have to handle the readers letters, or they leave to become P.R.s on record companies or, more sinister still, disappear entirely. *Call the cops.*

The rock press, namely *N.M.E., Melody Maker, Sounds* and *Record Mirror,* is this subterranean world employing perhaps

300 people if you count in the secretaries and part-timers and the guys selling space to C.B.S. and E.M.I. and W.E.A., a world of music industry gigs followed by ligs and review copies and record company lunches and Backstage Passes and being *really close* with, say, Iggy Pop or Dr Feelgood, and the star rock writer having his own groupies and being able to score on the strength of his Alternative Access card – being able to introduce the cupcake to David or whoever. From mid-1976 to mid-summer 1978 this world crossed in a lurid way with what was *actually* going on out there. Out there was the benighted world of Twenty Golden Greats, football and chips and Celebrity Squares which, for most of the rock press, meant something you made a freaky little *montage* from – Modern Life – something like John Heartfield, the 1930s political montage man who was really having a revival with the Large Format Paperback set. From 1976 to 1978 the rock press went full tilt for relevance.

Punk really blitzed the rock press, put them onto the Secret of the Universe track for the second time around and keyed them to the pattern of the future – mainly the point that there *wasn't one*. No future created more career opportunities in the rock press than for years. And what was so exciting about it – after all the *Mirror/Sun/News of the World* shock horror Punk Quickies died down at the end of 1976 – was that basically no one else knew about it. (The hippie counter-culture had been interpreted to death in the quality press within a year.) After the basic induction course of a couple of Sex Pistols singles and the Clash album and some Roxy nights – quite scarey some of it – you got the picture which would be, prototypically, a couple of kids with ratty white potato diet lumpen faces and spikey barnets set against a G.L.C. tower block, with a lot of graffiti sprayed on the wood-rendered concrete New Brutalist sixties finishes that were so hip in 1962 to those middle-class architects who lived well away from the damage in Highgate or Blackheath. The picture was the middle-class liberal nightmare, zombie flesh-eaters ready to turn the Fulham Road into a meltdown. This is the Modern World.

The rock press didn't invent punk, or its spikey barnets or its original aesthetic and politics – which were fashion-edited by a little art-school Situationist breadhead collective called Glitterbest, the Sex Pistols management company – but the rock press substantially controlled the Word on punk from late 1976 on. They provided the sustaining theory, the interpretations that mattered to anyone who thought punk mattered. In interpreting punk, of course, the papers changed it, and it changed them.

In the slough of the mid-seventies, you could have put a good case for the notion that 'youth culture' in the old, commercial, mid-sixties sense, was *over,* kaput, off the boil, and rock culture – the notion that any sort of rock was in any way important *and could change the world* – was absurd; the whole thing was tamed, incorporated petit bourgeois bohemia, the New Showbiz. Punk, therefore, represented nothing less than the biggest opportunity the rock press had had in ten years – a *growth* market – and the steady circulation growth of three of the four main rock papers from 1976 to 1979 showed it. But it also gave their *morale* a leg-up – it made them Custodians of the secret culture, the new oppositional culture. This culture, of course, started off from precisely the same areas and social mix as these things always did, Notting Hill/Ladbroke Grove, Soho and Camden/Islington/Round House. You saw punks where you used to see hippies. Punk London 1976–78, like hippie London, was recorded in the editorial/gossip pages like *Sounds, Jaws* and *N.M.E.'s* 'Teasers', though the new material was often difficult to manage . . . it was hard to get the right hip jokey note for broken bottle fights, squat ejections. Getting the tone right was a big editorial problem for the rock press – one they didn't solve till they got *the kids* on board themselves. The rock press generally played their sacred role fairly serious, however, which for *N.M.E.* and *Sounds* soon became a kind of Forward With The People populism which, in 1976, was a period notion of how working-class people looked, talked and carried on generally.

The other side of the Secret Culture in 1976 was every thinking rock press man's pet hate – *Ritz.* The rock press hated *Ritz,* this wanky, gossip knock-off of *Interview* – or the brighter ones did because it was the guide to the other new world: Gossip Narcissism and withdrawal. *Ritz* took Bondage Chic and said where the clothes came from, and how much and who the model and photographer were and all that. Art-business. There was quite a bit of crossover between the New Rock Press world and the *Ritz* one though – people like Caroline Coon who mixed high. The national dailies, in any case, couldn't tell *Ritz* and punk apart – any clapped out rich hippie in bondage pants and a haircut was the same to them.

The fact was, *Ritz* and the *N.M.E.* represented alternative options for the new leisure class. But *Ritz* had more in it for girls and the rock press was mainly for the lads. And for those boys, *pale* boys the advertising manager of *N.M.E.* once described as 'a nineteen-year-old clerk in Middlesbrough who wants to be one up on his mates with his inside knowledge of the rock world', it was heaven. From 1976 the rockers and the rock press fought the law, fought logic, and any issue of *N.M.E.* 1976 – 78 had some of the most inspired writing, incredible pictures, sharpest, funniest captions, the brightest themes – it was ten years ahead of Fleet Street, enough to send the pale boys to bed thoroughly unsettled. It took till 1980 for even a feeble acknowledgement that 1976 had meant anything to appear in the national press when a few 'legacy of punk' articles started appearing. Up till then the rock press had it to itself.

In America, there's nothing between the teeny fan-mags and *Rolling Stone,* now selling Pioneer hi-fi to the Frye boot generation and all the little Arty Jazzers Journals and fanzines like *Trouser Press* and *Creem.* But here, everything that matters in the sub-cultures goes into the national rock press, which is solid business. It's also good business. *N.M.E.,* the biggest seller at around 230,000, is reckoned to be I.P.C.'s most profitable specialist title.

The rock press is organized by conglomerate corporation publishing – no independents – in the interests of conglomerate leisure corporations of the E.M.I./C.B.S./W.E.A./Polydor variety. The rock press is a handy little thing for the record business – not so much to *sell* records any more but to maintain the flame of the rock culture, spot the fast little trends, the new scenes, and develop the appropriate hip vocabulary and generally act as a cheap freelance R and D department for sensibility. By 1976, the record companies were doing so much for the rock press – facility trips, enough review copies of albums to keep up a journalist's *habit* (you sold them back to the store), ligs after gigs, places the new writers had never been inside before – some writers were practically supported by the record companies, but they were more valuable *off* the payroll, *independent*. And this handy P.R. vehicle also had its subversive side . . . scale and coverage. It reached the kids – lads, rather – who never saw *Time Out* (London only, 100,000) or *Private Eye* (100,000) or the *New Statesman* (40,000) or the *Leveller* or otherwise came across any remotely radical, subversive, anarchistic or generally leftie reading from one year's end to the next. Malcolm McClaren, the Sex Pistols' manager, said it was only students and workers who read the rock press – but in practice, it was student manqués – pale boys who'd done four terms at the Poly, or sixth formers, quite ordinary working and lower middle-class kids who nonetheless wanted to be in touch with *something else*.

Come 1976, the rock press had a little . . . management problem, a new market out there and no one really to cover it. This is the second time around – the first personnel crisis had been hippie and, since things didn't happen so fast then, the papers didn't have to react so fast. Like most of the late sixties things, the real implications of hippie didn't hit the rock press till the seventies. It didn't hit *N.M.E.*, which had gone right through the sixties as a pop paper, until 1971/2, when the great divide between the teeny fan culture and this big new market that the 'progressive' groups had opened up – what the marketing men called 'the college market' – meant a new kind of coverage. In 1971/2, *N.M.E.* was being undercut in a really big way by *Melody Maker*, which had gone 'progressive' first – meaning it treated the music as serious, and *Sounds*, which was *new* and somehow hipper. *N.M.E.* still looked poppy.

N.M.E. got a big six-week makeover. The Class of 72 introduced the new *rock scribe* to the new reader and the hippie legacy came onstream in *N.M.E.*; it was quite spectacularly successful.

N.M.E.'s Class of 72 introduced the rock writer superstar – rock writers who were personalities, musicians who wrote, who were obviously *part of the culture*. In particular, it was Nick Kent and Charles Shaar Murray. Kent was so right for 1972, it was dazzling. He was late-hippie, fleurs du mal to the power of N and he looked like he'd crawled out of a Lou Reed song – talk about decadent.

Kent was the thinnest man on Wardour Street. His leathers were peerless, the leather trousers on pipe-stem legs, meatless thighs, bone shanks, lapping tightly over pointed black boots with the little spur strap round the instep, boots so *matt* it looked like they'd been rolled in oil, soaked in petrol, the anthracite look. The most exquisitely grimy, neo-decadent get-up in London. When he walked, which was everywhere, these boots moved in a curious way somehow, his ankles knocked together painfully with these little chunks. You couldn't miss him anywhere in London. You'd see Kent walking down Piccadilly at night, with a girl as fabulously thin and pale as himself, in a white wet-look mini-skirt and black stockings. You'd see him pacing up Oxford Street, down the Kilburn High Road, anywhere, and around his fabulous thinness the sulphur gloom of 42nd Street.

This, you have to remember, was the period just before *the cocktail hour* of 1972/3 when all these young dudes were into Keith Richard's elegantly wasted thing and his *problem,* and all this other New York decadent stuff like Lou Reed and Iggy Pop and other back of beyond creatures like that. Kent looked the part but, better still, in 1972 everyone knew he was doing a lot of drugs and that he was really obsessional about those guys, he had the real stuff on them. Kent had a unique grip on the early seventies aesthetic. There was, for instance, this story that Keith Richard had been sick on Kent's leather jacket once and *he'd never washed it.*

In the great clear-out of 1972 Kent was pulled in as a freelance from *Frendz* and told he could do what he liked.

Charles Shaar Murray came out of broadly the same

background – *Schoolkids Oz* – but he was complementary to
Kent, being altogether less of an aesthete. He was a stocky
Jewish boy from Reading with a *Time Out* Afro then. He'd
come out of the underground press with a lot of ideas, this very
vigorous, logic-chopping style and the *new vocabulary* which
was at a premium on the *N.M.E.* then, where it was still largely
suburban jazzers and enthusiasts or careerists who'd come off
local papers and saw the rock press as a step up into the Smoke
and Fleet Street. If Kent was an aesthete, Charlie Murray was
about a different element in the underground legacy – the idea
of rock as authentic, the community music, particularly this
English mainstream rock 'n' roll tradition, a hard driving,
bluesy, rather more home-grown tradition than Kent's, not so
heavy on the Baudelaire and Rimbaud.

Between them they covered the waterfront and between
them they had the suss and style to deal with Bowie, Roxy and
glam rock and neo-decadence when it broke in 1972/3. Kent
knew all the people, the styles and antecedents and Murray
weighed in heavy about the implications of it all. Murray was
given to moralizing; he didn't like the Roxy audience, for instance, all that nostalgic *posing* meant there'd be no seventies,
nothing real for anyone to remember. Between them, *N.M.E.*
was quite unbeatable. By 1973 it's circulation was right up and
they had a line about being the largest selling rock paper
against the title.

Kent and Murray both had their moments. First they were
mainly Kent's because of the decadence number, he's the only
rock press boy who knows what it is to wear make-up himself.
In 1974/5, as all that goes flat, Charlie Murray starts in heavy
to the next big little scene which is pub rock or *real* rock 'n' roll
and he makes new sightings in the quest for the authentic in
bands like Dr Feelgood, this gang from Canvey Island with a
guitarist with great jerky nutty movements called Wilko who,
as it turns out, is also an English graduate with a particular interest in Wordsworth.

But by 1975 it's gone flat again and everyone knows it.
There's no big new things and the kids are turning out like the
dullest, most conformist numbers you ever saw and Bowie is

into *disco,* a really sick joke, for God's sake. Everything's fallen apart, fragmented, contrived.

However, in the summer of 76 there does seem to be one scene, which is that the *Kensington contingent* – Caroline Coon who's doing some freelance pieces on *Melody Maker* and John Ingham on *Sounds* – seem to have a little conspiracy going. Ingham and Coon are, without a doubt, the best-dressed, most socially clued writers there have ever been on the rock press. Both came out of the hippie stream, but Notting Hill not redbrick, up-market. Coon, whose father's a Wiltshire landowner, has literally been everywhere. You can't fault her timing. In the sixties she set up 'Release', and then in the early seventies you see her modelling at the neo-decadent benefits – she looks fantastic, that anorexic campy, Vampirella look, that everyone's getting to in the early seventies. They say she's been Ferry's girl. She mixes high, and she's a kind of missing link with the Performance Play-power rich hippie world.

Ingham is this pale, thin, sandy New Zealander, a son of the manse who's run this little conceptual sci-fi magazine in L.A. and has exactly the right pleats on his trousers, the right art work on his T-shirt. Whenever he sees anything really dumb and frightful, out comes a 'look at these creatures' grin.

Coon and Ingham are into something very strange. It looks as though they've copped a sub-culture. They've got some spreads on some really weird looking kids who go down the 100 Club for the punk festival in the summer of 76 and the little gangs/contingents who follow the Pistols round on their first gigs. And it really stands out, this stuff. Ingham's quoting Sid Vicious saying 'In the Summer of Love I was playing with my Action Man.' Sid Vicious especially sets Ingham grinning – he's so frightful, the best cartoon character ever. Coon's interviewing Johnny Rotten who is on about throwing bricks down from the top of the council prison block and a nerve starts to throb in the editorial forehead which says 'get a load of that' because what Coon and Ingham seem to have discovered is, by the lights of the rock press, quite bizarre. You have to remember it was a different world in mid-76, the world of Elton John's Greatest Hits and still hustling for interviews with Led Zeppelin or Queen. Most people in the music business had a really big gut. What Coon and Ingham had discovered seemed to be the home-grown, working-class, submerged 10th who, so they said, were throwing the old showbiz supergroup rock culture back in the record companies faces. The romance of the council block was so devastatingly original, so *right*, and, as Coon and Ingham played it, so visual and shocking there *had* to be something there: what goes on down those clubs? I mean, this is really weirdness. Plus, of course, it's 'political' – which is what the editors mean by real things – class, money, who's running the show. It leaves the old stylized 1972 number standing. In a time to come, Coon was to say that punk was the hippies' revenge, capitalism hadn't heeded the hippies' warning and look what had happened, these wild mutations had crawled out of the woodwork and shown us how it would be in 1984. This stuff is making the best spreads you ever saw, particularly for *Sounds*, where they've also got this obsessional boy called Jon Savage – his copy's impenetrable but he does these fantastic John Hartfield style photo montages and they're totally 1976. They give *Sounds* that edge because they're so – and this is not a word one could use at the time, you understand – chic, cut-ups of fifties consumer goods and the council block death factories in South London and advertising lines. *Sounds* looks like its got an edge on something new.

This is all a big problem editorially though, because most of the writers have a heavy investment in all the styles and groups the punks are gunning for, but it's a problem particularly for *N.M.E.* since it looks like *Sounds* is stealing a march. Everyone's been looking for the *next big one* but punk looks difficult to cope with at first, because the kids have a sensibility that leaves most of the staffers standing, they don't like it and even Murray and Kent are a bit equivocal about punk. Kent knows the Pistols, even rehearsed with them, and there's a story that everyone's heard that he's been chain-whipped by Sid – but it's not *quite* them. When Nick Logan, Ilford ex-Mod, who's editor of *N.M.E.* looks round in the autumn of 1976 nothing looks quite right, which is why they run an ad for 'hip, young, gunslingers' in the paper itself (which is 1976 code for *are you one of the kids?*). Within a couple of weeks of each other they've recruited Tony and Julie, the Bash Street Kids, and nothing is ever the same. Once they've got Tony Parsons and Julie Burchill on board, it's quite obvious why everything looked wrong now – it was wrong. Tony and Julie had come to put *rock* out of business.

The main thing about them was the *class* thing. In rock press terms, they were 100 per cent un-reconstructed, inner urban prole, which in late 1976 was just about the most exotic, lurid, transcendentally right thing you could get. They also look the part, which is important for editorial atmosphere. Tony wears Doc Martens, the young workers' big boots with the huge domed toe-caps that the skinheads used to wear, and shifts. He's got these big white hairless meaty arms coming out of a shift. Later on he wears the original Seditionaries 'God Save the Queen' T-shirts – it's the badge and there's no one else on the rock press then with the front to wear it – and the leather jacket, no rock star tailored leathers nonsense, the correct form, zippered kind. He's from Billericay via Plaistow and done a couple of years at the Distillers gin factory and they say he's written a paperback in the Richard Allen style called *The Kids,* although no one's seen it. All of this adds up to the most tremendous barrel load of Street credibility you ever saw.

And Julie looks a fairly wild mutation herself. She's wonderfully pale and thin and looks like a bad girl *circa* 1963, which is to say totally 1976, with this bright red mouth and black dye job Cleopatra do, which is all scrungled up so you've got bits of brown showing through at the back. Plus a West Country accent and the fact that she's *seventeen*. On their own, just as *props,* they would have seen the *N.M.E.* through. As it turns out, though the first general impression is Tony is macho randy and Julie's into girls, within a couple of months three things are apparent – namely that they can write, they are a team and they're totally uncontrollable.

A stylish young working-class couple with street credibility who can spend nights over the Clash's rehearsal rooms in Camden Town – it's every editor's dream. But a lot of what

Tony and Julie write goes a bit close to the bone. If you were
anywhere near the rock press circuits, you heard it all the
time – *that* Julie Burchill, *that* Tony Parsons, and *what they'd
done now*. One evening at Hammersmith Odeon I was with
this clutch of Modern girls, Caroline Coon, Judy Nylon, Kate
Simon, and Vivien Goldman who was then doing the features
on *Sounds,* and Vivien had overheard Julie somewhere in the
interval. *That* Julie Burchill had said 'people aren't really very
interesting, there's not much to be said for individuals'. You
could see it *worried* the girls, individual-not-very-interesting,
what *did* she like then? What she was on about was bourgeois
rock individualism and this was a real *political* note, a tough bit
of vocabulary that I hadn't heard in years. Tony and Julie
brought the most basic class politics into the rock 'n' roll fantasy community.

From late 1976 onwards, it became standard for any serious
rock writer to check out a performer's class credentials. For
about a year, being a son of toil counted. This all knocked the
sixties unifying hippie classless mythology but, worse still,
Tony and Julie had the knives out for the whole rock
mythology itself. They had it in for students, record companies,
old stars, Artists, bohemians and particularly – and this was a
new mood for the rock press – Americans. Americans, in Tony
and Julie's line, were slack-gutted, old, over-indulged, hip easy
listeners, Big Babies.

Burchill-Parsons came on like a moral scourge. They were
anti-drug, save for speed (a fast, energetic, *urban prole* drug,
Tony and Julie liked a quick Do-Do between meals), they really went in hard, particularly on performers they used to like.
Julie said Bryan Ferry was a *worthless person* – think of it, a
worthless person, I hadn't heard that kind of language in
years – because of the social climbing and because he'd
deserted the kids who'd made him. Bowie was a 'toothless
piece of old burnt meat . . . a dead man's brain flouncing
around the stage' because he'd gone so esoteric, he'd believed
it when people said he was an Artist. Tony said The Ramones,
the world's most perfect group, the hip critics' choice, the conceptual cartoon group who'd had a spread in *Interview* – the

very best of the worst – were just dumb right-wing thickos and
junkies, out of touch with Jubilee Britain 1977.

All this is great stuff; it gets the readers letters going. In
1977/8, Tony and Julie get more hate mail than all the other
writers together. But they're writing themselves out of a job,
and they know it. The worst thing is they want to be writers not
rock stars, nor to make it in petit bourgeois Fleet Street, and
they know the rock press is an elephant's graveyard. After
thirty, what can you do? Go into a press office or do little cult
numbers in the specialist sections of *Melody Maker* or *Musicians
Only*. Rock writers are pulp at twenty-nine. They aren't worried about going for the big kill, namely the idea that music
matters. They're saying it's no big thing. A good rock star is a
good rock star only if he's a moral person.

But it all comes down to sales, whatever they write the sales
go up. Here they are writing themselves out of the picture and
Logan wants more copy and the readers hate them and the
record companies hate them and *it couldn't be better*. In 1977, it
was all go. This was the year that the *Leveller,* the Socialist
magazine, advertised itself in *N.M.E.* and the year of the
Cockney Voice Over – if you'd got any radio spots for New
Wave records, you had to have some kid with the really heavy
Sarf-East London voice over. Somebody the listener could
imagine looked like Tony. Move those old plates of meat down
the old Virgin Store and get a load of this.

This was pretty much how other editors saw them and
N.M.E. had them, which meant more frantic recruitment went
on for anyone who was it, the real thing, out of it, part of it, the
real pumping, hundred per cent Cockney, concrete hard-nuts.
Hey kid, can you write? This meant some confusion, not least
when the editors started looking to the original punk centres
and the fanzines. This recruitment didn't always go quite like
they'd planned, punk wasn't what it was cracked up to be, a lot
of these kids turned out to be pale boys in the grey Conceptual
Mackintoshes and berets who were a bit on the arty side. Far
from being the voice of the people, these boys, from Manchester or Ulster or wherever, were into some of the most
arcane things you ever heard. *Sounds* had this Jon Savage, who

was Cambridge would you believe, and stylized in a big way. Later they got Gary Bushell who was leather-jacket and cropped hair and off the White City Estate and, so it seemed, could cover the Tony number. Quite soon there was a whole gang of new writers competing for air space and by-line photographs and jumping feet first into . . . legend.

The other big post-punk opportunity was for *girl* writers and there was quite a little post-hippie, counter-sexism number mixed in with the newer class politics. Caroline Coon wrote up about these delinquent girl types like the Slits (actually very much the Holland Park types) who, so she said, were upending all the old stereotypes, and Vivien Goldman on *Sounds* cornered the dreadlock market in reggae features and Jamaican round-ups. And this was really radical because rock had always been boy's stuff.

Tony and Julie were a problem in the office. They didn't just look the part and add to the atmospherics. They acted it out. For a start, they didn't really get on with the other writers – not Kent nor Charlie Murray or most of the new pale conceptual class of late 77. They sat together in their own partition box – the Kinder Bunker – and stuck broken glass round the top, which was worth a couple of thousand a year in itself. They flicked cigarette butts in Charlie Murray's Afro. They sent the old lads up, which is a turn-up for the book since Kent and Murray know what it is to have the monopoly on enfant terrible-hood. There were even some real argy-bargies in the class room, like the time Monty Smith, who was long-term staff, was lecturing Julie – 'now look here, young lady' – and Tony grabs him round the neck and . . . *you've really done it now Tony*. Because Tony is the fantasy prole and there's a lot of worry about those pale meaty biceps and Julie's supposed to carry a flick-knife (she does) and *there are limits*. But, some hope, because whatever they do they *can't* get themselves expelled from progressive school.

These are times when a party line on something goes through the rock press in about two months. There's a real dialogue going on, they're all reading each other and going after the feature of the week. If one of the major leaguers has a line on somebody, you couldn't write about them next week without taking up what, say, Tony and Julie had said, and adding a little grace note. In another week or two it's coming back at you from the record company's press office because it's been played back by some third liner, who's a rock press old stager anyway, so you find these new little àttitudes to cop turning up in *Record Mirror,* which is the teeniest of the four, and even the *Evening News* pop column. When it turns 1978 the scribe competition is running really hot and there's a circuit of boys and girls focussing on . . . the New Wave musical community. Lost in music, caught in a trap. By the end of 1978, Tony and Julie have brought out a book, an *Obituary of Rock and Roll,* and they move off the *N.M.E.* staffers list. *Two years, then off and out by 1978.* By the time they went, a lot of Revisionist stuff was going on, it was getting really difficult to grasp what exactly 1976 was all about, whether punk was an Art movement or a political one or, indeed, just a big con, put on by the Pistols manager, Malcolm McClaren, who by then, was the most unfashionable person possible in rock press circles. With Tony and Julie easing themselves out, the class of 77/78, the pale boys in the macs, came out of the closet in a big way and the critical theories literally flew. There was one I loved called Power Pop which started in *Sounds* in spring 1978 and ran for about two months before it was *denounced.* The idea of Power Pop was the *essence* of pop, the People's music, all those twinkling, twangy, bright guitars and melodies, that 1964 sound; and boys in suits. It was a low camp haberdashery idea with no wind in it at all – a sweet little memory of *N.M.E.* around 1964, a pure critical theory, and a great read.

Then there was the whole German synthesizer avant-garde thing which came on in 1978. This meant you could be more than just alienated, you could *play robot.* It suited the Conceptualists because it was chic and Modern and made the barricades and the class war a little redundant – and it tied in neatly with that kind of post-hippie sci-fi sensibility that goes into video and computer games and synthesizers, and develops a little aesthetic about them. There was new American weirdness too, like Devo, jokey little chaps who came on in specs and

shorts and plastic kneee caps looking like psychopathic suburban wimps. Devo had a little college circuit theory about
themselves *ready made*, and a little Devo anthem, and they were
a lot of fun to write about.

The more you read this stuff, the more it struck you how far
Theory had taken over – what an Artistic type of person you
were getting nowadays in the short-haired underground. The
little theories seemed to come almost before the bands. Rock
was producing commentary rock, critique rock, reference rock,
rock about rock. It was like the sensibility of those smart
American kids who leave their comfortable suburbs and the
T.V. soaps and make the pilgrimage to the Village and Soho
and C.B.G.B.'s down the Bowery in New York, the multi-
media capital of the world, and produce: hyper-realist pictures
of fifties Chevys; montages of muscle-beach movies; and Art
rock bands with girls who aim to look like Leslie Gore. They
get out of the suburbs just to get even with them, doing the Art
Rock dance. It was as if the notion of mass-culture commentary in Art – once so different, so appealing – was the only
vocabulary these kids actually had, they didn't know anything
else. All those American Studies, those PhDs on 'I Love Lucy'
come home. The vocabulary of petit bourgeois bohemia had
turned upside down in the last ten years. Warhol had taught a
generation one easy little trick – the aesthetic of boredom, and
how to re-work mass culture. By 1978 the word was out, namely that rock could be real Modern Art in the sense that it started
from critical ideas and Artistic people.

Early in 1978, Danny Baker, who'd joined *N.M.E.* as the
New Model receptionist and went on to write, did the singles
review and made a *disco* number his single of the week. If he'd
gone for the Eagles or Des O'Connor he couldn't have been
more obviously spoiling for a fight because, right then, disco
was just about the most unfashionable thing out – studio
machine music. In this review Danny said how all the pale boys
were knocking disco as mindless, consumer fodder – all these
theory boys – and how they were contemptuous of the real
People's music, 'the joyous, whirling, throbbing music' disco.
'Bird shit', he said, on all the art rockers and West Village

fancies; here was the real thing. He meant it perfectly straight, though of course he was paying off a few old scores, since here was somebody who really had worked up a sweat to Johnny Bristol and the Philadelphia Sounds in the mid-seventies and who knew the whole white-suited world. It was one of those pieces that makes you want to send a telegram. Anyone with half an eye who'd heard 'Shaft' down the clubs in 1971, or had ever noticed what *the kids* actually did, knew that disco was the People's music. (The year before I'd said to one of the pale boys that a Donna Summer number, 'Love's unkind' – it was in the Top 10 then – was the record of the year. He'd never heard of it, he never looked at the top 20.)

This piece really stirred it up, here was the People's music, said the People's writer, and *how to get a grip on it,* get into that Polyester look, especially when, like most of the Conceptualists, you couldn't dance. Within a month, however, there was a Theory of Disco and the pale boys were writing on Donna and Abba and the Bee Gees as if they'd been keeping tabs all along. It was amazing. Enough to put you off. Disco had gone *ideological.* You could set it up as this very *manipulative* thing, a kind of futurist music of consumption, the real 1984 (punk was just *naive*), full of synthesized sounds that hit the brain patterns, made you jump or slow down. The um factors and the ohm sounds or some such, as one smart boy in *Melody Maker* explained it, and these ums and those ohms worked the different brain processes and moved the poor troggs around. This kind of thing meant you could admire disco and despise the consumer at one go, do this critical double-track on it, keep your distance.

The problem came when you interviewed the disco people, the *manipulators,* the record producers and their cute little disco clone groups. They turned out to be either one-dimensional businessmen or thick as planks, and they usually couldn't talk; you had to go to an Art Rocker for the chat. The disco producers were tough little businessmen in open shirts with the big collars – very non-conceptual that – and the chest hairs and medallions, and the singers were usually hacks who'd been working around the studios for fifteen years and the only thing worth photographing was the mixing console. It was difficult to work out these little theories about the *really* commercial music like disco and pop, this critique of mass communication. It all started to look a little oblique once you got into something that didn't *need* explaining.

By 1979 the rock press was right off the boil again. Danny Baker said it was hard to see which side you were on – as if *sides* meant anything in the great rock 'n' roll Phoney War. Rock 'n' roll was, after all, 'just a little Western luxury' and rock writing was just a job. If they were honest, said Danny, they'd have packed it in two years ago while it meant something, died before they grew old, that sort of thing.

The rock press itself disconnected, went back to showbiz or Art at precisely the time that 1976 started to connect commercially. In 1980 the little kids who'd been ten and eleven in 1977 and watching on the sidelines and reading the words in *Smash Hits* actually went hell for leather into the real next big thing. The great tiny craze which was – escapist, revivalist, relevant, short-haired, *teenybopper* dancing music from an independent multi-racial collective out of Coventry. Two-Tone, full of contradictions, like things really were.

In March 1980, *Melody Maker's* U.S. News pages reported the Sex Pistols film *The Great Rock 'n' Roll Swindle* opening at the Los Angeles Filmex Festival to a sold-out local mob. At the premiere were Barbra Streisand, Cher, Diana Ross, and Starsky from Starsky and Hutch. Cher arrived in a Fiorucci rig on roller skates and told the press that she was looking forward to putting several 'New Wave' songs on her album. The same week the Clash opened at the Palladium in New York. In the audience were Bianca Jagger, Debbie Harry from Blondie and, so they said, John Lennon. After the post-gig party, Paul Simenon from the Clash, once Caroline Coon's boyfriend, flew to Vancouver to start work on a new movie.

The Clone Zone (Night of the Living Dead)

This P.R., courtly, somewhere between the George Sanders and the Lord Carringtons, i.e. the gent and the actor gent, and in the big league – an office down Bond Street and £50,000 a year retainers from the kind of directors of *The Times* 100 companies who'd just pass muster down St James's at a pinch, and organizing lunches with Royalty around – i.e. knows how it works pretty much. One morning he calls with this discreet 'just might interest you . . . don't bother to reply or anything', and he can't resist telling me a little story about the previous evening, with some idea that I know about these things and may be able to set it right for him. What's happened is this: he's been walking outside the National Gallery fairly early in the evening and he sees this spectacular gang of . . . *punks,* coming towards him, and you could tell from the tone that if he'd had a sword stick, old D.S.O. and Bar, he'd have been gripping it pretty firm with the knuckles white. He's obviously been quite prepared for the worst, even though there are plenty of people around. This is his first active contact with any punks anywhere. 'And d'you know, they turned out to be American and the most charming young people you could meet' and they're asking him the way to the *Festival Hall.*

This business thoroughly rattles him in more ways than one. For a start, he prides himself on being a pretty sharp old bird and being able to clock most of the styles and he's mastered hippies and Teds and so on. But he feels he's lost his touch and somehow the rules have changed. Besides which there is a more practical matter: if this lot's turned out to be nice as pie, how does one know, well . . . which ones *do* bite?

Of course, it could have been *anyone* – the range of styles that these old gents call punk means just about anyone under the sun with short hair or a strategic touch of Day-Glo. But American? And looking for the Festival Hall? He's lost me there. So I'm trying to explain to him that he's right, the rules *have* changed and that it's difficult to tell and there's no way you can get up an Observer's Book of Teen Life Forms . . . *dangerous when aroused.* My advice is keep off the streets after six, George, keep the chain on the door, and write to David Jacobs.

He'd hit on something though. After 1976, not only did this lurid, Day-Glo, 1984 acid trip, Arty boot boy thing called punk emerge – and at least was photographed a lot so that the ordinary person could see the fiendish cult that was sweeping the nation's youth – but also something rather subtler and odder was happening to the whole teen style picture. For a start, there were *more* styles and more kids doing them. In the early seventies, teen styles had been in general spectacularly dull; by the late seventies, it looked as if there were new wilder mutations all over the place.

Punk had this curious effect of catalyzing other styles, even things that seemed to be its complete antithesis – like that very *shiny* neon and Lycra disco style you got in 1978 – so it was hard enough to keep track on the styles which were brand new. What was harder still for Average Reader was taking in the fact that in the late seventies there seemed to be pastiches, *reflections* around of every youth culture style since, well, since it was invented in the country – i.e. the mid-fifties. The pastiches of these styles were running around *at the same time* and anyone who'd been a Mod or a Ted or a greaser or an early hippie would feel thoroughly unnerved to see the oddest versions of their own styles reappearing in the wrong way, on the wrong people, with the wrong friends.

One afternoon, at the Virgin Record Store down Ken-

sington High Street, I see this group of little mates which is like
one of those mixed assorted liqueurs, because you've got a
rather bad one of everything. There is, for instance, a Nouveau
Mass-Mod, 1979 style, who's got on every obvious thing you
ever saw, from the fish-tail parka with the target on the back,
with the 'H' of the 'WHO' going back up into an arrow, the
short crop and the Ben Shermans, the Hush Puppies and the
parallel trousers in iridescent lovat. His mate is Two-Tone,
which is to say dressed exactly, but exactly, like the boy on the
cover of the Selector E.P. in a suit with a short straight jacket,
the peg pants, the white socks and the flattest black shoes possible, plus the short hair with the parting almost scored out,
and the loopy noon-day-sun shades. One girl is plasticine
punk, i.e. bondage strides, black monkey boots – a kind of
cross between Doc Martens, the big worker's boots, and running shoes with the lacing going right down almost to the
toes – and a little black leather jacket and the mohair spider-
web sweater over her haunches with a little nappy coming out
of that and 'CRASS' in whitewash painted on her back. Plus
the scrungled, blonde dye job with the black roots, and the red
lipstick. And *her* mate is a high yellow girl with the most enor-
mous bouffant, a B52, who looks like a bad girl trying on
the Motown look for size in 1963, and has a mini skirt with
black stockings and black suede winkle pickers with the stilettos
going in at this angle where you think they're going to snap
off.

And the point is not all these little details which may or may
not mean everything under the sun, but that they're all mates
and by any of the laws of nature ought to be at each other's
throats, for any of a hundred reasons to do with the old inex-
tricable laws of Teen society and *dressing the part*. The problem
is that the old laws are clearly being mucked about with
something criminal.

What has happened actually is that the repertoire of teen
style is now pretty well open to *anyone*. Above all, the jumble
sale habit, once something that one never saw below the *Time
Out* middle-class waterline of bohemia, has gone down to
ordinary teenagers with a vengeance, and they're picking up

the strangest things and changing the meanings of what they wear . . . and, of course, putting a lot of clothes shops into a lot of trouble. .

In a time gone by it was fairly easy to set out the guiding principles of obvious youth style. There would be the same three fundamental groups at it, whatever it was. They were: *the lads,* the inner-urban working-class peer groups, camp followers who went for the delinquent styles, whatever they were, and they *all* wore them; the middle-class youth culture contingent who went for something droopy and expressive; and this tiny little fringe of sharp stylists and art school weirdos and other media trendies who were just a curiosity. And once you'd got your eye on the basic principles, you could pick them out easy as winking. Punks shifted the focus quite a bit because they seemed to be *working-class bohemians,* i.e. they were artful and sharp and expressive but they seemed like bother at the same time. It seemed as if there was just a millimetre of nuance between outright loonies and nice kids.

Did they bite? You couldn't always tell. What had happened was that there was a whole big new world. Kids who should have gone to Polys but didn't, ordinary working-class kids who lived in squats or slept rough – once an unthinkably middle-class approach, save for the submerged tenth. This world *echoed,* in the oddest, most sophisticated ways, the real styles of all the rooted, straight-down-the-line brotherhoods of teen there had ever been. Unless you knew what they were you could mistake them for the real thing.

By 1980 punk had become a vague period word for a whole range of people. In 1980, a judge sentencing boys for an attack on some punks described them as an *endangered species,* not knowing real punks had been attacked on the streets by every other jungle creature around from the moment they appeared, in precisely the same way that the first hippies turned into a target for skins and mass-mods and everyone else. And when Neasden Tube station was spectacularly vandalized, the London evenings said punk gangs . . . whereas if you checked you found there hadn't been a real punk in sight – only skinheads and nouveau mods. And a cross punk girl wrote to the *Standard* to protest the way their lifestyle was being vilified by journalists who didn't give a toss.

The original punk look was *jungle stylist,* and the jungle materials were, of course, the real jungleland stuff, i.e. leather, vinyl, Day-Glo, nylon, jersey or anything that anybody's mum thought dead common and dated.

Being a millenarian sect, punks looked like they'd picked up the bits after the earthquake. The way to tell a proper punk was that every item he or she had on was *utterly out of sync,* a style from a cut-up of every other youth culture since the war and thus did injury to them and was a mockery of the whole wonder world of teen. The whole aesthetic was *perverse;* getting the dye job thoroughly wrong (since Clairol had got the blonding hints so piss elegant and subtle now). The colours were either Northern barmaid black or tow rope bleach with the roots showing. The actual range of styles was very wide and exotic. Something leopard – but not too much for that was Roxy art school – a touch of the Day-Glos; and for the boys, *hefty shoes,* either big Doc Martens with the dome toes or the real big thick-soled creepers in black or white, like the Teds. Of course, there were wonderful variations, like the boy who had musical notes dyed into his crop, or even the odd black punks with the green dye jobs etc. There weren't many black punks, however, because most black kids thought punk was . . . *madness.*

The original punks were the most absolute works of art you ever saw. There's hardly one of them wearing any of that stuff now. The torch has passed to younger and more provincial kids out at the back of beyond; you see the style followed to some degree of faithfullness, though it's been fading out fast.

Within a few months of punk 77, the earnest middle-class version appeared which would be, typically, a nice little fifth former from, say, Muswell Hill, who gets his hot tips from *N.M.E.* and *Sounds,* and three years before would have been a hippie. This kid, like every middle-class dreamer since the war, had seen punk as a mandate for the 'poor boy' style – which is to say *dull.* He's got a black jacket loaded to the gills with *badges* – the Clash, the Pistols etc. – and tight jeans and some kind of dinky little baseball boots (just like dear old John Lennon used to wear) and cut his hair and looks like the drabbest, most sincere thing you ever saw and probably he and some of his mates will join Rock Against Racism and start a fanzine, i.e. a ten-page xeroxed rave-in for his prole heroes. And while all that's going on, his elder brother, who's a *Time Out* subscriber, goes transitional in about 1977 and invests in a pair of dungarees, a pair of Kickers in dark blue and some kind of deadly naff T-shirt and crop and thereby ensures himself a thumping any time he goes anywhere further afield than the Round House. Which is understandable because he looks like a big toddler who's been shaved for summer.

The other style that came out of punk – and it *did* bite – was the pinhead, the post-punk thug rocker. These kids appeared as a kind of transitional type just between punks and the re-emerging skinheads. They despised what they saw as the posey elaboration of the original punks and kept to *basics*, i.e. spikey cuts, nothing too fancy, the jeans and Docs, and they went straight for the Reactionary Populist groups like Sham 69 who made it all sound like Phoney Class War on the football terraces. The pinheads did over the Students Union at the L.S.E. in 1977 . . . *fuckin' students*. Within a year pinhead was pretty much back to skinhead base.

Whatever happened to teen was in fact one of those sci-fi stories where something . . . *gets into the soil,* and produces very odd mutations. Supernature. The creatures down below grow up in the most peculiar way.

In the late 1970s, teenage style groupings lost their innocence. They became self-conscious. They knew who they were and they also knew *why*; the legend and the theory. If you asked any group of teenage types (not lacklustre mainstream youth) what they were all about, they tended to play back to you, at one level or another, a sort of folk/pop sociology *theory* about it. The skinheads and the residual working-class punks said it was all about *class* because they'd read it in the music papers and how they hated these hippies and posers. By knowing too much they lost their real certainties, however. That was why some of the groups became so extreme, huddling together for comfort. *Mass paranoia set in.*

Throughout the seventies, everything was onstream. First, there was a vastly greater range of style options, the repertoire was huge, and it was available all the time. It was quite easy to get eclectic and move across groups and lose your *commitment* in just a year.

Second, there was comment and analysis all around – some of it quite sophisticated – right down to T.V. and the tinies' papers. No sooner would kids do something than they had it played back to them and explained, like one of those Art shows where you walk in and they video you and you see yourself as you walk out. You didn't have to read all that well to know what people thought your group was all about. The sociology habit had spread right down.

The other big repertoire thing was the past, which was always there, always accessible. Every year throughout the seventies a bit more of this pop cultural archeology went on, forging through the forties, fifties, sixties, and a bit more – American Graffiti, Quadrophenia – was exhumed for the Large Format Paperback Set, for magazine features, for revival movies. It was all there for parody or quotation; you couldn't avoid it.

The oddest thing of all was to see the same style working on two or three levels just next to each other. You'd have people from the sixties and even the fifties who'd got stuck in a teen style and just moved it on a bit, like the guys about thirty-five, with the neat hair and the red V-necks, and you'd see, basically, Ilford Mod; and the little kids, thirteen and fourteen, who'd just taken it up – it was new to them and really exciting, though they knew a *bit* of the history; and the *stylists* in their twenties who knew *all* about it, the references and the meanings and the dates and so on and read *Generation X* and collected the old Top of the Pops Annuals 1964. This doubling and trebling rather took the edge off things. This style archeology developed an arcane language all its own. You'd hear Art Students talking about doing a number with a fringe jacket *like Sonny and Cher,* or 'a touch of the Bobby Vees'.

Along with this there was an enormously hyped-up rate of change – not just fashion detail but the *whole attitude* you could cop – so fast, in fact, that the styles never got a chance. Except for the really 'rough kids' peer group styles, the *paranoids,* it was difficult to make a commitment to a particular style. This meant a lot of what was around had no depth to it. The styles didn't get a chance to mature and their owners didn't get a chance to grow into them. What was happening was. . . *cloning.*

Punk brought it all together and pulled it all apart. Punk undermined traditional notions of what teenage culture was all about, it introduced some pretty highbrow ideas directly into the reservoir of ordinary working-class youth culture. The main thing that punk introduced was the idea of *cut-ups, montage* – a bit of Modern Artiness – to an audience who'd never heard of eclecticism. Punk was about changing the meanings of things.

At the same time, however, punk re-introduced a lot of the old styles. Punks were mucking about with everything from ted to mod, skinhead and rude boy and, here and there, some hippie ideas (quite a lot of hippie, though it took a while to be recognized). Punks, of course, scrambled it all up, but bits and pieces were there if you cared to look. A lot of the *tiny* kids, nine, ten and eleven, who were sitting on the sidelines when punk broke through in 76/77 couldn't have cared less about the big idea. They zeroed in a few years later on some of the particulars. The kids picked on the *shoes* and built their styles from the ground up. Doc Martens – pinheads and skinheads; Creepers – rockabilly; Jam Shoes, the black pointed jobs with the white vamp – nouveau mod. And they wore them as a *clone uniform.* Arty punk also caused big *reactions* and the biggest was probably skinhead. New skinhead, which started to emerge in a big way from 1976 onwards as one of the major themes in inner-urban working-class life in every big city, was both a development out of punk and a reaction against it. Skinheads were originally white, working-class, no-hoper kids who generally felt threatened, cut out by the classless word-processing disco New World, bewildered by choice. Skinhead was mass paranoia to a degree unmatched by any other youth group. If you saw a skinhead on his own, he'd always be doing these little side to side head movements and the eye flickering, looking like British soldiers on the Derry streets. Skinheads took punk paranoia *seriously.*

Similarly, the new disco stylists who came up in 1977/8 often turned out to have emerged very directly out of punk – but out of its stylish, latter-day Bowie components. The world of shocking pink and footless tights developed as directly in and out of punk as laid back L.A. developed out of one strand of hippie.

When things appeared to have settled down in 1978 – when it looked like they were going 'back to normal' – the reality was that they could never be the same again. Kids had seen certain things. You could never get out the guidebook and say *look,* easy polarities like mods and rockers. You'd need a whole Identikit to move and bend the old themes this way and that. There weren't five types but something like thirty. A substantial group of teenagers, you see, no longer believed in the future, but they'd lost any real links with the past. There weren't many *real* traditional styles left. The fact that you could 'revive' a style showed that it was dead at the roots. All this meant that the consensus Strawberry Statement, Youth Village, Our World Today onward and upward ideas seemed totally hollow.

If punk was a watershed, the one most persistent single influence on youth style groups throughout the seventies was Bowie. Bowie's importance was consistently under-rated. His own mythologizing publicity worked against him, so the analysts couldn't see for looking (and because he wasn't that great a record seller, never up there in the Guiness Book league with Presley and Wings). The fact was, however, that Bowie had a more intense influence on the perceptions of an important minority of kids than any other rock performer. Bowie's fans are *obsessive,* and they're obsessive about style.

Bowie was the connecting link between hippie and punk. What he did to teenage style in the seventies was introduce the idea of conscious stylization – Oneself as a Work of Art – and ambiguity to a wider audience than ever before. Bowie, so the journalistic ready-made went, *recreates himself* every couple of years. This wasn't actually true but the idea has had a huge effect upon a dedicated minority of stylists who've grasped on the central Bowie theme – *immortality through style, invulnerability through style.*

The special thing about Bowie fans and Bowie concerts is just how many of them are really involved with the Master. They want to be him. And this goes for girls too. You could spot a Bowie casualty anywhere.

Bowie had this avowedly Art Attitude from way back and he started mixing styles very early. That's why his influence extends across from punk to glam-rock to freaks to soul boys, all of which reflect one or other part of David's Presentation of Self and cop some Bowie attitudes. Bowie's last but one incarnation for instance – baggy Aladdin pants, snob sweat shirts, hair parted to the left in that heavy bob – is the basis of a whole group's style: the *Soul boys.* The Fiorucci baggy jeans, white socks, sneakers, snob T-shirts and *The Wedge,* the haircut Bowie had in *The Man Who Fell to Earth,* on the cover of *Low*; the most persistently influential haircut of the decade.

Taken together, the Bowie and the punk thing, things aren't what they seem. Kids are dressed in confusing ways because the language of teen style has been subverted. For every *real* teenage style group, every one that bites, there's a shadow group – somebody knocking it off, picking it up, doing it ironically, styling it up, people who don't have the thoughts to go with what they're wearing. And a really *big* movement can come and go in a *year* because mass exposure destroys a style's basis, makes it into a teenybopper thing. And, of course, everything's going younger and younger.

During the seventies, the Earth brought forth a series of clones and hybrids. The streets were alive with the jangly sounds of golden hits . . . just out of register, not quite right. The reservoir had been poisoned. The results are very odd.

Gary, thirteen, is a Two-Tone Tiny, part of the Specials badge set – except he's too cool to actually wear the badges which you can get with the little kid's papers now. He's got everything the Two-Tones have, starting with the hefty tassel loafers with the squarish toes (like Saxone 1969; the older perfectionists have the *Royals,* the real Mile End American look, heavy wing-tips with the massive welt and the double-

layer leather soles) and the white socks and the two-tone
trousers and the Slazenger crocodile V-neck over a black
T-shirt. Gary was the youngest punk on the Orange Hill Estate
in Burnt Oak in 1977. Burnt Oak is Edgware, but it was also
the overflow re-housing for North-East Londoners in the fifties.
Gary was into punk long before there was *real* trouble with glue
sniffing on the estates; he got his mum to make him the bondage strides. Gary was pop crazy – the *Top of the Pops* level – till
1977 when he started spending his money on *Record Mirror* and
then *Smash Hits,* where you could read the song *words.* He
pored over the words, and he used to cut things out from
magazines and stick them all together like a picture, very
strange. By the end of 1978 he was going New Mod and he had
a parka for Christmas 78, and by the end of 79 he was Two-
Tone. This Christmas his mum gave him the *This Is Soul* compilation album. She's thirty-four and she remembers the old
Mod stuff herself and still dresses a bit fast – high heels and
tight jeans. She's very proud of him, she's with him all the
way. That year he also got his own budget music centre.

What about this, George, this . . . Teddy type, this delinquent silhouette.

At the Zanzibar, happy hour, Friday, on the Pina Col-
adas – it's the oldest leather trouser straight in Richmond.
Nick is creative director of this medium level ad. agency, and
his look is very . . . *Fonzie* – leather trousers, black cowboy
boots, slightly palm beach, button-down shirt and this shiny
Johnson and Johnson Ted/Mod Showbiz mohair jacket and the
Teddy hair that the ad. agency, American Graffiti set and
record company liggers go in for. In 1976 Nick did one of the
first jean commercials to use all that stuff, set in a diner; he's
generally reckoned to be a bit fast. Like Henry Winkler,
though, he's getting on, nearly thirty-five. His face is going
somehow and the under-eye bags are really coming.

Nick's credentials are O.K. He's secondary modern from
Harrow. He was down in Brighton in 64 and wore all the stuff
and he got to art school – the London College of Printing – and
in 68 he did Marrakesh. Until 76/7, he'd been really heavy on
Jerry Lee Lewis re-plays and Steely Dan and Ry Cooder. In

77, he developed an enthusiasm for Elvis Costello, then Police and now he's gone Joe Jackson. For the last two years he's been thinking: *can he take the crop*. Some friends have had it and they look like 1958 Polish scientists, not so good. One of the new assistant Art directors he's hired on the jeans account – twenty-four – has the proper crop. *He has to do something about the hair.*

The Sloane Rangers

Harpers & Queen, October 1975

Two girls get into the Tube at South Ken and sit opposite me. They're not together. They both wear: Gucci shoes (navy); a navy blue skirt, navy tights, a printed shirt (Cacharel, or Jaeger?), a jacket (one has a velvet blazer, the other a wool blazer), a Hermès scarf knotted under the chin (one's is knotted on the point of the chin), a small patent shoulder bag on a gilt chain. One has another scarf knotted through the chain. Their hair is straightish, shoulder-length, pushed back. One has a velvet headband.

They don't look at each other – don't even rake each other up and down. If this is a sisterhood I want to know how it's acknowledged. I imagine myself leaning over and saying, 'Look Caroline, there's Caroline.' I imagine both saying 'Really, where?' They are Sloane Rangers and Sloane Rangers are famous for reliable responses. Sweet girls, if a little . . . predictable.

The Sloane Rangers, usually known by other regiments as the Headscarf Brigade or the Knightsbridge Knotteds, after what they wear on their heads, are a cavalry regiment. 'She looks marvellous in uniform.' They are the nicest British Girl. They wear Gucci not because they want to seem international girls, Eurogirls, but because there's something archaic, pageboyish, about them; and Hermès scarves because they too are archaic and unmistakable and really no more French than a picture of the Sun King in a history book. They like navy blue because it Always Looks Good. But on the basic uniform there are always decorations of snaffles, curb chains, stirrups or other reminders of the country, where they grew up. When the uniform's right it looks very good. It has to be right or it can seem boring, even sleazy. Good shoes are worn too long.

After the Queen closed her doors in 1958 to girls wanting to be presented, the ladification business, instead of declining, became a growth industry fuelled by successive waves of New Money. The girls' Sandhursts had never had it so good: Winkfield, Mrs Russell's, the Cordon Bleu. After the passing-out parade, Sloane Rangers look for jobs in their preferred firms: Sotheby's and Christie's (art without artiness), the merchant banks (a young Hambro or Fleming), Knight Frank & Rutley, John D. Wood or another good estate agent, J. Walter Thompsons, C.A.P., Vernon Stratton or Rupert Chetwynd (some advertising agencies are just too pop-y), directors' lunches (good for a giggle), Bond Street galleries (Cork Street's wares are not so sympathique).

But in the sixties, a host of slightly similar organizations – fringe banks, property companies, travel agencies, P.R. firms – were setting up smooth new offices in the West End and the City. Art dealers were multiplying, advertising billings were up. Men who had made it in ten years wanted girls who added tone and authority to the business: well-bred colleagues, prestige secretaries.

The Sloane Rangers always *add tone*. They never put on prole accents, like self-conscious Oxford boys in the sixties.

Their way of talking, behaving, is always crisp. Their way of dressing is always crisp: they wore in those days tweed, cashmere, pearls and a Jacqmar scarf with a racehorse on it. They are never pretentious or ingratiating, like many of the new businesses who were using them as totem Upper Class.

In fact, Sloane Rangers, as a group are more likely to be upper middle-class. They are not conspicuously smart, not regulars in the social pages. They come from manor-houses, farms, and Army and Navy backgrounds – the daughters of colonels and admirals, whose naval crowns, crossed lances and so on they often wear. Of course they would never talk about class, except to suggest that certain sorts of people would really *rather* do different things – like eating packet food and spending their money on holidays.

All Sloane Rangers are ladies, but by no means all ladies are Sloane Rangers. In 1967 and 1968, a great many young People Like Us deserted Us for the style of their own generation: went in for higher education, became actresses or social workers or counter-cultural. Good sense itself was threatened by mind-expanding drugs. Bells were even heard in Jermyn Street and Ovington Gardens for a while.

The Sloane Rangers, however, were the crack corps who knew the form and could be expected to bear the burden of the defence. The flower people beat a retreat, and the Sloane girls came back stronger than ever. The early seventies was the new rational Age of Extravagance when people were greeting the Return of Elegance, Back to the Classics. Suddenly other groups took up what had always been exclusively the Sloane Ranger style. French and Italian designers re-did the skirt and scarf. Magazines ran articles about the 'Rich Girl Look' or the 'Jet-Set Look' or 'Paris Shows Le Style Anglais'. The Sloane Rangers themselves took to the French and Italian designs with enthusiasm. And perhaps they got slightly swept away by the convergence with themselves of the jet-set. Anyway, they became not only more chic but also more recognizable. People started getting a bit irritated by them, started talking about them as a breed, the headscarf brigade.

Then came 1974. As the great job cut-down began, employers were galled by the Rangers' British amateurism, by their unspoken feeling that one has a private life and one always has one's hair properly done on Friday if one is going to a dance, and catches the 4.40 for the country. The Sloane Rangers know that typing speeds really don't matter all that much. But they can do shorthand. Sometimes they found themselves in the *wrong* office – the kind of office where some-one wanted them to type with a machine in their ears, messing up their hair. When the Sloane arrived and was shown the machine she would say she had never seen one before; she didn't *do* audio. Someone would patiently explain to her how simple it was, which knobs to press. She would wait, smiling thinly, until the demonstration was over and then repeat: 'I don't do audio.'

The prestige office world had been hit rather harder than the rest and the art trade had a nasty drop last year. There are other attacks on the nice Sloane girl: higher education for one – or rather the idea of higher education, and T-shirts and *Time Out* and Chou en-Lai. There are now so many ways that a Sloane Ranger could be lured and tempted into leaving the Army. Once a Sloane marries and moves to Kennington and starts learning sociology through the Open University, she is off the rails. And once she flirts with Euro-style, has her hair streaked, goes out with Italians instead of nice boys from Lloyds, she is off the rails on the other side.

Sloaneness, some people would say, is a track to be liberated from. Most Sloane Rangers however, are perfectly happy. They love a giggle, a bit of a giggle, and they manage to find it most days. And they really like the classic. They have certain *sayings*. About clothes, for instance: 'I like to keep up to date, but I wouldn't like to look . . . well . . . way out. I think it's appalling, when people just look at your clothes.' About politics: 'A lot of Labour people are stinking rich anyway.' 'I can't bear to watch Harold Wilson on the telly. He's just so evasive, he's an absolute fox.' 'Keith Joseph's a bit of a drag.' They haven't a big vocabulary, though they heighten the effect of their few adjectives by exaggeration – 'the most', 'utterly', 'riveting', 'spastic', 'blissful', 'draggy'. They don't need to be wordy. So many things are understood.

The less important the matter, the more they exaggerate. 'The most ghastly thing – the fridge isn't working.' But a broken neck is 'rather a bore'.

They always call things or people they dislike boring, 'a bit of a bore'. Strangely enough, this is exactly what the outside world says of the unevolved Sloane Ranger. But the outside world is careless, amusement-sipping, whereas the Sloane Ranger is highly trained in a general way, a disciplined girl ready to go to some frontier.

The habit of discipline can lead to being led . . . is this the hanging and flogging brigade, potentially? Private Army types? Certainly not. These girls are truly good-hearted, and, always, sensible. They are the marrow of Britain, willing to have a go.

The goal of a Sloane Ranger isn't necessarily marriage. They are enterprising – starting businesses, going to Canada for two years. But most of them do get married. (They are what is called marriageable.) A Sloane Ranger meets men (to add to the boys she grew up with) at the many drinks and dinner-parties she gives and goes to, or on skiing parties. Her phrase is 'lots of sexy men'. These men are in the Army, or Supertravel, or just out of Cirencester, or in the Middle Temple, or a management consultant, or on *The Times*, or in the Conservative Research Department. They are *nice* men. These nice girls might hanker for, or go out once with, a jet-setter or a 246, but it's not really their style. (The 246s wear those caps and drive MGs and TRs and Dino Ferraris, the Ferrari 246. One of them came up to Stirling Moss at a Cygnet Ball and said, 'I say, what do you make of the 246?' Stirling Moss has used the line ever since.) Sloane Rangers are funny about sex, or, more correctly, they are strictly motivated towards marrying well. So those who don't marry immediately, or (nowadays) have a three-year relationship with a man, might do it, but some of them are rather hot on technical virginity. This brings all sorts of new skills into play, since they are not keen to seem unsporting or old-fashioned.

At evening parties, they wear long print dresses from Valerie Goad with a lot of front showing (their generous bosoms are one of their best features. Not for them the summer's bra-less T-shirts). With the Valerie Goad frock, they might wear a velvet choker. The look they are going for is somewhere between Tom Jones and Georgette Heyer. They are keen on Georgette Heyer.

Otherwise they don't read much – the Personal Column and the Angélique books and things like *The French Connection* and *The Day of the Jackal* two years late. They always put Krook Loks on their minis. Nowadays many have a bicycle instead.

They seldom wear scent. If they do it's Calèche or Miss Dior.

Before marriage they share flats in S.W. (except a few in W.8) – S.W.3, S.W.1, S.W.7, S.W.6, S.W.5 or S.W.11, in that order. They like Georgian and Regency things, those which are unexceptionable and bland. They admire, but do not really like, the extreme or baroque like the Royal Pavilion. They tend to make their houses ever so faintly bijou, like doll's house versions of stately homes. (They are uncertain about the meaning or spelling of the word Bauhaus.)

A Sloane Ranger is almost certainly looking for a tall, dark, handsome man, actually the same sort of man as her mother found: safe, reliable, amiable, Protestant, dependable, with a bit of money of his own, and the brother of another Sloane. She finds him, a landowning farmer in Cheshire, who trades in his racehorse to marry her. They get married surrounded by bridesmaids, and are given hunting-scene table mats and silver pheasants and things from her list at General Trading and Peter Jones. She gives him a gold lighter with his initials on it.

This is where she goes off to her posting on the frontier.

She has mahogony dining-room furniture and Peter Jones kitchen chairs. Her husband drinks a bit too much and she soon has a son called Charles who is down for a decent school and she runs a largish house without enough help and still gives super dinner parties and has the Lord to tea after hunting or shooting and her still unmarried Sloane Ranger friends to stay. She will teach Charles, Emma and Lucinda about standards.

You will not get anyone to *admit* belonging to the Sloanes. Some have even adopted mufti (jeans). But nobody need feel ashamed of being a Sloane Ranger.

SLOANE RANGER HEROINES

Princess Grace of Monaco, the Duchess of Kent, Lady Churchill, Princess Alexandra, Lady Elizabeth Shakerley, Margot Fonteyn, Lady Jane Wellesley, the Begum (Sally) Aga Khan, Celia Hammond.

SLOANE RANGER PET HATES

Princess Margaret, incense, Norman Mailer, *Interview* magazine, Vanessa Redgrave, Alice Cooper, Harold Wilson, queers, Wedgie, Ted Heath, football, intellectuals.

SLOANE RANGER QUARTERS

Cornwall Gardens, Cadogan Square, Cadogan Gardens, Pelham Crescent, Onslow Square, Onslow Gardens, Ovington Gardens, Pont Street, Walton Street, Ennismore Gardens, Egerton Gardens, Thurloe Square.

WHERE THEY LUNCH TOGETHER

The Petit Café in Stratton Street, La Campagnola (Lucansville), the Loose Rein, the Dress Circle in Harrods, Cranks, Fenwick, the Spaghetti Houses, the Granary, the Loose Box, anywhere in South Molton Street.

SLOANE RANGER COUTURIERS

Belville-Sassoon (especially for wedding dresses), Gina Fratini.

SLOANE RANGERS CARS

2/Lieuts: mini, Fiat 500 or 127. Lieuts: M.G.B.G.T., Scimitar. Capts: Volvo, Alfa Sud. Majors up: Triumph 3000, Saab, Rover 3500, Range Rover, B.M.W., Peugeot.

SLOANE RANGER DECORATING

Elizabeth Eaton, Designers' Guild, Hammond's, George Spencer, Peter Jones, Brother Sun, Nina Campbell, Parrots, Treasure Island, Laura Ashley, Home Decorating, Casa Pupo.

SLOANE RANGER CATERERS

Searcy's, Robin Brackenbury, Mrs Payne, Party Planners, Justin de Blank, Cordon Bleu friends.

SLOANE RANGER ENTHUSIASMS

Cocktail parties, house parties, skiing, Scotland, thrillers, Pimm's, point to points, Goodwood, blanquette de veau, Annabel's (sometimes called the Bells among themselves), Hickey, fine art courses, contact lenses, *Watership Down,* Floris pot-pourri, Raffles.

SLOANE RANGER MUSIC

Early Beatles, Neil Diamond, Georgie Fame, Barry White (they think he's black and funky), Juliana's discotheque, the Dark Blues, Nilsson Schmilsson, Bach, John Denver, Stevie Wonder, Vivaldi, Frank Sinatra, Andy Williams, ballet music.

SLOANE RANGER SCHOOLS

Cheltenham, Downe House, Benenden, Wycombe Abbey, St Mary's Calne, Tudor Hall, North Foreland, St Mary's Wantage, Heathfield, St Maurs Weybridge, Battle Abbey, St Mary's Ascot, Heathfield. Not Cranborne Chase! Not Dartington Hall!! Not Bedales!!! (disturbing places).

SLOANE RANGER ACADEMIES

Queen's Secretarial College, Byam Shaw Art School, Constance Spry Winkfield, Mrs Russell, Cordon Bleu School of Cookery, the British Institute in Florence, Eastbourne School of Domestic Economy, Beech Lawn, the Oxford & County Secretarial College, ('the Ox and Cow'), Madame Havel-Dare, Look & Learn, Lucie Clayton, St James's, Brillantmont in Lausanne.

SLOANE RANGER TREASURES

A good key-ring, a Gucci felt bag, a King Charles spaniel, a Smythson diary, Ken Lane chunky ear rings, pearls restrung at Jones, a Yorkshire terrier, a valid cheque book, an Asprey's address book, a signet ring.

SLOANE RANGER HOLIDAYS

Chalets, villas or relations in Val d'Isere, the Algarve, Florence, Bembridge, Greece, Scotland, Cornwall, Gstaad, Zermatt, Sardinia, Kenya.

MEN SLOANE RANGERS LIKE

Prince Michael of Kent, Robert Redford, Simon Ward, Peter Jay, Dudley Moore, Illie Nastase, Colin Davis, Peter Sellers, the Vestey brothers.

MEN WHO LIKE SLOANE RANGERS

Peter Sellers, John Anstey, Stirling Moss, Tommy Sopwith, Prince Charles, Nigel Dempster.

RANGER SECRETARIAL AGENCIES

Norma Skemp, Senior Secretaries, Masseys.

SLOANE RANGER TRAINS

On Fridays: the 16.48 to Cheltenham, 16.40 to Hampton-in-Arden, 16.36 to Horsham, 16.46 to Lymington, 16.20 to Tunbridge Wells, 16.00 to Edinburgh, 16.53 to Newbury, 16.30 to Westbury, 16.38 to Gillingham, 16.50 to Woodbridge.

HONORARY FOREIGN RANGERS

Queen Anne-Marie (Greek squadron), Lady Porchester (U.S.), Princess Mary Obolensky (Imperial Russian), Mme Giscard d'Estaing (French).

This piece helped start the second great Class Boom. People took it very seriously. A lot of checking out went on against the lists and it set me wondering about what I call Wasperanto, the language of things mutually understood. You really only get it in this country and north-east America, though they try in Australia, etc. It's all about a very subtle responsiveness to certain class sounds and, like those dog whistles, *it's out of human hearing*. Accent is the thing, particular tones of voice, a certain palette (faded), some smells . . . they know where they are. Summoned by bells.

It isn't what it was of course. There are too many options around. It's difficult to square things up when you've got King Khalid's brother – who is undoubtedly an aristo – living in *Stanmore*.

It's very American, very Seventh Avenue and Women's Wear Daily, this habit of talking about groups and naming them and that's where I got the idea. The fact that it's caught on here in a big way shows that things are changing. People *aren't* that secure, and the whole spate of 'society' cheque-book journalism – Dirty Dai in the *News of the World* etc. – shows you how Class Traitor-dom is big business.

Sloane Ranger Man

Harpers & Queen, March 1977

I am in the San Martino in Walton Street with a woman dress designer. Opposite us is a table of eight very big boys. They *all* wear pin-striped navy blue suits, the trousers with turn-ups, narrow at the ankle but loose around the seat, and Bengal-stripe red or blue and white shirts. Two of the striped shirts have detachable white collars. The plumper, blander four wear black oxfords. These have specs and look like lawyers. The other four wear Gucci loafers – the plain kind, without the red and green ribbon. They *march* across the floor, snap to attention, slap each other, horse around. One says of another that he's the best mucker he ever had.

They start laughing and don't stop. The wave goes round the table. The Italian waiters laugh too, faking it that they've caught the wave. The youngest waiter, obviously new, can't believe it. He's giggling and sniggering *at* the Sloane Ranger boys openly. The others push him back into the kitchen.

Then the boy nearest us falls over in his chair. The pine alpino chair overbalances, and he goes flat on his back, still in it. He isn't hurt, he's a big healthy chap, so he waggles his feet in the oxfords with the dark grey ribbed socks concertina'd round his ankles. The wave goes round again. The staff ignore it this time – they're used to this kind of stuff. Having discovered the trick, this boy repeats it regularly; they'll just be talking and – whump – over he goes, and the other Sloane Ranger men have these braying very ci-vi-lized conversations with the horizontal Jamie. My companion, severely chic, not young, who lives for changes in style, can't take her eyes off them. '*I hate them,*' she says. 'I *hate* them.'

Fashion people generally do hate Sloane Ranger men (so do

aesthetes and socialists and intellectuals). They think of them as boring, and all the same. There they are, talking to each other in that accent and that language. Sloane Ranger men speak Wahwah, their expression for their particular hooray tone of voice. They call non-U people charlie. They call weekends play-aways, drinks snorts or big wets, whisky nut-browns and gin and tonic Ranger's Delights (since October 1975 they've registered their new name. They used to be called Hooray Henrys or, by Mayfair Mercenaries, Right Nigels). They build one a drink rather than make one a drink. They call pound notes pondos, greenies, crispies or vouchers (drinking vouchers if in the pub). Those lads who come up to their standards of fun are known as players. Those who don't are kicked out to touch.

Like their girls, they don't need a big vocabulary as they speak in a code mutually understood. They try to make it more effective by exaggeration and repetition. 'The hotel was utterly ghastly. *Utterly* uncivilized.' For more serious mishaps, understatement is in, a military atavism. (They all saw *Bridge over the River Kwai.*)

While the world, the Cortina-driving, systems-analyzing, Euro-salariat, Honda and Colonel Sanders world rushes by, these boys continue lifting their eyes to the hills, to the Real Thing. The Queen herself is the Colonel-in-Chief of the Sloane Ranger men, and not only because she's boss. After all, who did she marry? What are her children? Who did her daughter marry? S.R.M., S.R.M., S.R., S.R.M., S.R.M., S.R.M. The Queen's all right. S.R.M.s are actually courtier types, for all their heartiness. They are very keen on royalty and titles. They represent what could be called the Brideshead syndrome, the thousand-year infatuation of the English upper middle-classes for what it imagines is the style of its betters – which is still, as in 1067, the Norman horseman style.

People in the real world, in Sutton Coldfield, in departments of sociology, suppose that the Sloane Ranger man they see in Osbert Lancaster or films about the army is an obsolete caricature. But the group is still amazingly intact, marooned in a curious time warp. From Dr Arnold of Rugby (1795–1842) on, a group man was produced by prep schools, public schools and the Army to run colonies and things and win wars. A man who knew the form.

Sloane Ranger men think that *knowing the form* still counts, having failed to observe how few recent big-time successes have cared to know *that* form at all. By keeping together they ignore the real social changes of the last ten years. If you ignore it, it'll go away.

What exactly *is* the form? That's no longer sure. But the S.R.M. tries to find out and then sticks to it like a book of rules. A hostess writes: 'I gave a dinner party for twelve. Every single man wrote a thank-you letter but only a few girls bothered to telephone.'

'Yes,' says a less friendly observer. 'They are assiduous writers of bread-and-butter letters.'

The fact is, Sloane manhood cannot be strictly defined. There are general qualifications of private education and the Queen's English, but S.R.Mhood is a state of mind. A public schoolboy can be all sorts of things other than an S.R.M. If you're one it's because you want to be. A man can get out by becoming too well-educated, specially at a plate-glass university (an S.R.M. pet hate is Lord Melchett, who went to Keele for his M.A.). He can make too much money (Pretty Boy Bentley was a normal Harrow lad until, *on, up and out* – Cannes and Mynah Bird and Vivienne Ventura). He can be influenced by the wrong job, when you rub up against oiks; or the wrong wife. He can smoke too much grass. He can even take a liking to the modern – to towns and modern architecture.

Like their female counterparts, S.R.M.s take reference at every point from the country. There are country references in the weekend gear worn in the Fulham Road, in the atavistic (or new-found) affection for houses that are large, old and draughty. In the appreciation of dignified putrescence in game, cheese and socks. They like or will watch *things equine*. They have hunting prints on the walls and on the table mats. By no means all of them have been on a horse but they all stand as though they had a good seat. They shoot – or any any rate identify with the real guns.

Cradle to country churchyard

Or, as S.R. families call it, hatched, matched, dispatched. Sloane Ranger men usually show their stripes at about sixteen. Affecting eighteen, they stay with an aunt in Cranmer Court or Chelsea Cloisters for a few days at the beginning and end of the holidays. Or they arrive on day pilgrimages from Newbury, Basingstoke, Horsham, Tunbridge Wells. Sloane Square is their Mecca. Junior Sloane Ranger men are the urban form of the unreconstructed public schoolboy. They are as keen to be in London as their seniors are to get to big country houses. They hang around Smith's basement record department, carry their suitcases to Harrods and queue for a cup of coffee in Way In – all the while looking out for friends from Oundle, St Mary's Wantage, Harrow and St Michael's Petworth. They want to go to an S.R.M. pub. But pubs open at 5.30 and the J.S.R.M.'s train to Kent leaves forty-two minutes later from Victoria or Waterloo. Hassles with mother on the telephone. She mentions the 'spoiled dinner' and goes on to 'Where are you staying? Is their mother or father in London too? How can you when you haven't got your pyjamas? Well, we're very cross.'

After school, S.R.M.s try to move on to the deb scene. They love all cocktail parties and dances and balls (called bollocks), and are very competitive about engraved invitations. They try to be on Peter Townend's list, the man from *The Tatler* who seems to run the young men 'coming out' side of things. They say they don't like him because he's common, but they're very two-faced about it.

Most of the clever ones go to Oxbridge, where they aim to belong to the Pitt Club and the Beefsteak or the Bullingdon. They always have a car – a V.W. or an M.G.B. They are all very keen on being in the shinies (Jennifer, *Tatler*) but are secretly scared of Nigel Dempster and the *Mail*.

While at university, they are responsible for a good deal of archaic heartiness. One smashed four thousand eggs with his friends in Oriel Square in Oxford on his twenty-first birthday. Another removed all the garden gnomes from suburban houses in Salcombe. A third group of night workers cemented up the door of a pub they didn't like.

Most don't get educated. They are the public school proletariat. Their main university is Sandhurst.

S.R.M.s talk about money all the time (but call other people who do vulgar). It's an orgasmic macho subject with them. However, they're shy of taking jobs in commerce (very few work in the big retailing groups) or in industry, which actually produces the stuff. They want it to be *old* money and they want to marry it, or get it, untainted – cleaned by the magical laundry of the Stock Exchange. They don't fancy 'selling brushes'. (In youth, they have, of course, all sold toys in Harrods or aprons in the General Trading Co. or Peter Jones – anywhere where Mummy had an account – or worked in the Post Office, good fresh air, at Christmas.)

They go, above all, into the City – the magic words are Lloyds, or a merchant bank, and failing those, a chartered accountants or stockbrokers. But the City is that much more competitive now than when their fathers went into it – full of outsiders. Rangers now have problems with the job market. Their style works against them. One management consultant (headhunter) told me that Rangers looking for jobs outside the net were coming up against employers who felt they wouldn't buckle down and might not mix. In fact they do work, most of them, and do their best to mix. Their verbal xenophobia (of oiks, peasants, huns, nips, gollies or nignogs, hook-nosed gentry, dagos, frogs and wogs) is more style – a pastiche of their fathers – than substance, because when they come up against these people (not often), they tend to behave quite decently.

Part of the difficulty they have with personnel directors and managing directors is the thinking, fashionable since the early sixties, that it's important to be clever and qualified. This rather puts a damper on all those *intangible* qualities of character – integrity, honesty, loyality etc. – to be discerned from vowel sounds alone. Modern managing directors ('chief executives') seem to have rather lost their ear.

Many Sloane Ranger men are emigrating to America because they see no future here as a stockbroker. They go off to try the Chicago Corn Commodity Market or Wall Street.

Sloane Ranger men also go into the law, into wine merchanting (the last gentleman's profession) and the O.K. brewers, and into estate agents and estate management. Some have trained at Cirencester, because they have farms to run, but far fewer have farms to run than you might imagine.

S.R.M.s are verbal M.C.P.s, anyway till they get married. But they are very sentimental. They fall in love a lot as bachelors and get hurt a lot. They love their mothers, sisters, dogs, war poets. They always visit their old nannies at Christmas. They call their mothers Mummy, Mum or Ma, and refer to them when with friends as Old Wrinkly or the Aged Bat. Some S.R.M.s ring their aged bats up in the small hours to tell them they are pissed. Mummies love it.

They drink a lot, particularly the idle squadron called 'the Lads': headquarters, the Australian pub in Milner Street. The answer to the question 'How are you?' is often 'Feeling a bit silly' (has a hangover). Waking up to a hangover is 'going through the pain barrier'. 'I went over the hill in a very senior way' – got drunk.

When the Australian closes, or the cocktail party finishes, or the dance becomes too boring, the Lads go to Françoise (Frankie's), opposite Peter Jones, or Raffles, in their Fiat or Mini. As they drive home, stereo blaring 1965 Rolling Stones or the band of the Blues and Royals, they are stopped by the police. They get breathalyzed and are taken off the road again. This makes a welcome change of topic at the Australian, which is getting a bit bored with hearing about the usual day when they did sod all and night when they rogered a new deb.

As for marriage, S.R.M.s want if possible to *move up a notch*: a Ranger with a handle..A girl who knows the form and helps the Old Wrinkly with the washing up and asks what to do with her bed on Sunday. The ideal deb has a father with a big estate, is fond of animals and will raise a few children (howlers or kiddi-winks) and not run out of cheese (from Paxton and Whitfield) or walnuts.

S.R.M.s lust, of course, after Mercs and at some point might have a crack at a trainee Merc, but in general, Mercs make them nervous. But most terrifying of all is the Home Counties girl. She sends their mother's warning, N.O.C.D. (not our class, darling) into their heads. An S.R.M. I know got seriously involved with a girl from a large stockbroker mansion in Guildford. She was very pretty and astonishingly good at it – new party tricks – and they were richer than his family, but something about the Maples ormolu and the father's vowels worried him. He never dared take her home to Gloucestershire (where, like most S.R.M. families, they lived in an old rectory).

After he marries Caroline, the S.R.M. begins to put on weight and life is rather hard. The cost of the basic upper middle-class London life goes up and up. Ten thousand goes nowhere, with one child at prep school and a Volvo or B.M.W. to run and a bit of private medicine and decent shoes. The Sloane Ranger pair in their little house in Pimlico or near Hurlingham give candelit dinner parties for their muckers with *Sunday Times* food, the good silver coasters reflected in the Peter Jones repro, talking about cars, prep schools, shared holidays in the nice part of Majorca, au pairs, *not* the arts. . .

The general feeling about the arts is that their finest flowering can be seen in the grander English country houses. It is called Georgian, or eighteenth century, and nothing worth having has happened since. Luckily, one can buy reproductions.

Art at auction is much more macho. Sotheby's and Christie's have a similar place in the pantheon to Berry Bros and Rudd. However, au fond, S.R.M.s feel that the life of the atelier or the conservatoire is the sign of a sick mind. They would far rather see *Murder at the Vicarage* than *Equus* (and indeed they'd *never* take Caroline to *Equus,* because you know what happens in that!)

It's amazing what they don't know. Like the judge who must have practised for hours before asking who Diana Dors was. And the more expensive life gets, the less they want to know. Their clever sensitive cousin who liked acting at school is now at the B.B.C., but we-live-in-different-worlds-I-don't-really-see-very-much-of-him. They have a curious Toytown

language to describe people and jobs outside the known world.
'Systems analysts' and 'social workers' are always mentioned
as though they had inverted commas.

S.R.M. kit has altered little in the last twenty years except
for the arrival of Guccis and jeans (worn with tweed
jackets – 'change coats') and the departure of the bowler hat.
In the country they wear Huskys (anorak art!) and flat caps
from Herbert Johnson (Herbie J). It is le style anglais but it is
totally different from what smart French or Italians do with the
same ingredients. Wogs look too elegant by half. What really
annoys the S.R.M., subconsciously, is that with foreigners it's
a look, not a badge of faith.

S.R.M.s assimilate some marginal trends, a few years late.
They are thinking about wider trousers now, and slightly fatter
tie knots. Some of course make a *point* of knotting their ties very
thin in the *old* way, just as snotty young S.R.M. lawyers carry
battered old brief cases.

S.R.M.s are ambivalent about the very rich, especially if
they are jet set (Gunther Sachs, Michael Pearson) or politicians
who say uncomfortable things (they are coming to dislike Peter
Walker as much as Ted Heath, as he takes up the baton of centrist Toryism), or arty, or Jewish. But the really vexed question
is the Home Counties – Sunningdale, Gerrards Cross, the
whole of Surrey. Every S.R.M. can pick out charlieness across
a crowded room. But the secret reason the S.R.M.s know and
hate the charlies is that they themselves usually come from
similar roots, though a generation or two back. The carriage-
lamp houses with fayke beames that make the Rangers shiver
are copies of the Ranger style which is a copy of the stately
home in Wiltshire built in 1760 with the proceeds of the
medieval equivalent of lawn-mowers. Oik into aristocrat.

Sloane Ranger men at the moment face the world with some
puzzlement. They suspect that solid worth is not being
recognized. And they have a point.

And while S.R.M.s can be noisy, snobbish and Philistine, in
the context of the international war of all against all, their faults
seem venial to say the least. They don't posture about things
that matter. They say 'ghastly' and 'civilized' too much, but

that's to be expected of the socially insecure. They may be moving rightwards through disgruntlement, but by many people's standards they are positively Socialist. They actually treat lesser breeds quite well. When they grow up, around thirty-three, they mellow into good husbands and fathers. They have a sense of humour. And who would you like to have behind you on the road when you break down?

Save the whale!

THE NAMES SLOANE RANGER MEN HAVE

S.R.M.s are called by 'plain English names' (their definition – actually, Norman Conquistador names), thus: Charles, James, Christopher, Richard, Timothy, William. See *The Times*. Never called Saxon (Harold) or Celtic names unless Irish or Scottish, and then few: never Kevin, Keith. Never called 'poncy' or N.W.1 names: Lancelot, Torquil, Jason, Oliver. Never called footballers' names: Bobby, Frank, Les, Terry, Dave. Nicknames are nursery 'ie' diminutives: Timmie, Jamie; or prep school surname nicknames: Smitty, Dodders, Tolly, Cobblers. Simon is now In, Mark out, Henry and William creeping back. Surnames: many S.R.M.s have brewers' surnames, but Farquharson is the ultimate. Failing that, a double barrel is convincing.

THEIR JOBS

Lloyds, merchant bankers (merchant wankers): Guinness Mahon, Kleinwort Benson, Warburg's, Hambros, Baring's. Insurance brokers: Sedgwick Forbes. Solicitors (but S.R.M.s don't like Divorce): Slaughter and May, Freshfields, Clifford-Turner. Barristers. Chartered accountants: Peat, Marwick, Mitchell. Estate agents: Knight, Frank and Rutley, John D. Wood, Hamptons. Farmers: Cheshire, the Shires. Stockbrokers. P.R.: new hotels and Grand Met chain and clubs catering for Arabs. The army: Guards, Greenjackets, 17/21 Lancers, Royal Hussars, Queen's Dragoon Guards (Mark Phillips' mob). Sherwood Rangers, H.A.C. In fact, any regiment that sounds as if it's either in the saddle or carrying weapons obsolete by the seventeenth century. But 'S.R.M.s haven't joined the army since the troubles in Northern Ireland,' says a critic. Wine trade: Peter Dominic, Morgan Furze, Justerini and Brooks.

JOBS THEY DON'T GO FOR

Theatre ('After all, you've got to be jolly good to get to the top'). Journalism ('Jolly hard work, and you might be invading someone's privacy'). Richard Compton Miller an exception to this. Advertising ('awfully spivvy'). Conservative Central Office (too intellectual). Civil Service (exams are too hard).

THEIR SCHOOLS

Eton, Harrow, Marlborough, Charterhouse, Gresham's, Stowe (for dud S.R.M.s), Downside, Ampleforth (for the left-footed), Rugby, Gordonstoun, Radley, Wellington, Oundle, Lancing, Fettes, Portora. *Not* Winchester (too intellectual) or Millfield (common) or St Alfred's (progressive).

THEIR UNIVERSITIES

Oxford (Christ Church, Trinity, rugger-bugger Brasenose, Magdalen, 'Teddy' Hall – 'Get your oar in'). Cambridge (Trinity, Sidney Sussex, Magdalene, Emmanuel, Queen's). Durham, Exeter, Bristol, Southampton, Edinburgh, St Andrews (which all have next-best social life and rich, clever girls).

FATHERS

'The Old Man'. Always treats his sons as adults, even in infancy. When son 16, father offers bribe not to smoke or drink until 21. Offer gracefully declined, as expected. Success rate only assumed among daughters.

HEROES

Military and Empire-upholding, i.e. Churchill, Mountbatten, Douglas Bader. Sporting and torch-carrying, i.e. Tony Greig, David Hemery. NOT John Curry. Men of action, i.e. Lord Hesketh, Freddie Laker, James Bond (and Odd-job – look what he did for the bowler), Humphrey Bogart, Freddie Forsyth. Bastards you have to admire despite yourself, i.e. Lord Lucan (they *know* he's alive), the Shah of Persia, Jimmy Goldsmith. Current fancies: John Cleese, Jamie Hambro, James Hunt, Muhammad Ali, Nigel Broackes. Fictional: Tigger, Tonto (preferred to the Lone Ranger because they can see all of his face; they hate mystery), Dan Dare, Inspector 'Give me a rheum' Clouseau.

HEROINES

Bombshells: Maria Schneider, 'Emmanuelle', Joanna Lumley, Joanna Shimkus, Angie Dickinson. Nice girls: Nicola Paget, Leonora Lichfield, Jilly Cooper, the Queen Mother.

LOVE-HATES

People 'on the box' (which they loathe, but watch furiously on Saturday afternoons after the pub): Dr Who, Eddie Waring, unfashionable football teams, i.e. Ipswich, Norwich; Angela Rippon (groan), Reggie 'Keep your hair on' Bosanquet. Off box: Mark Phillips, Heath ('at least he had the guts to . . .'), Bernard Levin.

MUSIC

Carole King or Genesis from girlfriend. Beethoven's Fifth and Ninth, Mozart's greatest hits, the Messiah, Vivaldi. Early Beatles, early Stones, Dylan, Elton John. They will 'discover' people the weary world has forgotten ('Have you heard this really good stuff by Mike Oldfield/Nina Simone?'). Grand March from Aida ('I'd like that at my wedding').

SLOANE RANGER MAN HUMOUR

They get a laugh from: old Tony Hancock and Tom Lehrer records. East Cheam is a spiritual home. The *Beyond the Fringe* crew (becomes helpless trying to splutter out the old jokes), and all the funny voices: Goons, Monty Python ('That parrot is dead'). Love *Dirty Linen, Gunner Rommel, Playboy, Private Eye* (they *say* the Grocer, never Heath). *Punch* (of which they must comprise 95 per cent of the readership). Pig French amuses them ('mercy buckets') and pig Latin.

EATING OUT

Go with muckers to: Mytton's ('Gloves'), Sweeting's, Simpsons (not in-the-Strand), Green Lion, Motcomb's, the Loose Box, Charco's. Sometimes Fortnum's, Sloane Wine Bar, Searcy's, Borshtch'n Cheers. *Taken by bosses to:* Scott's, Wheeler's, El Vino's, Le Poulbot. *Go in braying crowds to:* Drones, La Popote, Kalamaras, Bistro Vino, 19 (Mossop Street), Hungry Horse, Santa Croce, Daphne's, GAD, Charlotte Street Greeks, the Ark. There's nobody else in the Ark. *Take a woman to:* Ma Cuisine (where they discover gastronomy), La Croisette, Walton's, Poissonnerie de l'Avenue. *Taken by parents to:* Brompton Grill, Hyde Park Hotel. Stag night at Scott's. They go in for breakfast. Breakfast on wedding morn at the Connaught, of course.

PUBS

Admiral Codrington, Windsor Castle, the Australian, Finch's (Fulham Road), Duke of Wellington (Belgravia), Grenadier, Jamaica, Denmark, Hereford, Green Lion, Princess of Wales, Antelope (pronounced like Penelope), Marquis of Anglesey. Girls go to all except the Australian.

NIGHTS OUT

Raffles, Annabel's (the Bells, Mabel's, the Works Canteen), Françoise (Frankie's), especially among younger Rangers (who also go to Hatchett's). They long to know somebody who really is a member of Tramp. Charity bollocks. Scottish dancing at Wandsworth Town Hall.

TREASURES

Old Poohs and pandas they had at prep school, old school photographs, cricket cap/bat, grey plastic model of H.M.S. *Hood* stuck together at age nine when getting over measles (the UHU is still in yellow bobbles on the super-structure), pair of Purdeys given by godfather for twenty-first, flat gold cuff-links, Scalextric set, gold signet ring, grandfather's half-hunter, a stamp album. Love letters tied with elastic band.

WOMEN THEY LIKE

Mummy, Nanny, trainee Mercs, Hons and Ladies, girls with no discernible make-up, Hamburg women with lots of make-up, a girl who doesn't talk in the butts, 'a dumb bird who adores them'.

THEIR DOGS

Labradors, red setters (usually left at home with Mummy) called Stinker or Purdey. Pups then called Holland, Cogswell and Harrison. Springer spaniels called Cholmondeley (Chum) or Wellington (Boots), boxers. Some S.R.M.s run over cats on purpose.

FILMS THEY LIKE

They go to laugh, or to see a bit of action. Thus: Mel Brooks, Woody Allen, *Carry On, Pink Panther,* etc. And *King Kong, Raid on Entebbe, Straw Dogs* (howl with delight at the man-trap), *The Exorcist.* Wriggle and moan if dragged to foreign films. Wriggle and curse throughout *Death in Venice.* Girls take them to *Lady Sings the Blues* and *The Passenger.*

TRAINS

It's a fiction that they would not be seen dead on a train; at least, since the breathalyzer. Race train to Newbury, night train Inverness (they get off at Perth), picnic train Glyndebourne, Monday-morning Paddington, Waterloo.

LANGUAGE

They know they are damned for Hoorayness; they can still sound like caricatures of themselves in emotional extremis. Mark Phillips: 'I say, you know, a horse, I mean, is a very heavy animal, what?' after his wife's cracked vertebrae. Expressions (need to be read aloud with forced emphasis): EXcellent, a GAS, TOO RIGHT, ABsoLUTEly, a BIT of a giggle. Words: soggies (breakfast cereal), fast black (taxicab), a dinky (big car, say, B.M.W.), motoring racer (smaller car), greasy spoon (pub with food).

HOMING IN ON THE RANGE

Observers who have helped with research on the S.R.M. include Victoria Mather (chief reporter, S.R.M. desk), Nicholas Coleridge, Paul White, and 'A Lad', who wrote with Parker 51 on pages tied with a Gucci ribbon. (Will this writer please identify himself if he wants the odd greeny for his goonery.)

The
Mayfair Mercenaries

Harpers & Queen, April 1976

Written with Emma Soames

A Renault estate swings sharply into Berkeley Square at lunch-time, slamming Jasper and Oliver, the King Charleses, across the seats. It stops outside Morton's and a red-eyed Sloane Ranger gets out. Her brother Henry, decent stockbroker, stays in the car. Once inside, blinking against the unfamiliar in that state known as culture shock, she asks in a controlled tone if Mr Bignall-Price, her husband, is in the club. They are not sure, but they think he may be. She wonders whether to go further in, or have him called out. Her dilemma is solved by Jonathan himself coming through a door, dressed in jeans, with a girl so thin, so blonde, so brazen-eyed in her sunspecs, so generally *defined,* as to cause Caroline to lose her resolve and leave Morton's in front of them. She collapses into the Renault – while Jonathan and Linzi make a noisy exit in his new Porsche.

The streaked blonde destined to be known forever around Sloane Street as the girl who snatched Caroline's husband (*'literally* from the polo field at Cowdray') is a Mayfair Mercenary (also known as a Penge Pal or Chelsea Gobbler), a breed known for its voracity, its fun and guts; but mainly for snaring rich upper-class men.

It's not surprising they can do this. They are more attractive than the girls in the young men's own circle (particularly when

73

the young men have greying hair and thickening waistlines),
and they are *more relaxed* – it used to be only demi-mondaines
who were guaranteed to provide the ultimate in fun, but since
the sixties, the Mayfair Mercenaries and many other girls have
known there is nothing wrong in it. Only some Sloane Rangers
don't seem to have heard.

The Mercenaries, or Mercs, would have beaten the Sloane
Rangers in the sex war long ago, except that they weren't
allowed In Society. Then, in the classless sixties, they got in,
and are now seen everywhere except in the houses of the most
ancien régime. This isn't to say that they are the modern version of earlier sirens, different only in that they are admissible
and there are lots of them. They lack the weight (in both
senses) of the grandes horizontales (one cannot imagine a man
being ruined by a Merc). They lack the humour and honesty of
the good-time girls of the twenties and thirties (one cannot imagine a Merc being played by Ginger Rogers). Nor are they
hustlers (hustling is a downer – other people are hustlers), nor
kept women (kept women are old fashioned and the Merc
counts herself as modern and free). Mercs *live with* men. Mercs
are pals; mates; spontaneous; *fun*. The Merc is the apotheosis
of the semi-liberated woman.

In the fifties and early sixties, some men saw classlessness coming and introduced Society to its first Mayfair
Mercenaries. Some people consider that Tara Browne invented them, as he invented so many things, like long hair and
velvet suits. He liked these girls because they aren't disapproving. They don't ask impertinent questions like 'When are you
going to get a job?' or 'Why don't you get your hair cut?'
Michael McCreery was another who seemed to be able to make
Mercs into ladies. Lucian Freud, perversely, was making
ladies into what seemed more like Mercs in the same period.

The great Merc years were those of the King's Road. Their
high point was the property boom of the early seventies ('asset-
strippers' delights'). Life is harder for them now, but they're
resourceful – survivors. (Now of course they regard the King's
Road with disdain. They occasionally use its amenities but
their attitude to it is definitely de haut en bas. 'It's been

ruined.' 'It's draggy.' Gone are the Pheasantry, and that sixties mecca of the Chelsea Gobblers, the Aretusa.)

They are seen in Society now, but they are not part of it.
This is one of the fun things about them. Sloane Rangers have
so many Sloane Ranger friends, and their boyfriends were at
school with their brothers, and then comes the invitation down
to Clayshire on a non-shooting Saturday to meet Poppa and
Mummy and how do you get out of the whole entanglement?

But Mayfair Mercenaries don't have parents when they're
with you. Since they think like you think – a male, go-getting
philosophy adopted with the zeal of a convert at about fifteen – they know almost as well as you do that you don't want
to find yourself just good friends with the granddaughter of the
hall porter at Bratts. And they don't have girlfriends – they are
loners. Many of the top Mercs at the moment are foreign
anyway. They come from Somewhere in Germany, or
Nicaragua, or India, or Africa, or Scandinavia. Their origins
are glamorously obscure, unlike the Sloane Rangers, whose
background is boring, but impeccable in all those unfakable
details. The Mercs hate it when the Sloane Rangers and the
Sloane Ranger men start talking about Poohsticks and Mrs
Tiggywinkle and apple charlotte.

There *are* upper-class Mercs, Merc-hood being taken as an
attitude of mind, but the Mercs who *need* to climb look upon
their well-born rivals as little better than whores.

A native Mayfair Mercenary has usually been educated by
the State. She knows quite a lot ('She's too well-educated to be
well-bred'). But the idea of being someone in her own right did
not take on. Instead, she felt an unfocussed desire to be where
it's at. Later, she came to recognize how where it's at relates to
money. She began to understand the workings of fame, and
gave herself an exotic name, something ending in i or a, or that
could be a man's name – Vivian, Sam, Micki, Sasha. She
acquired a working knowledge of class; although she remains
equivocal about it (some Mercs have made a line out of
berating their man's anachronistic style even as they move into
Belgravia's antique embraces). She began to set herself targets,
and secretly fixed for marriage (for better, for richer, in health)

or something else really solid, though continuing to play the pal thing for all it's worth.

On the way up a Merc isn't a real careerist working in a job that makes demands. She is an actress/model rather than in the R.S.C., a receptionist rather than a P.A. She's in a beauty salon, the music business, fashion photography as an assistant, a press officer of one of the newer hotels which get lots of Arabs, the rag trade. Some sort of job is essential, both for amour propre and to fill in the lean times. Mercs don't have their own money. But they like a job with high exposure and low work content. A job whose *definition* owes a lot to the girl herself. These days, several Mayfair Mercenaries work for rich Arabs, doing their London shopping and so on.

The fact that Mercs are man-reliant, not self-reliant, terrifies the mothers of eligible sons and gawky daughters. Here they are, actually in one's own house, what one used to call little shopgirls, praising one's things to one's face, commenting on one's 'sofa' and 'drawing-room' in the capital letters of someone who until a year ago said 'couch' and 'lounge', and running their hands down one's son in full view of everyone on the walk back from church.

Mayfair Mercenaries don't like these family weekends either. They are town girls. They 'can hack' the very short country visit, just for the party – one night, or not a night at all. They like travelling by helicopter (especially Michael Pearson's helicopter) to someone's grand house for a really spectacular dance. They weren't really invited, but Simon brought them along. As the day draws on, they will sit at the end of a large room on the sofa, flicking through magazines, waiting.

The Mercs think their lives have moved forward man by man. If you are an old and trusted friend, she might show you the albums she has in one of the smart suitcases she takes round from flat to flat. First, there she is at a nameless school, now a comprehensive, in Chorleywood, or Didsbury, or Hatfield. A little out of focus, nothing special, hair darker; Kodak Instamatic. Next, eighteen, at an advertising agency party, blonde but still a little ordinaire, standing near the client, forty-five; Zenith. In the third, St Trop 71, she has, in her own phrase, got it together. She is thinner, blonder, browner, almost luminous, in large dark glasses; Pentax Spotmatic. She has met a man: in her view, her first man. They are on holiday *together*. His name is Bobby and she met him through the client in the earlier photograph, who is now a *pal*. From this point the photographs come thick and fast. There she is in a horizontally banded red fox coat at an airport, with capped teeth, on an Italian millionaire's arm. She is both photographed and photographer now; she does a little with a Nikon herself.

In maudlin moments, she will talk about Bobby as her only love. However, this is not her usual style; more commonly, she will refer to 'having a thing' with 'a guy'. He is her 'fella'. If the 'thing' lasts too long or becomes complicated, it will be described as 'heavy' or a 'heavy scene'. Merc language has a *period* flavour. It is a sanitized version of sixties drug and sex slang – 'getting a buzz', 'scoring', 'hanging loose', 'letting it all hang out' – with a few new expressions from Madison Avenue, like 'no way', and those words like 'loo' and 'what?' that seem to be what her fella prefers to what she used to say.

There she is, in her jeans – such well-cut, hand-ironed, heavily gauged jeans they look as though they had been made for her, fitting exactly her narrow, almost boyish hips (she wears no knickers with trousers – they spoil the line). Over the jeans she wears an extremely expensive French sweater. (Mercs diet *viciously*, are always scoring appetite-suppressants, and anyway haven't that English-rose pear-shape which follows good nursery food.) Her hair is streaked blonde (Mercs have decided that since they have only one life it should be lived as a blonde). Or henna red. Whatever it is it has been worked on and come out a success.

What the Mercs look like is what they are. They came in at the same time as the trendy hairdressers, in the sixties. Many of them actually got their first jobs in hairdressing, as Saturday shampooists in Chorleywood, or Didsbury, or Hatfield. Then when they left school they started in a small way as models. Photographers' studios and the fashion trade lead to knowing the gaiety, who are useful in their way: although Mercs, unlike some fascinaters, are not full-scale fag hags. The homosexuals

Mercs know actually buy many of their clothes for them, on trips to Paris or wholesalers in Milan.

Their little crowd pores over *Elle:* they are anti-British snobs. And the reason their clothes fit so well is that they all have a plain friend who takes everything British they buy to pieces and puts it back together stitch-and-seam perfect (the Mercs could do it themselves, having learnt Home Economics at school, but they're too grand by now).

At the beginning, the Merc's eagerness to get where the action is, to be in fantastic houses, at the most private parties and in the weirdest scenes, leaves her open to exploitation. In the longer term it makes her both more willing and more able to exploit. The technique of the Mayfair Mercenary can be stated in terms of her rules for herself.

Look good

Mercs are utterly professional at looking good (their much-tanned skin can look . . . *hard*'s the only word – and battered without their make-up, but when *are* they without it?). Their knowledge of cosmetics and skin care is encyclopedic, their fishing bags are full of tackle (also a toothbrush and toothpaste tube without a cap. Also a spare packet of the Pill). They are preternaturally fond of all-over sunbathing, and if they haven't had their quota, they substitute Guerlain's Teint Doré. They have been known to wear other things besides denims, such as Laurence Corner khaki shorts or a Yuki. They *never* wear freaky clothes like those art student types. They wear a lot of real gold, in chains, watches, rings etc. – too much, in fact.

Be fun

Mercs' fundamental assets remain tangible. They will minister to special needs. They dance extraordinarily well. There on the floor of Tramp's, both in their jeans, Jonathan will feel younger than he has for years. Drugs and their effects

are another Merc area of expertise. They know where to score
for you. In their flats you will often see rolled up pound notes,·
little spoons and torn away Rizla packets. Generally, however,
they steer clear themselves nowadays.

Teach fun

One Mayfair Mercenary is called Maggie the Mouth. Their
professionalism is daunting, so daunting that the target man
feels obliged to take the Merc to San Lorenzo and Tramp's; the
Sloane Ranger would be content to go Chinese round the corner. Continued friendship with a Merc may cause a man to
change his car. If it is his first such liaison, it may cause adjustments in his life. He will learn about bracelets for men, the
Philadelphia sound, the value of vitamin E.

This is the modern Mayfair Mercenary. The prototype
Merc-fancier of the early sixties saw himself as a Professor
Higgins, or even a purveyor of Mercs to the nobility and gentry. But whereas he taught the prototype Merc not to say 'ser-
viette' and hold her knife like a pencil, now the Mercs teach
men things and purvey themselves (Stephen Ward was one of
the earlier type, though the ladies he knew were not quite as
nice as Mercs).

Have male chums

Mercs know a lot of people whom they peck on cheeks, all
the while searching the room over their shoulder for someone
more interesting. They know a lot of men from twenty-five to
forty-five, all of whom they describe as boys. Though they do
not have women friends (or, perhaps, one successful fellow
Merc who is a semi-ally) you do sometimes see a group of successful Mercs lunching together, which is an impressive sight.
It used to happen at places like Mimmo's or La Popote, then
came Drones, then Morton's.

Be seen

Mayfair Mercenaries go to places with high exposure. If sixty per cent of their income is spent on clothes and make-up, the rest goes on taking themselves to the right places. If no one takes them, they go on their own. They are 'into' all the saints: St Moritz, St Tropez, San Frediano, San Lorenzo, Saint Laurent.

When she arrives at a restaurant, a Merc doesn't wait for her escort to open the car door, perhaps doesn't even wait for the restaurant door to be opened. She advances boldly, greeting the waiters by christian name.

At the table, she will drop a few foreign aristocratic names, and English aristocrats' and celebrities' nicknames, and perhaps recount something she's been to, with all the brand names: 'We had Beluga caviar, and Dom Perignon, and Roman was there . . .' Three people mentioned in most Mayfair Mercenary conversations, in London or New York, are Roman, Victor and Marisa.

But the Merc doesn't talk much on dates. the inexperienced man worries that he is boring her. She will not do it the first time out, for that would be literally to make herself cheap. Once the ice is broken, however, she is almost embarrassingly tactile. She is literally all over him. 'Let's leave the light on . . .'

Later, having no Sloane Ranger hang-ups about these things, the Merc may move in. 'They never ask,' said one Merc-fancier, 'but first there are flowers around, then your fridge is full of food . . . and then the Vuitton suitcases arrive.' If the man is a major catch (peerage for instance), her acquaintances will remark: 'Amazing!'

The Merc has a lingering fondness for aristocrats, although as money is the first quality, she usually finds herself with a would-be film director whose father makes electronic components. There are perhaps four aristocrats who also have the money and reputation she wants. Illogically, she yearns for the ladyhood of the Sloanes, the crippling boredom of whose lives she delineates amusingly. Once she has got a peer he will become an *invisible* aristocrat, except that everyone will know exactly who he is.

Mercs sometimes have their own flats. These are done up like restaurants, all cane and rattan and palms. The tiles are laid by a decorating contact. The loose covers are made by another less-pretty friend who once worked as a machinist. On off nights the Merc sits there, near the white telephone (though she is not intending to answer it on the first ring), flicking through magazines for the hair and make-up credits, waiting.

Sometimes, Mercs live at home between 'sharing an apartment with my girlfriend'. You see them waiting for the London train at Ilford and Great Bookham and Carshalton Beeches and Croydon. But unlike Sloane Rangers, who have a London and a country telephone number, you only ever get a London number from a Merc.

Men sometimes like to keep their Merc on in their flat, if they have several rooms, even after she has become a pal. Mercs are excellent housekeepers and of course decorative. They know about mange-touts. They always have plenty of liquor and Fortnum's tins in the fridge and can produce an expensive meal in no time. They don't mind seeing other girls at breakfast (that is, when it's over). One man kept a pal Merc on in his penthouse above Green Park, and lent her his Mercedes when he went away. When he came back she had smashed it up, but he only said, 'Never mind, darling.' That is the sort of man Mayfair Mercenaries like.

Knowing people as they do, Mercs hear about husbands and wives and friends and sleeping arrangements. Since they feel no loyalty to the families of their natural prey (their motto could be *No loyalty given or expected*), gossip columnists find them invaluable.

Not knowing the form, behaving badly, is one of the Merc's appeals. They are, for instance, honestly, paranoiacally jealous. They are the cast of those Nigel Dempster vignettes about confrontations in clubs. They enjoy fights and scratches. They table-hop, they call out to acquaintances, they are always moving. They will slash tyres in moments of excitement, or throw a man's clothes out of the window.

Tension can run high if a Merc wants your man. One Sloane
Ranger found herself up against a Merc on holiday. 'He was
very good-looking and rich, and I was being terribly cool about
the whole thing. Which was entirely the wrong thing to do,
because she was getting all the attention – she was bolder and
brassier and tougher than me. *She washed her hair every morning.*
She never ate a thing. So I fused her hairdryer – they get very
upset about that sort of thing. But she won. She made him
spend the whole day finding someone to fix it.'

Merc-hood has by now quite a well-trodden path to success.

Stage 1: Go blonde. First man.

Stage 2: First major move-in, new non-job.

Stage 3: Featured by William Hickey (brief write-up,
photograph) in 'Gobbler's Corner' – or even the *Sun*.

Stage 4: Mention by Nigel Dempster as 'constant companion' of significant figure.

Stage 5: Becomes generally known by first name alone.
'Nikki.' 'Nikki who?' 'Don't ask me.'

Stage 6: She has made it. She can now become either a fully-
fledged celebrity, like the recent escorts of a well-known finan-
cier, which will put her outside the limits of ordinary striving
Merc-hood, or she can become a companionable rich wife – a
sort of jet-set Worthington E person – or she can go one further
and become a ladyship; most terrifying of all, she can seem, to
everyone but the still-resisting ancien régime, a lady.

Most likely, however, she will then get divorced. As was
recently said of one sundering: '£250,000 – not bad for a begin-
ner.' The older type of Merc used to go in for several mar-
riages, like Mrs Storm in *The Green Hat*. The younger ones tend
to settle for one, as a rich man's second wife, without too much
to do for his children. Another outcome is for a Merc,
stimulated by money and success, to complete her evolution, to
become at last *someone in her own right*: a successful business-
woman for instance, with a couple of shops and something
sunk in property, her boyfriends becoming progressively
younger and younger.

Are Mayfair Mercenaries in fact old wine in new bottles?
Some are, some aren't, but Mercs aren't clear thinkers

anyway – something to do with the conversion to rich young men's values in their early youth. 'They're tarts and they don't know it,' said one photographer. 'Like alcoholics who don't know it.' There should be a list of questions like the ones to help you discover if you're an alcoholic or not. Do you dye any other hair on your body the same as the hair on your head? Does your underwear cost more than your outerwear? Do you keep champagne and a record player within reach of your bed? That sort of thing.

What a thing to say! Mercs are perfectionists. They try to perfect the moment and they work hard at the surface. Is there anything wrong with being good at things? And trying to increase the sum of good times? Anyway, they don't care what ordinary people think of them – they feel that the spirit of Bianca approves. Jonathan likes them even if old Lady Bignall-Price can't understand what the world's coming to these days.

Curled up on the sofas of the future, flicking through magazines, the Mercs wait.

SOME EARLY MERCS

Becky Sharp, Julie Christie in *Darling*, nearly all James Bond's girls, Rita Hayworth in Gilda, Josephine Beauharnais, Desirée, Lady Hamilton, Amber St Clair, 'My Lovely' in Peter Sarstedt's song.

MERC HANG-OUTS

In London: Morton's, Mimmo's, the Alibi, the Brasserie, San Frediano, Meridiana, the Clermont, Chelsea Rendezvous, Scotts with a man friend, Tramp's, Walton's, trichologists, manicurists, health farms, Dukes Parfumerie, the Factotum, Mr Chow's, the Montpeliano. In Paris: Régine's, New Jimmy's. In Madrid: the Jockey Club. In New York: Doubles, Le Club. In Los Angeles: the Roxy, the Rainbow.

MERC HAIRDRESSERS

Leonard's in Grosvenor Square, Ellishelen, Michaeljohn, Gotama.

MERC KIT

A ginger fox coat worked in horizontal bands, a wolf coat, a boiler suit, Y.S.L. blazer (nothing underneath), khaki shorts from Laurence Corner, jeans from Fiorucci, Jean Machine or Pooh, Sun and Sand T-shirts, Janet

Reger underthings, shoes from Chelsea Cobbler, Kurt Geiger, Maud Frizon boots, clothes from Browns, Jap (sparingly), Stirling Cooper, Missoni, Yuki, Bill Gibb, Elle shops, Ossie Clark, Janice Wainwright, halter necks, peeptoe shoes from Charles Jourdan, a Cartier watch, capped teeth, painted toenails, much Vuitton luggage and Fendi bags and a general impression of ceaseless travel, Gucci belt and wallet (in fact anything initialled V., F., or G.), Jones hoop earrings, roll-on lip gloss, Mary Quant mascara (waterproof, love-proof), a current passport in a Gucci case.

MERC CARS

Lancia, Porsche, Mercedes, Corniche, Maserati, anything white (such a good frame for a tan), a Mini-Moke.

MERC DÉCOR

Albrizzi, Bayswater rococo, Zarach, cane, chrome and anything else that would look good in a restaurant, Valentino's bamboo, new taps, Badedas beside bath, Rigaud candles, contemporary graphics framed in glass with chrome edges or clips, sexy drawings by Willie Fielding, huge photographs of lions or other wild animals making love (male's tongue sticking out), a photo of Them on the beach in Montego.

MERC SCENT

Calendre, Imprévu, Bal de Versailles, Fracas, Alliage, Chloe (any new one is a must), Monsieur by Givenchy, Vetiver by Guerlain (men's scent for during the day), Calèche, Y, and at a real pinch, Charlie.

MERC DRINKS

Dom Perignon (corny but true), Tequila, iced Perrier water, citron pressé, Bucks's Fizz (the first upper-class glamour drink they learn about, so they try to drop its name: 'I'd like a Buck's Fizz').

MERC HOLIDAYS

Marbella, St Tropez, Gstaad, Jamaica, Sardinia, Lyford Cay, Malta, Mombasa, Mauritius, Porto Carras, Rio, house-parties and yachts almost anywhere; but they draw the line at Scotland or Bembridge.

WHERE THEY LIVE

They prefer a cubbyhole at a good address to a palais in Hammersmith. Getting there: Prince of Wales Drive, Portman Square, Montagu Square, the Water Gardens, Fulham. Got there: Eaton Square, Eaton Place, Chester Square, Cadogan Lane, Markham Square, Cheyne Walk, Montpelier Street, Montpelier Place, Brompton Square, anywhere overlooking Green Park, anywhere off Berkeley Square (so convenient).

MERC PET HATES

Germaine Greer, attractive au pairs, all girls under twenty (especially if under twenty herself), the Pre-Raphaelites, point to points, horses generally, London in August, 7.30 a.m., opera, weddings, Customs officials, parking meters, traffic wardens, the Marx Brothers, the Paris Pullman, writing thank-you letters, prostitutes, trade unionists, parties in S.W.19, travelling by bus, his wife, his children, his mother, country walks, Sloane Rangers, Laura Ashley, fake gold, fake coral, fake tortoiseshell, Courtelle (Mum wears it), Festival of Britain décor, charades, criticism, discussions about ethics, discussions about socialism, evenings alone, Merc-fanciers who turn out to have little money, and even worse, who are not members of Tramp.

MERC HANG-UPS

His alibi; pregnancy; press-cuttings on his wife.

MERC ENTHUSIASMS

Keeping a diary (partly in code), yoga, Tarot and all other fortune-telling (Mercs are 'into' things), dancing, water-skiing, backgammon, swimming topless, riding bareback on beaches (usually purely verbal), *Lady Sings the Blues*.

MERC TREASURES

A gold Charlie Brown pendant, a crystal flower on a fine gold chain from Jones, Cartier gold love rings, a Tiffany gold or silver heart, Barry White's latest album, Hesketh racing stickers, real gold, real coral, real tortoiseshell, a gold cigarette lighter, the latest bestseller such as *Ragtime*, two telephone lines, a Shih-Tzu, a Lhasa Apso.

MEN MERCS WOULD LIKE TO GET TO KNOW

Michael Pearson, William Pigott-Brown, George Moreton, Gareth Browne, Spiros and Philip Niarchos, Jonathan Bulmer, David Davis, Rupert Dean, Dai Llewellyn, Willie Fielding, Jake Morley, John Bentley, Gilbert Lloyd, Richard Johnson, Piers Weld Forester, Rod Stewart, Alexander Hesketh, David Metcalfe, Lee Davies, Charles Benson, Roman (Polanski), Victor (Lownes), racing drivers.

MERC-OBSERVERS

José Olivestone of Models One, Jackie Collins, Chris Collins, Nigel Dempster, Richard Compton Miller, Jeremy Lloyd, Paul Callan, Mara of San Lorenzo.

WOMEN MERCS ADMIRE

The Duchess of Windsor, Pamela Digby, Nicole Nobody, Dewi Soekarno, Bianca Jagger, the Gabor sisters, Nicky (Samuels, Waymouth) Lane, Marisa Berenson, Aldine Honey, Caroline Cushing, Anita Pallenberg, Patricia Wolfson, Vivian Ventura, Anthea Redfern, Jackie Rufus Isaacs, Charlotte Rampling, Marjorie Wallace.

SPIRITUAL HOME

If Sloane Square is the spiritual home of the Sloane Rangers, Morton's is where all good Mercs go to when they're alone in their bed.

Now that was a very sixties/seventies thing, and although they're hanging on till grim death, I don't see another generation of girls making it quite like that; they'll want a bit more still out of life. Also, there's quite a big backlash coming up against the sixties glamourosi among the young.

New Model

Spectator, May 1976

Earlier this month Margaret Thatcher had her hair re-styled. Her familiar waves and the upswept 'wings' on either side disappeared to be replaced by an altogether smoother job, one which apparently caused cartoonists to complain that there was not much left to latch on to.

It was, for anyone who believes in the portents of small behaviours, a significant political act. Why did she do it? What does it *mean*? The *Daily Mirror* had a go at explaining it recently in one of their front page shockers, where they said that getting her hair done had been her only definite act since taking office. The implication, facetious as it might seem, was that Mrs Thatcher's presentation of self was somehow a cover up for a political vacuum, a standard politician's trick.

But it goes deeper than that. A change of hair*style* in the sense of a movement from one consciously created look to another has a powerful symbolism. To chart the move that Margaret Thatcher is making you need to understand the messages implicit in her original frozen fronds, and those in the new simplicity. You also need to ask what kind of a woman Mrs Thatcher really is.

The *old* hairstyle would have suited a rather kitsch rococo shepherdess. To be less fanciful it expressed – and was widely seen as expressing – the quintessential nature of Tory womanhood. It was hard and set and classy and old-fashioned and ceremonial. In its rigid 'femininity' it was a sort of hat substitute. In fact this is precisely what it was, because until very recently Margaret Thatcher was a *hat woman*; in this once again she conformed to the popular conception of a Tory *lady*.

If you were to do an association test on Mrs Thatcher with the average man or woman you would find replayed to you across the board all the clichés about twinsets and pearls, about well-bred women doing good works, about the opening of fêtes, about posh patronizing voices. The perspective would change according to the respondent. The more upper class the more likely he/she would be to identify her as middle-class and suburban; the more working-class you went the more likely you would be to find the image simplifying into one of irritating poshness.

The hair, like the hats, like the voice of Margaret Thatcher, is one of a series of mistaken signals. While to most people in this country Margaret Thatcher and Raine Dartmouth are practically sisters, Mrs Thatcher is not a *Tory lady* at all. She is a highly educated, highly intelligent upper working-class/lower middle-class girl of considerable application and resolve, a science graduate, a trained lawyer. In 1976 it is not insulting to suspect that if she were to complete a psychologist's masculine/feminine personality rating test she would probably register as having a strong, logical – in fact a *masculine* – intelligence. Equally, one might suspect that it is the traditionally 'feminine' qualities – impressionistic grasp, sensitivity in human relations – that she is short on. In other words, in neither of the archaic and now pejorative senses of the word is Margaret Thatcher a 'lady'. It is an interesting question therefore why she took on the protective colouring of a type of Tory womanhood that was fading even when she entered politics and interesting to speculate as to whether she did it consciously or unconsciously.

Did Margaret Thatcher just think that the suppression of a very considerable self was either a way to get on as a woman in the Tory Party, or was it that, at the grass roots, it was indeed the way to get on then.

That it was protective colouring is strongly suggested by the simple fact that in the sixties, when she herself was only in her thirties, she wore *flowered hats*. The same rigid suppression of self tends to show up in her voice, which is controlled to a degree; so controlled as to come out quite monotonous. She speaks in the tones of a woman who is finding it hard to control her irritation that other people are much stupider than she is. This is why she repeats things s-l-o-w-l-y and carefully. The net effect is one of immense care and precision; a place for every hair and every hair in place.

But winning the Tories and winning the country present entirely different problems. To win the country you have to project, in the words of the professionals, a more *inclusive* image. The very image qualities which served so well at the party grassroots are a positive burden at the top. With what distress must Mrs Thatcher's advisers and chartists have watched the centrist appeals of Shirley Williams; the image of a somehow classless, modern woman who is female without being in any ritualized sense feminine. A woman whom men might consider they would like to know as a *person* and of whom women, while tut-tutting about her untidyness, could remark approvingly she did not spend all day on herself. How they must have noticed her *hair,* falling untidily forward, *moving as she moved.* Mrs Williams is a woman who seems utterly without contrivance. How unfair, how much the usual paradox then that Mrs Williams comes from a comfortable upper middle-class background, while Mrs Thatcher comes from the hinterland which produced Heath and Walker.

When did Margaret Thatcher or her advisers grasp the nettle, realizing that Mrs Thatcher would quite literally have to *woo* the centre? If one were to trace the steps of the way Mrs Thatcher is being represented to the world one would have to go back to her triumphant progress – or so it was reported here – through America. This allowed Mrs Thatcher to appear on a world, rather than a parochial, stage. It allowed her to wear a black, merry widow sort of dress, which, while in no sense really see-through, was in fact rather attractive. Truth to tell, Margaret Thatcher is a very good looking woman. The hairstyle could be seen as representing the crowning move in this gradualist programme, for Mrs Thatcher is out to scotch the crisis of confidence among the Tories, she is out to answer the question of whether the Tories can ever govern again. Not, as yet, by means of a statement of intent but by the use of symbolic devices.

The new hairstyle is an upswept job without waves or curls, and swept back too; it suggests that she is a fairly determined figure looking into a gale. It is clearly more modern, more classless, but above all a more *active* looking sort of hairstyle. Rather like early streamlining, however, it *suggests* movement rather than actually moves. It is not, of course, in the least like Mrs Williams' Lib./Lab. flop, for that would be going too far. (But then, consider the fact that Mrs Williams seems recently to have gone in for a rather neater, shorter coif, somehow *tidier* and less inclined to fall around her face.) What Mrs Thatcher has taken up is a hairstyle of the early 1960s, instead of one better suited to a star of Gainsborough films. This hairstyle is one favoured by smart middle-aged ladies of a powerful kind, like Katherine Graham, Majorie Hurst of the Brook Street Bureau; it has power and authority without the deadly Tory overtones. It expresses the real Mrs Thatcher very much better than the original.

If anyone supposes this is fanciful, let him consider how they order these things in America. In America every major politician is surrounded by a circus of P.R.s, researchers, hairdressers, cosmeticians, and dental mechanics (how else to explain the acrylic bright-work and atavistic quiff that decorate Ronald Reagan's poor old face?). With that in view who, we might ask, debated Mrs Thatcher's change of style? Which of her advisers was called in on the job? What was the strategy brief they agreed on? Did the Research Department run split-run comparisons with Mrs Williams? Is Mrs Thatcher's P.P.I. (Personal Popularity Inventory) being monitored at this moment?

However, it seems quite straightforward and unconspiratorial. Michael Rasa of Michaeljohn (in Mount Street), her hairdresser, tells me that Mrs Thatcher simply came and said she was looking for something more *modern*; apparently she did not like herself as she appeared on television. She left – as all good managers should – the specifics up to Michaeljohn's specialist skills.

The problem for a woman politician in the West is to find an appropriate role at a time when all the prescribed role uniforms are in flux. Mother figures like Mrs Ghandi or the original Mother Courage, Golda Meir, aren't on, and nor are goddesses like Evita Peron. Mrs Thatcher can't stalk about in tennis shoes, or raise jewel-encrusted arms to the crowds. She has instead to compromise, to try and be *more* things to more people; in doing so, oddly enough, she has a better chance to be herself.

Gradually breaking free from the constraints of Tory ladyhood it looks as if she could become a real woman/person. The new Maggie is issuing an implicit invitation to Peter Walker – and perhaps eventually Jack Jones – to run their hands through the flaxen strands. The lady known for being far too precise in every part is trying to get away and do a bit of bewitching.

I've put back what the *Spectator* cut out. Patrick Cosgrove, who was deputy editor then, was very close to The Leader and I thought he'd censored it. Her position was a bit sensitive then. I could be imagining it, but they promised me they'd restore the cuts, but whole chunks disappeared and I thought, I'm not doing that again. There's no point in writing for those little magazines unless you can get what you want through – because they give you about £25 a piece.

Discontinued Models

London Collection Magazine, April 1978

Girl Model joke: First girl model to second girl model 'where did you get those Biba Boots?'

Boy Model joke: First boy model to second boy model 'where *did* you get that souwester?'

The first Trad Anon, told me by the first fashion photographer I met. The second, of course, is *Beyond The Fringe:* It was around 1963 that I first got the hang of the word. ('Good morning Miss Keeler and is your father still making his excellent marmalade?' Randy Mice-Davies, Swedish model, Swedish modern. French model second floor.)

Rather later I constructed a model joke of my own which ran roughly. 'I am model – show me your wallet' and had to be acted out in the Tarzan and Jane manner. This was silly stuff but it got me going.

Later still when friends of mine were starting to make a few quid as fashion photographers, I got to meet models. It was strange: after shoot suppers where everyone looked good, in fact looked how God meant people to be, a better configuration of limbs, superior fittings. The girls were raucous. The boys were the colour and finish of glazed carrots. This was the early seventies, the period of the Dancing model, the Tacky model, and Donna Jordan and Pat Cleveland, the Screaming models. This is the life, one thought. It wasn't.

Models themselves, I learnt, have an extraordinary set of rationalizations about the job: it's for the money; they're putting their husbands through college; they're learning archaeology by post. They seem vaguely ashamed of what they do, ashamed to admit to liking it. (It seemed like the life of Riley to me.) There's often an impression of excessive spiritedness, like off-duty nurses – scream and scream again. Models aren't dumb. Nor, usually, are they stupid, there is a real cleverness involved in understanding looks and presentation. If beauty isn't genius it usually signals at least a high level of animal cunning. This is why I like models better than actresses, who suppose themselves to be Artists and thinking women. Models talk about food, health, Health food, restaurants, parties, famous people, things that happen on sessions. Gossip stuff. Ambitious but usually unpretentious, save when they get onto the subject of the Designer as Genius. Then some of them go bananas, explaining and interpreting their heroes. . . 'Billy's really a very shy ordinary person – but I can talk to him . . .' 'Zandra's absolutely schizophrenic. . .'

But the best ones get on with the job, go to bed early, save their money, marry the proprietors of mini-cab firms and don't believe in *Superstars*. They settle down as anonymous unsung heroines.

The early seventies, in fact, was the beginning of the end. In the sixties, a model seemed a particularly exciting kind of person; by the later seventies she – it was mainly she – did not. Their role was analagous to that of, say, computer programmers or air hostesses; they were the visible face of a new industry. Models haven't been done away with – any more than air hostesses, but they are part of the furniture now, and Adel Rootstein has got the look off pat.

One day someone will make a documentary about the fashion industry in the didactic Soviet style, showing models as assembly line workers of the world. Because of course, the industry *is* massive, although its Great Leap Forward has come and gone. Fashion, like the music industry, is settling down to schedules and flowcharts. There is a devout wish to be boring in the air. Stodgy Chic Rules.

The other factor in the decline of what Jonathan Aitken called 'The cult of the Photogenes' in his *Young Meteors* (*very* 1967) is the general urge for fifteen minute stardom – which means a discontent at the idea of token people living out your fantasises for you. Modelling isn't enough when a girl could be a terrorist, a brain surgeon or a host on an intimate problems talk show on Capital Radio. The real emphasis in fashion today is on the *consumer as artist,* and the creation of what fashion writers call an individual look – a sort of manic eclecticism. Anti-fashion is, of course, a fashion in itself, and often drearily predictable, but it serves to mark the end of universal looks: (A lines, H lines) and the end of the mentality that could announce, as one fashion writer did of Twiggy, 'This is the face of 1966'. For 1978 you would need *at least twenty faces* for twenty separate but equal looks.

In *Harpers'* fashion room, which looks like a draughtsman's office, but muckier, four excessively well-dressed women choose other women to demonstrate clothing in the manner of architects picking components from the Barbour index file cards. In another cubby hole, the Men's Fashion Editor (another woman) is picking boy models from similar cards giving dimensions in English and German, the colour of eyes and hair, and noting skills and *peculiarities* (Equity member, hands, teeth, swimming etc.).

The London Model Book 1978 under 'Terms and Conditions' tells you that 'the overtime rate is 150 per cent of the normal hourly rate between 1800 and 2400 hours' and that travel time 'will be charged at 50 per cent of the hourly rate for travel . . . outside of Streatham Hill and Tooting Bec in the South'.

On Seventh Avenue, focus of soap opera, people veer wildly between believing that the fashion trade is like the auto industry, the back-bone of capitalism, and believing it is Fine Art to be exhibited in the Met. I suggest we go for the industrial version; it will give the girls a break.

We have all grown used to models, so now we can settle down to thinking of them in their new role as production workers, grist for the national mills. The girls can relax by the fire in Pirelli slippers, go shopping dressed as Hampstead housewives, forget Tramp. Goodbye San Lorenzo, goodbye Beauchamp Place. The Models' Ball will be held in Hounslow. The after-hours glamour part can be left to amateurs.

You, Me and One

Harpers & Queen, February 1977

The *New Yorker* of 5 April 1976 ran a cartoon showing a door, apartment 8B, covered with the labels Bio-Energetics, T.M., e.s.t., Rolfing, Vegetarianism, Gestalt Therapy, Hypnotism, Acupuncture, Yoga, Psycho-Analysis, Tai Chi, Zen. The impression is of the side of a suitcase covered with luggage labels – London, Paris, Geneva, Athens, Rome – or the window of an electrical appliance dealer – General Electric, Philips, Pifco, Braun, Westinghouse.

The *New Yorker* sells far beyond Manhattan, but its editors knew that the average reader in, say, Des Moines, Iowa, would understand the names and get the point. The point is the relationship of the surging wave of Me-ism, described by Tom Wolfe in last month's *Harpers & Queen,* to the mainstream of American life. A commercial relationship. The Me organizations and cults and therapies are brand names.

Me is big business in America. Tom Wolfe's article, 'The Me Decade and the Third Great Awakening', first published in *New West,* 30 August 1976, plus a whole raft of new books on self-scrutiny and self-fulfilment, plus the seal of factuality, a *Time* piece, in September, on narcissism, all confirm the economic and social trend towards what is called, pejoratively, narcissism or privatism. But if you show the *New Yorker* cartoon around in London you draw a blank. More than half the names, with the exception of psycho-analysis, vegetarianism, hypnosis, acupuncture, yoga – are only dimly understood. London has not got Me yet, nor has Manchester, or Aberdeen.

Economic and social prophecies tend to be self-fulfilling in

America because of the very eagerness with which reported trends are monitored. The habit of seeking to contain the rough magic of a new movement by finding a word for it is very American. If you talked to the reader in Des Moines about the Me decade, he would focus his attention on 'the narcissism trend' – the *Time* brand name – and try to be in on it, much as his wife thirteen years earlier adopted the interior decoration style Mrs Kennedy was said to favour, 'French Provincial'.

In New York in 1974 I had the virtues of T.M. (logo of transcendental meditation) and e.s.t. (Ehrhart sensitivity training) extolled to me by two limpid blonde Upper East Side girls of advanced sensibility I had met through a photographer friend. One of the girls took me to her leader, the T.M. organizer for the East Coast. He was young, and pure Wall Street – shortish hair, grey striped suit, Brooks Brothers Oxford shirt. No, he explained, T.M. had *nothing* to do with religion or politics or George Harrison. Great corporations across the country were putting their executives on to T.M. simply because it does you good. It had no ideological significance at all, no after-taste.

The following day the photographer and I were forced by the girls into a jogging session round Central Park. Trembling at the knees from the rush of raw air to the chest I began to think of writing a piece on this self-improving aspect of American life, tentatively called Transcendental Jogging.

A picture taken that day of the girls achieving spiritual growth in their tracksuits appears in a book by Caterine Milinaire called *Cheap Chic*. Both girls, Sue Murray and Ingrid Boulting, were more or less British, refugees from the cloud of unknowing that hung over London.

In 'The Me Decade' Tom Wolfe comes to grips with a fact so startling in the Californian light as to create a demand for a whole new set of goods and services: 'You don't live forever.' The immediate reaction to that thought was 'I don't have to put up with it . . . my wife, my husband my haemorrhoids . . . none of it.' In the rush for life that the realization has brought, wheelchairs and geriatrics in caravans – trailer sailors – are competing for freeway space with Zen bike boys all over America. Somebody could get hurt!

Why isn't it happening here? Why aren't the British, too, light-headed with the fever of self-realization? Why isn't the left-hand neighbour in Wimbledon into T.M., the right-hand one into Primal Therapy?

The answer lies partly, as Rambling Sid Rumpold used to say, in the soil, in the bedrock of English cultural life. But it's even more a product of economics.

The Me decade in America is the result of thirty years of what Wolfe calls go-getter bourgeois boom. Middle-class America is heavily into stage three consumerism: not goods (stage one), or services (stage two), but stage three – experiences. This country, stopping and going from Butler to Maudling to Healey, never really wiped up stage one. Tertiary – or terminal, depending on your perspective – consumerism demands a large, new, *mobile* middle-class, one neither in thrall to Connecticut WASPdom nor Nancy Mitfordism or eat-up-your-chicken-soup. Stage one is a new house on a new estate with a well-stocked freezer. Stage two is an American Express card (cut loose, see the world). Stage Three is thinking and talking about Me.

The Money pump has never worked well or long enough in this country to create enough of these people – Weybridge pales beside California, or even beside Rose Bay and Double Bay in Sidney (Sydney being the centre of Antipodean Meness). The celebration of Me is a party at which the British are all shabby-genteel relations standing huffily aloof.

A further brake on the growth of Me-ness in Britain is socialized medicine. The British are no more used to taking their psyches to an entrepreneur than they are to taking their bodies to an acupuncturist. Americans are used to it. Since the Fox Sisters set spiritualism going in America in the 1870s with their catchy toe-tapping there has always been a market for a *new product; we* tend to think that the state will provide.

In any case people in Britain *do* live forever, or at least those people who have always set the prevailing cultural tone. The King is dead, long live the Queen. The Queen plants trees: garden is a verb in English. Investing is something the last generation did, economic editor Peter Jay remarked; but the demise of continuity in English life is overstated. In *Accident,* a 1966 movie about Cambridge made by an American director, Joseph Losey, an aristocratic student (Michael York) tells a don (Dirk Bogarde, smoking a pipe) something like 'I have to die . . . I'm an aristocrat.' But there's always an heir.

And here is the crux of it, that a significant number of people in this country who had the money and the education to make a run for Me now actually subscribed, and continue to subscribe, to a most mysterious and wonderful form of serial immortality, that of *One.* When Tom Wolfe describes the 'high-class psychological cabinet work' of European finishing schools, and their being dedicated covertly to talking about Me, he is confusing two separate aspects – the aristocratic pleasure principle and the working of gentrification.

Remember the Bourgeois Gentilhomme, crushed into shape by a succession of sadists and pedants who tell him what one – a gentleman – should do. The gentleman is an obedient, polite, dutiful person. It is gents who *hold it in.*

The Royal Family say 'one' all the time, though we only noticed it after Mark and Anne's cosy interview. Princess Anne is, we realized, just another upper middle-class person like the folks back home.

And 'one' represents in the purest form what the sociologists call an internalized reference group – a reference group crossed with a beau ideal, the gentleman or gentlewoman – the lady. The English probably developed the lady and the gentleman in greater numbers and to a higher degreee than anyone. The ideal of the gentleperson is at one and the same time the most stabilizing and civilizing cultural influence in this country and the greatest constraint on the Wheatgerm Liberal Self-expressive Progressive Middle European Upper Bourgeois ideal that, in America, crossed with the go-getter bourgeois boom and Californian sunshine and Vietnam, finally bred Me.

Before 1920 there were perhaps seven progressive schools in Britain for the original wheatgerm liberal upper middle-classes to send their children to learn about Me – and analysis and pottery and finger-painting. Now there are six. (Possibly

Princess Margaret – always more Me than One – sending hers
to Bedales will make it a growth market.)

The remainder of the genteel sections of the middle-classes
have all this time plunged straight for One; for different grades
of public school that turned out gentlepersons. Religion was
taught at these schools and along with it the notion that it was
not a thing to get worked up about. And along with this came
an aesthetic in whose terms encounter groups and primal
screaming and all those situations that demanded spontaneity
to order were either funny (see how Anthony Powell or Evelyn
Waugh deals with the original wheatgerm belt, see how
Nicholas Bentley draws them) or, in the case of the newer cults,
silly and jejune and no more on for one than regular Tupper-
ware parties (less, far less). After all, one is what one is, more
or less, in the serial immortality of a class that doesn't believe
in fighting against the dying of the light.

But what of the new money, the new 'classless' classes and
the affluent workers?

The problem about the new money was that there never really was enough of it in enough places working in a polyglot
enough society to produce America's kind of volatile hetero-
geneous mix. What Tom Wolfe can, justifiably, call the
middle-class, which begat Me.

And in America there never was a consistent reference group
for the better sort of middle-class person across the country to
copy. The Episcopalian East Coast anglicized upper middle-
class style didn't stretch to the rest of America. Now, anyway,
WASPdom is in positive retreat.

But in Britain, most new money went public school. And,
despite a real shift of disposable income downwards, the
affluent workers were never affluent for long enough; they are
still moving from stage one, a new house on a new estate with a
well-stocked freezer, to stage two, see the world with Thomson
Skytours.

There are *patches* of Me in Britain: in the south-east, to the
north of London, in Old Highgate and Hampstead – Me in its
original upper middle-class wheatgerm liberal form – and in
the movie-star belt of Weybridge and Esher – Me in its

thrusting new-money form. Wherever you get a high concen-
tration of people working in the entertainment industry or its
cousin the liberal professions – in places like Maidenhead or
the streets between Hyde Park and Hampstead in London – Me will be talked about (Weight Watchers do especially
well in these areas, too). These sort of people have tried the
made-in-U.S.A. original brand names of Me, just as they own
hot-wax imported Philly sounds. At Quaesitor, 187 Walm
Lane, N.W.2 you can get addresses of rolfers, and from the
Churchill Centre, 22 Montagu Street, W.1 (it always was
showbizzy around Edgware Road and Baker Street, even in the
thirties) you can get information about primal therapy. The International Primal Association at the Churchill Centre (a different, non-Janov brand of Primal) offers '(his) approach to
freeing us from past experience and relationships to live more
successfully and creatively in the present' (from an advance
notice by the Centre's Ken Holme for the talk which visiting American Primalist Dr William Swartely gave on 12
January).

'Free us from past experience and relationships to live more
creatively in the present' indeed! A life without continuity, in
the continuous present, to be Completely Yourself, whoever
that is. How unjustly disinherited. And 'creative' is the word
for a type of person who draws advertisements. Osbert
Lancaster would savour every word. But most intellectuals, the
old kind, find this kind of thing alarming, with its suggestions
of privatization and the trivialization of personal relationships.

In 1972, Jeannie Sakol, a New York journalist who works for
magazines like *Cosmopolitan,* wrote a novel called *I Was Never the
Princess* about a clever resourceful witty observant (Jewish?)
New York girl with a big hang-up: she isn't pretty. Miss Hang-
up loses her man to a dumbie who looks like Bianca Jagger.
Hysterical, she drives her car into a wall. She isn't killed, but
her face is mangled. Plastic surgery is necessary. And under
the knife Miss Hang-up is transformed into a girl of hypnotic
beauty. She returns to ordinary life to devastate her faithless
man and celebrate Me by *living for herself.* Shortly after this,
Jeannie Sakol wrote a piece for *Cosmopolitan* which described
her own feelings at not being pretty. And shortly after that,

following a televised chat with a plastic surgeon, Miss Sakol braved the knife herself. Then wrote and was interviewed about the New Me by magazines up and down America. She was a Make-over. Life imitated art on the alter of Me.

Cosmopolitan is perhaps the best Me magazine. The British edition sells vigorously on articles that dissect Me hang-ups in sensible ways. 'I read *Cosmo*,' one woman told me, 'because I know *next month* they'll get to *my* problem.'

At the heart of this is a Perfectabilist feeling that *you can change your life.* 'It changed my life' is one of the great American expressions, and only Americans can use it with a straight face. Only they have the drive and enterprise/innocence/naïvete/vulgarity/immaturity (depending on which British perspective you take) to believe that it is possible.

Among the ideas which Americans take to their hearts is one that postulates that the foetus, any foetus, experiences the total experience of mankind in rapid flashback in the womb, and thus is capable of anything provided this experience can be unlocked. Discover the Hidden Power within yourself is classic American advertising. Anybody can do anything. 'You can do it, we can help' says Diet Pepsi (the Power to be Slim).

The 'How to' book is a staple of American publishing, and has never sold better, now that Me has come out into the open. Books on sexual success and hang-ups, T.M. made easy, sensuous womanhood and dominant manhood have succeeded Dale Carnegie on how to win friends and influence people. This kind of book has never really sold here. It's an American dream to reinvent Me – to be both creator and clay. In this country one knows perfectly well who one is, and if one forgets, someone will tell one p.d.q. 'Americans believe they can reinvent their lives,' says Charlotte Gray, the editor of British *Psychology Today,* whose circulation is around 25,000, against several million for its parent magazine in America. Americans learn psychology at university, so a vastly larger proportion of Americans are familiar with the terms for the mysteries of the mind than readers in any other country, and many times readier for a *Time* magazine of the inner life.

The belief in Me Made New is nowhere clearer than in the simplest form of current narcissism, the cult of health and

beauty. The new psyche and the new fitness sell to the same
market. The girls who are into Primal or T.M. are also into
roughage and rolfing and aroma-therapy. The executive who is
reading about Me in the Mid-life Crisis jogs every morning. In
America a woman will spend $15,000 on a face and body
overhaul. This order of treatment has never really caught on in
Britain. Not only do Brits not have the $15,000, they are also
wary of the idea. Changing oneself is an implicit reproach to
family and common sense, something the flashy do. It remains
socially suspect among the county to dye, actually *dye,* your
hair. And some years ago, the *Sunday Times* ran a piece on
cosmetic dentistry, pointing out how few people in public life
here have it done. In America it is practically standard, not
only among politicians (new brightwork jammed in poor old
faces like Nixon's, Ronald Reagan's, Hubert Humphrey's)
but down home too.

Lately, however, the emphasis in American narcissism has
shifted from the cosmetic to the health-based, from teeth and
nose straightening to the elimination of interior pollutants,
gaining a *natural high* through diet and exercise (eliminate
toxins and rediscover the Real Me underneath). All this too has
failed to get up real steam in Britain.

France is more interested in this side of Me. France has
given Me a unique contribution – la cellulite. Several years
ago, a French girl (a French*woman* – twenty-five) astonished
me by starting to pull, literally pull, at her immaculate thighs,
giving little moaning yelps. What was wrong? *'La cellulite!'* she
explained. *'Peau d'orange.'* She implied that she would fight it
every inch of the way. From her I learned about Continental
Me – the notion of one's *duty* to Me. Dear dead *Nova*'s article
on Princess Pignatelli, revealing that she pulled out the hairs
on her legs one by one with tweezers, made an impression even
on committed Me people.

For this article, we sent 500 *Harpers & Queen* subscribers,
chosen at random, a questionnaire to fill in which asked them
the following things:

*Is there any person, kin or not, or humanistic cause that you would die
for?*

Have you ever been, or would you like to be, psychoanalyzed?

Which of the following would you choose to emulate: the Queen, Edna O'Brien, Golda Meir, Helen Mirren, Jimmy Goldsmith, Jimmy Savile?

'If I've only one life, let me live it as a . . . . . .'

'If I only had one year to live, the one thing I'd want to do for myself is . . . . . .'

'If I had to die today, the one thing I would be really sorry never to have experienced would be . . . . . .'

A hundred readers answered (anonymously). The overall impression from them was of quite extraordinary contentment and stability, despite the alleged current middle-class despair. Most of the women (and some of the men) wanted to emulate the Queen or Golda Meir. An important pleasure was gardening. Regrets were minimal. Some of the women wished the earth had moved, but the emphasis was on love, not sex. In general, serial immortality – children, gardens, spouses – was embraced. Only one filled-in questionnaire qualified as Me: the seventy-plus, upper middle-class, self-styled 'lady of leisure' who said she would wish to be a Beautiful Person and that her one regret was that she hadn't had her nose bobbed. But for the rest, all is silence.

Jean Gimpel, in a recent piece in the American weekly *National Review*, 'The Greying of America', saw in the surge of Me-ism – particularly Art, Mystery and the Cult of Irrationality – the signs of a culture that had run its course. The U.S.A. had peaked in 1971 and was now sliding downhill – the industrial investment figures, in his view, proved it. America was like Britain in the 1850s, when *we* lost *our* grip. America was in a bad way, Gimpel felt. It had lost its psychological drive, and Me showed it.

But one totters on, steadfastly ignoring the war of all against all. The national heartbeat, located neither at Ford's Liverpool plant nor in Morton's, thumps away. Auberon Waugh, probably meaning it, said in his *Private Eye* column in December: '. . . one realizes that England still survives. Beneath the notice of television or colour supplements there exists a whole world of quiet, intelligent people going about their daily lives pretty well as they have always done, untroubled by trade unionists or transistor radios or comprehensive schools. The secret is to take no interest in what people say is happening, and disbelieve everything you read in the newspapers.'

Slime Time

Harpers & Queen, September 1976

'I am the slime in your T.V. set.' FRANK ZAPPA

A favourite occupation of mine on a winter's evening was to lie on my leopardette bed cover, a bowl of Butterscotch Instant Whip to hand and turn the lights out. By the small phosphorescence of my Sony portable, I would surrender to a solitary passion for the works of Rod Serling.

A neat grey-haired Extra-Terrestrial would introduce a world of Henry James via Vincent Price. 'What happens,' he would say, 'when a beautiful model girl is obsessed with something . . . *evil?*' In the following quarter hour – for Mr Serling works to a tight timescale – the beautiful model has killed maybe five men in her early sixties/L.A. decorator kitsch/Washington Square brownstone-style set.

Our spirit guide would then reappear to introduce another quickie. A young psychopath (in the classic oedipal S.M. Anthony Perkins mould) has done in a similar number of victims, simply to regain possession of a necklace in the Hollywood Rococo manner which belonged to his late mother. A family portrait shows he has the mad eyes of his great-grandfather who lived and died mysteriously . . . the portrait, however, owing to the special time warp that attends the supernatural, appears to be in a style *after Annigoni.*

This is SLIME TIME – the special witching hour of T.V. segments when chronology is suspended. The programme was, of course, *The Twilight Zone,* and as we know now, it is tinged with the sweet sadness of trash on its way to becoming art.

Trash T.V., like Dell's *Modern Screen* comic when Louella Parsons was with us, like the Hollywood product itself, like early rock, all in their time, is coming up for deification. Curiously, few T.V. observers in this country appear to have seen the potential. Not surprising, of course, that the academics of television criticism Milton Shulman and Raymond Williams should have so utterly ignored the business of a *content* analysis of American entertainment T.V., obsessed as they are with endless post-McLuhanesque discussions of form and technology and political implications. Clearly not their cup of tea. And in any case they are very much the pre-television generation themselves.

But why have the kids fallen silent? I suppose it comes from the critical assumption that you can't decently reassess a popular art form until it is dead. This effectively necrophiliac tradition precludes looking at the great – and predominantly American – art of T.V. segment canning, since the machine is clearly still working. Ready-made half-hour chunks of brand-new pap take the place of old chunks with unfailing regularity. However, my feeling is that the process of disinterment has started and you can confidently expect:
– Festivals of trash T.V. at the N.F.T. after the style of sci-fi conventions.
– Art Necro glossy paperbacks on fifties/early sixties series and stars.
– Serious critical exhumations devoted to the *directors* of, say, *Maverick* or *The Munsters* in *Films and Filming*.

In practice the whole thing has been put under way by the television contractors themselves, starting with Granada, who for the last year or so have been showing a selection of revival time canned T.V. – all of it American – after what Leslie Halliwell, who buys series and films proper for the network, describes as 'a modest request for suggestions' brought in 3,000 responses. Some critics suggested unkindly that this was Granada justifying ultra-cheap television in rather imaginative fashion at a time of apparent financial exigency. (Things have changed since then for the television companies.)

Whatever the motive was, it worked; the programmes – *The*

Untouchables, Rawhide, et al – made the ratings. And like good retailers seeing a 'flyer' line start to move, the companies began to put more products on the shelves. Tyne Tees came up with *Those Wonderful T.V. Times*: a cheap midday panel game in which assorted British television mid-weights 'cast their minds back' over twenty-one magical years of commercial television. But the dross of British sitcom and armchair theatre sadly obscured the American real thing.

The idea spread to the network. A request for suggestions was run through *T.V. Times* earlier this year and a new series of network repeats was launched as 'Command Performance'. Number one was *77 Sunset Strip* starring Ed 'Kookie' Byrnes (for whom 'Kookie, lend me your comb' was created and 'Once more, in English Kookie', and of whom nothing has been heard since), Efrem Zimbalist Jr and Roger Smith, later to find a new career as Ann-Margret's husband. *77 Sunset Strip* could not have been more *right*. It had Hollywood and car lots and music and everything to endear it to American Graffiteers everywhere. Thus, the medium, for once, had been prescient – even if under financial pressure. It had anticipated the professional revivalists and done its own exhumation.

Of course, there was plenty of precedent with films, enough indeed for a statistician to draw a graph of the apparently chance workings of the *nostalgia factor*. And do it well enough to tell you what people of what ages would fall into their net, and when, rather like a doctor tracing the pattern of delayed side-effects from a once-popular drug – now withdrawn. Milton Shulman himself, in fact, once calculated for different age groups how much of the formative years would have been spent watching television. It seemed to hinge on people who were twenty-eight or under in 1974. . .

There is now an army of millions in their twenties, in this country alone, who took their cues to life from Ed and Efrem, who noted that Troy Donahue's success with women in *Surfside 6* sprang from his Botany 500 wardrobe. Think of it, more people than ever bought singles records, more potential than all the Revived Forty-Fives put together. A built-in high exposure factor and *thousands of cans of the product* lying discarded, waiting

around the world – for it was sold from here to Timbuc-
too – and it keeps. Who, one wonders, is already laying it
down?

Someone undoubtedly will have plotted the pattern of
household penetration of television from the early fifties. By the
sixties, I would reckon, all except the most benighted parts of
Hampstead had succumbed.

Thus the segments became in effect the first popular entertainment with well-nigh universal penetration. Once in the
house all sorts of curious things oozed and slithered out of the
set and crawled over even children togged entirely from
Rowes, children for whom the Saturday morning pictures were
not on, classic Midwich cuckoos with long, straight cowlicks;
their minds, too, were secretly possessed by an alien force.
These children entered into the Westworld of *The Fugitive, Bron-
co Lane* and *Sir Lancelot* (early Roger Moore), of *Robin Hood, My
Friend Flicka, The Munsters* and *The Adams Family*.

The best T.V. Slime gains immeasurably the second time
around. It has sense of period and limitless confidence. You
can spot the actors who went on to make good – everyone
worked in the machine at some point. *Peyton Place* is almost too
close for comfort, but how about *Dr Kildare?* Some is surprisingly well made and inventive in spite of – or perhaps because
of – the constraints it was made under. Aficionados will recall
the 360-degree whip pan used in *The Man from U.N.C.L.E.* to
denote 'meanwhile over at' effects. This was novel in its day.
What is so special about the best of American canned T.V.,
however, is that it is untouched by higher values. You get the
feeling – perhaps wrongly – that nobody concerned in its making got beyond primary school, whereas even the B-picture
men had, you felt, been to Europe at least once. There was no
concern for artiness, for Abroad, or for socially redeeming
qualities; in particular none of the social concern that has crept
in since the late sixties (probably starting with that excellent
middlebrow series *The Defenders*: the dawning of the liberal hour
on television, where an Ivy League pair of lawyers defended
the have-nots and explained Issues of Conscience). It is the
sheer confident tackiness of a time of chrome brightwork and

bolt-on accessories. The best of it is full of clues to a Mythic Age, pre-1963 America.

What I personally like best of all are the horror mystery segments produced by Rod Serling – the Russ '*Beyond The Valley of the Dolls*' Meyer of the Supernatural – throughout the sixties. First they were called *The Twilight Zone* and then *Night Gallery*. These curious series appeared to be set all over the place – *Night Gallery* was made on the transatlantic principle – but one could never quite locate the period, since everything was in perpetual time warp. Constrained by the small screen, Serling sensibly avoided Hammer Grand Guignol, and went for sick suggestion coupled with good musical effects, all played out against those timeless piss-elegant interiors. There was no one to match him at it. Rod Serling was born in Syracuse, N.Y., and is the *only* living writer to have been awarded six Emmys. Good, too, was *The Invaders*, a superior science-fiction series starring humanoid aliens who disintegrated when shot, and Roy Thinnes, who looked pretty peculiar himself.

A curious situation has arisen over the re-showing of *The Invaders*; originally promised for later this year, it has been rescheduled until no one seems sure when – or even if – it will appear. . .

The other really Extra-Terrestrial series is *Hawaii Five-O*. A magical opening sequence, plus Jack Lord, who is clearly *not a real person* and is only pretending to be Steve MacGarrett in order to win our confidence. Most of the current products seem less promising. How can we single out today's vintage potential – for who would exchange the unspeakable *Kojak* (memorable only for Telly Savalas's claim to being the *first* Greek-American to make it, excluding Jackie O) for Ed and Efrem? Look closer, ask yourself what series still holds out against authenticity and character development, which series still has the feel for a great tradition?

I nominate for eternal stardom: *Police Woman*, starring Angie Dickinson. Miss Dickinson has the bone structure of a white Diana Ross, and perfect early sixties hair. She once, so it is

said, dated President Kennedy and is now married to Burt
Baccarach. She has a lot going for her.

In *Police Woman,* Angie plays Sergeant Pepper Anderson, a
neurotic heroine who saves other women and cries frequently.
She is forever thrusting herself, in touchingly vulnerable
disguises, into cat-houses and women's prisons and even, once,
into a vast mobile gambling joint careering down the freeways.
All these visions of Hell have that timeless *acrylic* feel, that total
lack of verisimilitude that suspends disbelief. It is what we are
looking for in T.V. art.

SLIME RATING

Primal Slime. It came out first, and all copies and follow-ons can never be as
good.
Slime. Plain, simple, plotless slime.
Big-time Slime. Mere Slime – except that it rates audiences of 40 million.
Cult Slime. This is the mythopoeic stuff. People take on the mannerisms and
catch-lines and make them part of their daily life.

PRIMAL SLIME

Dr Kildare with Richard 'I can play Hamlet' Chamberlain as knight with shin-
ing stethoscope.
Dragnet with Jack Webb – four-twenny-two a.m., call from Homicide. . .

SLIME

Robin Hood with Richard Green. The corn was Lincoln green and nobody
ever made Marian.
Tenderfoot (*Sugarfoot* in the States) starring – if that's the word – the forgettable
Will Hutchins.
Jason King (British). He was Peter Wyngarde in wig; Mickey Spillane goes
Carnaby Street.
Emergency Ward 10 (British) with Dr Paula Byrne and Sister Jill Browne in that
extraordinary saga of hospital folk. Slime and slime again. British Slime takes
a star rating of nil on a one-to-ten scale.

BIG-TIME SLIME

Rawhide with Clint Eastwood in the days when he was working for a few
dollars less.
Hawaii Five-O with unreal Jack Lord. Good versus evil but with blue
lagoons . . . Aloha.

Police Woman with Angie Dickinson, she of the early sixties hair and humanitarian outlook.

The beast also rises in *Peyton Place*, with Barbara Parkins playing gay divorcee fit to bust.

CULT SLIME

The Avengers (British) with Emma and her Steed.

The Untouchables. Don't call them, Scarface, they'll call you.

Vaughan and MacCallum, the *Men from U.N.C.L.E.* The adversary was T.H.R.U.S.H.; the ladies loved it.

77 Sunset Strip. Ed 'Kookie' Byrnes sent us to hipsville. Wipe out, fade out. . .

One can take camp sensibility too far. In the seventies there was a critical time when it was clear that too many people were using the easy 'so bad it's good' number as a way of avoiding making any judgments about quality at all. Also, you found the *wrong people* starting to say they liked old rubbish in this cutesy N.W.1 way and you could see a mile off they were *fine tuning* – that *Sunday Times* middlebrow sensibility making all these little adjustments a couple of years too late and getting it wrong anyway.

It always put your back up, if, like me, you'd been the *original real market* for that stuff. I really watched all that T.V. *first time round*; just like in the early seventies, we'd have a special night in for Jason King. The fact is – and one should admit it – that when you get the wrong people picking up on things, the 35-year-old Kickers types, the Tony Palmers, the boys who were into Tangerine Dream when they were kiddies, taking an interest in disco, then it puts you off things you genuinely used to like. This is how the world goes round and it's one of the most powerful mainsprings of fashion moves.

Them

Harpers & Queen, October 1976

In the Rama Unit Superstore, a jumble of Pakistani traders in denim and cheesecloth parked in the shell of Biba in Kensington High Street, I see an exquisite yellow couple – Japanese, Vietnamese? Everything about the one reflects the other, though there is nothing unisex about them. The man is dressed in a shiny fawn cotton suit with narrow trousers, a black shirt and the very best quality English riding boots, the toe far too pointed actually to be English. The woman is in many layers of different finely printed cottons with an Occidental/Oriental look. They are perfect – not handsome, not beautiful, but elegantly, subtly, expensively yet unusually got up. Anyone with half an eye could see it. They don't knock you dead but are clearly Good Taste.

Their faces register the uselessness of the place for their purposes and they stroll out.

Later in the same store I see a pair of boys. One has two chromed safety pins set at angles stuck through his ear, a short-sleeved white shirt with tiny collar, a razor blade on a chain round his neck, peg-topped white trousers and green plastic sandals. His hair is parted in the middle and goes straight a couple of inches but ends in corkscrew curls. His friend is remarkable only for his unremarkable look. He has short hair, National Health spectacles, a too-big jacket, too-short, tight, permanent-press kind of trousers and plain black oxfords. He looks like a high-school boy from the Mid-West in the Hiram Holliday era. Save for the shock value of the razor blade no one would notice these two boys. There is little to astonish or offend. But think, who wears plastic sandals and do any Middle Americans really look like Ike now?

Both get-ups are really code messages. The boys are junior grade Them.

In the street outside is a girl dressed to . . . what? Everything about her is loud, harsh, artificial – Bad Taste. Her hair is flaming red curls, with a tonsure of shorter frizzier purple hair, her make-up is Cruella de Vil. She looks like Bette Midler, only worse. The people in the street – denim couples, sharp Italians, mucho macho Spanish boys looking for sixties girls – are looking at her. The unspoken question behind their eyes is: Is it on purpose or doesn't she know any better? It is of course on purpose. She is a middle-class girl with the morals of a nun who believes in what she calls 'vulgar sexy clothes'. She is a Them.

Further on (for Kensington High Street is a good sighting ground), I recognize a well-known fashion writer. He is wearing tight-legged unbleached Levis, a Lacoste T-shirt, snowy tennis shoes. No watch, nothing else. It is a clean, functional get-up, pared to the minimum. *Minimal,* for he too is a Them; big league.

All these people are Them; part of a mysterious aesthetic conspiracy. Had they seen each other they would have known instantly; each would have read the other's code. They are examples of a new breed, the creators of the dominant high-style aesthetic of the seventies.

These new aesthetes have in common a visual sensibility so demanding that they are prepared to sacrifice almost anything for the look. Yet the look is not necessarily meant to be attractive in any sense that most people would understand; the look is itself an ideal: a complex series of references. In this case, the Japanese couple (Exquisites) are a walking lesson in colour toning, the odd boys (Peculiars) are sense of period. The tarty girl (Peculiar) is l'aesthetique du shock. Michael Roberts (Exquisite) is 'I am beyond all that'.

Tom Wolfe explained in *The Painted Word* how modern artists ended up painting, instead of pictures, ideas about pictures which only other people who had read the books could understand. Thems are the word made flesh. Thems put the idea into their living; they wear their rooms, eat their art.

If this sounds like sophistry, ask yourself why most people dress as they do. James Laver has supplied the classic common sense answer: either to look socially acceptable – rich enough, couth enough, etc., or to look sexually appealing – as young and good-looking as possible. It is a mark of a Them that he/she does neither of these normal things. Thems are people who will make the supreme sacrifice: to look interesting rather than sexy. Like a book setting out to appeal to a small circle of other writers, a Them's clothes are meant to be interesting or original or allusive or clever or witty to his or her *peers*. Thems are excessively literate in the language of style.

How has this strange sensibility taken so strong a hold? At the back of it there are two dominating factors: the art school bulge and the assimilation of camp.

In the period from the early 1960s to the early 1970s, art schools both increased their intake and changed their nature. The numbers going into some kind of art education rose by about seventy per cent and some hitherto neglected or non-existent Applied Arts – principally and most obviously Fashion – took on a new importance. Instead of being split between Fine Art and obscure hack training, a sort of intermediate, newer and more attractive self-image was on offer to art students: the Applied Art media star, in particular The Designer. At the same time, dominant life-style references for the artist were changing from essentially fashion-despising nineteenth-century European ones to newer ones – principally American – which were more compatible with current chic. The kids were into clothes; and clothing was what many of them went into after they graduated. But many more spread their sensibility into all sorts of other things – music and films and magazines and restaurants – since there wasn't room for all of them to practise or even teach their own subject.

The art-school graduates of the late fifties and the sixties took as their starting point the idea of a nation crying out for design, excitement, colour. The problem in Britain, as they saw it, was not the wrong designers but no designers at all. Time after time these young bloods, many of them women, were quoted as saying that things were run by a bunch of boring old farts and what was needed was *their* vigour, talent, originality, sexual directness. What they really ended up doing was selling smart middle-class good taste to a wider audience of proles and wets. By 1970 their efforts had succeeded with a vengeance, and the world was walled by knotty pine and Mucha posters and clothed in blue denim.

Thus the inevitable reaction of the Them by the seventies was not against lack of design but against design overkill, boring mainstream trendiness, the assimilation of prole naivety into smooth compromises, etc. Thems took as their starting point the Bland Authenticity of James Taylor, Habitat and the Sunday supplements. The only jump ahead was Reaction and Extremism, the only defence the creation of a special language.

Pop Art in particular was important to the early Thems – and *remains* so, since culture lag means that new ideas take longer to work through the system than sophisticated people suppose. Pop Art taught Them how to look at things in a cock-eyed way, i.e. in the way that somebody else had already looked at them. Thus, a minority sensibility, an interest in 'popular art' forms and double-think, became widely diffused. This led to a widespread use of pastiche: the more accurate, the more derivative, the more like the real cliché thing something was, the more O.K. it was. Rip-offs were right. (Borrow it! Photograph it! Silk-screen it!) Pop Art reinforced America-worship and the reverence for prole and period Americana – a recurring visual theme among Thems. Euro and arty became démodé and middle-brow. Thems were cognoscenti of trash, aficionados of sleaze.

Then, to a generation and a sub-group already seeing double through pop art, and thus in the vanguard of the double-think revivals that marked the sixties – the Arts Nouveau, Deco, Moderne, Ultrakitsch, et al – was added another devastating factor. Camp. In a very acute article in *The Village Voice* last year, John Lombardi showed how the assimilation of camp – once largely a homosexual sensibility – had begun to effect the marketing of all sorts of things sold to non-queer people in America. At the beginning of the seventies, homosexuals became, as Lombardi says, the niggers of the time, the O.K. outgroup. Gay became lay. The result of this exchange was that:

a) 'Straight' people learned to think and look at things in 'camp'. It was the new ghetto sensibility.

b) A lot of homosexuals left the Boys' Town ghetto and became more relaxed and mainstream, and thus more influential.

The thing about camp is that it is a very confusing, over- under- sideways-down way of looking at the world, which takes as basic the notion that nothing is quite what it seems. To look at the crudest example – the deceptive pronoun. He and she: She's *bad* = He's wonderful.

Art school people and quasi art school people, post art school people, fashion business people and Applied Art media stars were of course in the forefront of this merging of sensibilities.

Double-think became treble-think: more cerebral and in-group than ever. Of course it was in the nature of things that some Thems and putative Thems *were* homosexual, although far more tended to appear so to ordinary people than actually were. In addition, there was the pansexual revolution and the women's one, both starting in America, which said these things were old hat anyway: what's a pronoun between friends?

British Thems were listening, assimilating all the changes into their styles and their behaviour. Camp and Pop put together produced what I call Art Necro: a quick-change revivalism which became very big business around the turn of the decade, when, as John Lombardi says, people were looking for something *silly* to take their minds off depressing things.

The shorter the revival span, the less sincere it seemed, not homage but one long giggle. This was new and strange. Had early Victorian architects built Greek Revival churches because they were amusing? Did the Pre-Raphaelites feel that their versions of the Renaissance world were a laugh and a half? But some of those old things the Thems revived *were* rather good; it was nice to have someone standing up for them. . . It became hard to work out what anybody thought about anything, there were so many ways to look at it.

The Necro industry gave employment to many Thems: designing new/old record sleeves, doing jackets for books about forties movie stars, working in Antiquarius in the King's Road, and so on. Send-ups or 'fun clothes' – fried egg appliqués etc. – gave us the Mr Freedom/Paradise Garage/Tommy Roberts look, which degraded into the tepid fun at the Rama. (In late 1970, Roberts started selling authentic-looking baggy overalls from Serena Shaffer's Electric Fittings. A harbinger of *anti-fashion* to come. Thems had been wearing real Osh Kosh B'Goshes and Pays-Days since 1968).

One of the main things about Thems is the belief in stylistic novelty and originality, which at its crudest means doing it first. They say 'I'm so bored with that Hawaiian shirt look' or 'I (or whoever) was wearing Mylar back in 1969'. This is a very important putdown, the implication being that the speaker practically invented it. Thems are mad to be first. First in and first out. The new fashions are always old to them. They know dates. They're historians of style.

Designing, art-directing, Necro-ing, camping-things-up. Thems moved into every corner of the visualities. Gradually two polarized streams of Themness became apparent: Peculiars and Exquisites – both representing a reaction against mainstream sixties trendiness.

The Peculiars were generally younger, shabbier, poorer, less made-it, more certain to have been at art school, and keener on outright shock value. Around the Peculiars hung the homemade, musty air of jumble sales. Peculiars collected Clarice Cliff's repellent rust-red, black and yellow ceramics in 1970. They had burr-walnut wardrobes, pussycat motifs, plastic jewellery. Peculiars were advanced. Peculiars were obviously odd – though, unlike the sixties people, they did not wish to make statements about matters of political or sexual morality; they wanted not to shock the bourgeoisie but to entertain and *confuse* them. From the early seventies both boy and girl Peculiars favoured henna'd heads, an odd palette of eau de nil and funny pinks, and floppy fabrics. Most of them looked

unhealthy. They didn't go in for Martini people's tans. The
girls – and for a time, the boys too – wore heavy obviously jam-
my make-up while the rest of the world was going in for the
natural look.

The Mercs called them 'freaky', though this was wide of the
mark. They were perverse, or to use a word much in currency
around 1970/1, they looked *decadent*. They were the antithesis
of everything the sixties people had bequeathed to the mainstream. However, when you looked closer, even if you did not
really understand what they were on about, you recognized
that it was, some of it, really quite clever and original. . .'

The Exquisites, on the other hand, simply looked exquisite – they were the first to zero in on Chinoiserie etc. You
would not necessarily get the hang of them either, but
everything about them was subtle. Even the loudness was
subtle – and well-made, and *expensive,* in addition to being
novel. It might have been unfamiliar, but it was immaculate. It
might have been artifice but it worked. Exquisites collected
Eileen Gray lacquer screens in 1970. They knew Karl Lagerfeld. They got around the world.

But strangely enough, when you looked closer, they too looked slightly odd. They sent the mind racing but not the blood
running. Girls whose appearance was so refined that it seemed
to elevate them above any real-life sexiness, who had faultless
taste – these girls had something a bit *peculiar* and unreal about
them, something you felt you'd seen before somewhere. . .

Every Peculiar has something exquisite under the skin; every
Exquisite, something peculiar. They are sometimes scathing
about each other: Exquisites say that Peculiars are tacky,
Peculiars that Exquisites sacrifice originality for finesse.
Generally the Exquisites discover, consume, endorse or retail
what the Peculiars work at.

Exquisites are more likely to affect the mainstream.
However, the line is very thin – some cross over. This year
Karl Lagerfeld, probably the ultimate Them couturier in his
time, had a wonderful scarf in his collection. On one
side – beautiful, clever, witty, perfect – was a Breughel
reproduced on fine wool. On the other – campy, tacky,

schlocky – were Lurex stripes. It was the quintessence of
Themness. Exquisite and Peculiar at once.

What kind of backgrounds do Thems have, you may be mut-
tering. What do Thems think about the Third World, the
Capitalist Ethic, Ecology and all that?

Thems are predominantly suburban middle-class, Bendix
and leaded lights, though some Exquisites have international
exotic upper-class backgrounds. (People from the standard
Sloane Ranger background find it hard to learn the language.
Few try, and most who do, fail.) What do Thems think about
capitalism etc.? Not very much – most are apolitical, save
when a politician excites them aesthetically. Overly rigorous
analysis depresses them. By instinct, of course, they are
élitist – though they would not see it that way, or be sure what
the word really meant.

How about sex? Gore Vidal attributed to Jackie Onassis the
sentiment that sex was a bad thing because it rumpled the
clothes. Thems are not all that struck on it either. They consider sex middlebrow. It doesn't get much airtime with them.
They would prefer to read funny 1950s pornography with those
wonderful pictures. This, however, is a *hard-line* Them value.

A real hard-line Them is consistent – the primacy of the
visual and the exercise of taste extends to every part of his or
her existence. This singlemindedness distinguishes true Thems
from surrounding social territories into which they may appear
to merge. The following sorts of people are not Thems.

1. *Extreme working-class street style.* Every year a new group of
wonderful kids appear in some benighted place. Their style is
spot-on. Professional commentators discover them, too late.
Last year it was the Puerto Rican kids in New York. This year,
it was the Canvey Island gang. These kids, a temporary freak
of nature, last a year. Then they metamorphose into perfectly
ordinary adults. (Thems keep at it for ever.)

2. *The straight fashion trade world* latch on to Them tricks fairly
fast, but in moderation. They never O.D. on it. They don't
have the feelings, the cultural references, or the way of life to go
with it. They want to look *nice*, they want to get on.

3. *Ordinary smart rich people and aristos* buy some things from

120   STYLE WARS

Thems, know some of the most established Thems. (Example – Zandra Rhodes, whose clothes are worn by society women and Daughters of the American Revolution.) This doesn't, of course, imply any commitment.

4. *Trad aesthetes, art frissonniers, scholars.* These people – over-educated as they are – can only manage double-think in small matters, preferably verbal. They really believe in Beauty, even if a somewhat purply slim-gilt sort. They are too classically biassed, *too* verbal, and most of them too old and well-bred to even get the hang of it. (Bevis Hillier and John Byrne are borderline cases.)

5. *Heavy Metal kids, bread heads, the rock business.* Most of the rock world is very unThem, although Thems have infiltrated important parts, particularly in the area where presentation is paramount. (David Bowie and the neo-decadents etc.) Rock people package former Them trends for mass consumption (Queen and Cockney Rebel – pansexuality for the people), or steal former Them looks as a presentational device. But what Thems really like is ethnic or récherché or ultra prole stuff. They are hot on Rasta, Kilburn and the High Roads – anything where the Sound is a Look. Many Them designers do sleeve covers and some do clothes for rock singers – Elton John for instance is Them-designed as an echo of Hockney, ten years after. Antony Price does his all for Bryan Ferry.

A real Them is a Them through and through like a stick of rock. Three examples sum up Themness: a Them singer (Bryan Ferry), a Them movie (*The Man Who Fell to Earth*), a Them event (Andrew Logan's Miss World contest).

The case of Bryan Ferry

'What d'you think of Bryan Ferry and Jerry Hall?' I asked a Them after reading of their engagement. 'Oh, Ferry and Jerry go together wonderfully,' was her response. I didn't need to ask whether she meant they had interests in common, voted the

same, had compatible temperaments. She meant, of course,
that they would photograph well.

Bryan Ferry, an Exquisite, is perhaps the best possible example of the ultimate art-directed existence. How right then
that he should be linked with a model, who looks as if she had
walked out of one of his album covers. (She has . . .)

Ferry is the most important pasticheur in Britain today.
That he is a big-time rock star and has gone rather too uptown
recently should not obscure the fact that he has a degree in Fine
Art, and a very demanding Them sensibility. Many kids take
the Ferry style seriously, not realizing, presumably, that Ferry
himself does not. His outfits, his album covers are all 'looks,
looks, looks' – from Art-School Glitter (1972) to Jerome Rob-
bins, to forties Tux, G.I. Slick, Odeon Spiv, Roma 1968
(1976). The Ferry style is none of them. It lies in a joke called
Master of Disguise. This trick of perspective was caught in a
brilliantly conceived and executed profile of Ferry written by
Idris Walters in the now defunct magazine *Street Life* (an
English knock-off of *Rolling Stone*). Walters described Ferry, set
against the background of his elegant house like a Hockney
drawing, talking about himself as an Artist, speculating, while
the light faded, whether he could make movies, describing
himself as the 'mock balladeer'. Walter ends by wondering
whether they're in a movie anyway. Ferry is a professional of
the highest order, and his records are very clever jokes, his
singing voice the ultimate put-on. He should hang in the Tate,
with David Bowie.

The Man Who Fell to Earth

The British Lion film adapted from a fairly lowbrow science
fiction novel by Walter Tevis, starring David Bowie and
directed by Nicholas Roeg (*Performance, Don't Look Now*), is a
Them movie, made by Thems but for a wider audience. Many
Thems profess to dislike it, perhaps because it is chock-full of
Them symbols and allusions. Spotting these relieves the mild
boredom of the movie itself. The most obvious Them thing in it

is Bowie; the film is a star vehicle (most Thems prefer that to a film d'auteur) in which Bowie reflects his own original mythic persona – Ziggy/the man who sold the world. (He has a new one now.) Other things to note are:

1. Sci-fi is/has been a Them cult.
2. Bowie wears Them kit: plastic sandals, the O.K. Them haircut, two-tone hair.
3. Prole Americana in the art direction (production designer: Brian Eatwell).
4. Necro/Retro moments (Candy Clark looking like Annette Funicello).
5. Homage to Warhol. In the scene where Bowie falls ill, his 'dead dog' playing resembles Paul Morrissey's *Flesh for Frankenstein*.
6. Suggestions of odd sex for the jaded palate.

There is more, indeed the film is overburdened with Themness.

Andrew Logan's Miss World

This party, held at irregular intervals, has men and women contestants; the men win. The judges in March 1975 included Gerlinde von Regensburg, David Hockney, Zandra Rhodes, Amanda Lear, Justin de Villeneuve, Janet Street-Porter and Kevin Whitney. It was held at Andrew Logan's Thames-side warehouse home, got up in ultimate Eclectic from jumble sales. (Logan produced the roof-garden decoration for Biba, the mirror-glass trees for Bombacha, Thea Porter's silver lily lamp, and, with Duggie Fields – key Them artist – the fifties foyer to the 1975 Mary Quant exhibition at the London Museum in Kensington Palace.) Logan is a Peculiar. Among guests at his hand-knitted Satyricon were Bill Gibb, Bryan Ferry, John Stefanidis, Molly Parkin (who got thrown in the pool), Noel Tovey, Teddy Millington-Drake, Sheridan Dufferin, beastly Barometeer Miles Chapman, Derek Jarman (who won) and Celia Birtwell.

The Pantheon of the Peculiar is under assault now, however,

for all sorts of reasons, economic and aesthetic. Art school education has already been cut back and Government grants are getting even smaller. The real high point of Themness was 1972/3. An awful warning sounded with the closing of big Biba in 1975. Big Biba had started with the idea of selling the complete Them taste – jokes with everything – to a mass market but ended as a venue rather than a shop. The mass market came, but only to look. The Pointer Sisters, Manhattan Transfer etc. all *played* the Rainbow Room. By then Biba's obvious camp had played itself out.

Thems are now going low-profile. Exquisites are into Minimal, Peculiars who follow the news have been going Punk for eighteen months. Back to basics. Retro is out.

A group who take a dim view of much Themness are the people who run the Sex clothing store at the World's End. They represent the extreme ideological wing of the Peculiars. The Sex shop people, untypically, have political views, of a kind which they describe as anarchic. The shop has produced a manifesto on a T-shirt, detailing the people they endorse and those they dislike. The *wrong* side includes, along with the names of straight-up-and-downers like Anthony Haden-Guest, and *Harpers & Queen*, a fair sprinkling of Thems, particulary Exquisites. On the right side are the heroes of anarcho-chic, street-kid style. The Price sisters and Eddie Cochran, Ronnie Biggs and Valerie Solanas. Their associated pop group the Sex Pistols are alleged to cause trouble wherever they go. The Sex people *hate* Retro, and seem perfectly sincere about it, yet they are working in a 1958 Council Flat Greaseball vein. In the graffiti décor sprayed on the sponge rubber walls of their shop appears the telling question: 'Does passion end in fashion?'

There are chapters of Thems in other countries – Australia, Japan, Holland (not rational France), and a considerable interchange between American and British Thems. New York was the original powerhouse of Themness, but the energy seems greater in London now. At the party Anne Lambton gave in London last November for Andy Warhol's book *From A to B and Back Again*, there was a crowd of Thems: the Sex Shop people, Little Nell, Andrew Logan, Kevin Whitney, Luciana Martinez, Amanda Lear, plus Bianca Jagger in her Florence of Arabia number. Andy, who had practically invented Them, was quite overwhelmed. He whispered to Christina Berlin, 'I haven't seen so many freaks since the sixties; and they think *we're* bad'!

ART SCHOOL ETC. INFLUENTIALS IN THE THEM MOVEMENT

Bill Gibb (who went to the R.C.A. – 'the College'), Duggie Fields (Chelsea), Andrew Logan (Oxford architectural school), Carol McNicoll (R.C.A.), Janet Street-Porter (A.A.), Brian Eno (Ipswich), Jack Miller (Slade), Mick Brownfield (Hornsey), Lizzie Carr (Kingston), Rae Spencer-Cullen (Oxford), Antony Price (R.C.A.), Michael Roberts (High Wycombe), Michael Chow (Hammersmith), Bryan Ferry (B.A. Fine Art, Newcastle), Hugh and Betty Barnden (R.C.A.), Zandra Rhodes (R.C.A.), David Bowie (Bromley). A full list would cover several pages.

THEM HAIRDRESSER

Keith at Smile.

THEM PHOTOGRAPHERS

Mick Rock, Tim Street-Porter, Tony McGee, Eric Boman (Exquisite), Johnny Rosza (Peculiar).

THEM PRECURSORS FROM THE SIXTIES

Christopher Gibbs, David Hockney, Ossie Clark, Yoko Ono, Molly Parkin, Gilbert and George. Hung On You and Granny Takes A Trip were important shops.

THEM MILESTONES

1970: the Kansai Yamomoto/Boston 151 fashion show at the Great Gear Trading Co, staged by Michael Chow; start of Japonaiserie.
1971: opening of the Hard Rock Café in June. Ritva produce art you can wear – sweaters by David Hockney, Elizabeth Frink, Patrick Hughes.
1972: in September, the David Bowie 'whale benefit' concert at the Festival Hall. Roxy gets going. Wembley Rock Revival Spectacular.
1973: Zandra Rhodes' show at the Round House, with Anjelica Huston and Caroline Coon modelling. Andrew Logan's first Miss World contest. Richard O'Brien's *Rocky Horror Show* at the Royal Court. Smile opens, Biba opens in the Derry & Tom's building. 'Almost any afternoon in 1971, '2 or '3

was a milestone of Themness at the Chelsea Antique Market,' says a member of the Gang wistfully.

1974: 'A Bigger Splash' – Art becomes Life becomes Movie.

1975: Biba closes. The Gang is photographed for The Calendar (of Them, by Them, for Them) outside Buckingham Palace by Tim Street-Porter.

1976: in January, Thems discuss their style before a largely Peculiar audience at the I.C.A. Fashion Forum.

THE GANG

are a group of ultra Thems who know in their hearts they are the definitive Thems. Andrew Logan and Duggie Fields belong.

THEM COUTURIERS

Zandra Rhodes, Chrissie Walsh, Ian Batten, Jim O'Connor and Pamla Motown, Karl Lagerfeld, Kenzo Takada (Jap), Kansai Yamomoto, Vivienne (Sex), Rae Spencer-Cullen (Miss Mouse). Walter Albini was, from 1971 to 73. Ossie Clark, then and forever.

THEM CLOTHES SHOPS

Hard-core Thems do not usually buy clothes from shops. They either make their own or are given them by Them designer friends or get them from second-hand stalls. For the occasional thing: Swanky Modes, Howie (a patron of Thems), Acme Attractions, Sex, Zapata (Blahnik himself is one of the definitive Exquisite Thems).

THEM INTERIOR DESIGNERS

Tchaik Chassay, John Stefanidis (so ultra Exquisite as to be stratospheric), painter Richard Gillette, designer Stan Peskett (both in New York), John Cairns, Olivia Brett (paints blinds for Thems).

THEM HATES

Mary Quant, Terence Conran and Habitat, Tuffin, Foale, all the Sixties made-it people, 'grey-haired blue-jean boys', vigour, other people pretending to be Them, the Sunday Times, Patrick Hughes, Kenneth Noland, Led Zeppelin, E.L.P., heavy hippies, Hermann Hesse, Kris Kristofferson, J.R.R. Tolkien, initialled fashion – Vuitton, Gucci (although the double-think, ultra Thems now like it because it is becoming a piety not to like it – hence the Vuitton rug), Gatsby, Sammy Davis Jr.

THEM HEROES AND HEROINES

Schiaparelli, Warhol (love/hate), Rose Sélavy, Grace Coddington, Cathy McGowan, Gala Mitchell, Charles James, Judy Holliday, Cocteau, Seifert, Thelma Ritter, Franklin Pangbourne, Irene Handl, Marcel Duchamp.

THEM GROUPS AND SINGERS

Bryan Ferry, David Bowie, Kilburn and the High Roads, Lou Reed, the Sex Pistols, Split Enz, 2nd Honeymoon, Brian Jones (R.I.P.), 10cc (in patches), Bob Marley, A.W.B., Ry Cooder, Smokey Robinson. Sparks look like Them – but are not, say the Gang. Thems remember The Rainbow, Tiny Tim and Van Morrison. The Pointers, Manhattan Transfer, Bette Midler and other Bibataste are out of favour. Thems are also discovering jazz.

THEM ADDRESSES

You will find Thems everywhere (except in Westminster). Some of the more important ones live in Earls Court, Marylebone, Limehouse, Shad Thames, Putney, parts of Notting Hill, Richmond, Brighton.

THEM KEY SONG LINES

'Looks, looks, looks': Sparks. 'You're still doing things I gave up years ago'; Lou Reed from Transformer. 'All the young dudes follow the news': 'Hymn to the Dudes' by Mott the Hoople, a band invented in his own image by Bowie. 'I'm in with the in-crowd': Bryan Ferry single, 1974 (a version of a Dobie Gray number of around 1965). 'Andy Warhol, silver screen, can't tell 'em apart at all': Bowie. 'New York, New York, it's a wonderful town' as rendered by Little Nell Campbell.

INTERNATIONAL THEMS (BASED IN NEW YORK)

Edie Sedgwick (R.I.P.), Tatum O'Neal, Penelope Tree (the Once and Future Them), Larissa (the leatherette), Paloma Picasso, Catherine Milinaire, Tiger Morse (R.I.P.), Andy Warhol (Them of Thems), Ara Gallant (Avedon's stylist), François de Menil, Luis Martinez, Ronnie Cutrone, Holly Woodlawn, Lou Reed (the François Villon of Themness), Antonio Lopez.

OBJETS DE THEM

All these have recently had intense Themness.
1. Dismembered pre-Adel Roostein shop-window dummies.
2. Black Fosters pottery 'hand' ashtrays.
3. A peach-tinted mirror with etched edges (usually eventually sold to a rich nonThem – good Deco is now hard money).
4. Woolworth's 1950 contemporary ceramic art, with splay-legged furniture patterns or African art patterns on it.
5. An old Anglepoise lamp.
6. Mid-fifties girlie mags, such as *Men Only*; Lilliput.
7. Something connected with the Festival of Britain.

8. Poodle art.

9. Specialized sun specs, particularly ones with red and green prism lenses for instant trips/migraines.

10. A pair of stilettos/winklepickers.

11. An example of Crawfie art.

12. Ultra-banal postcards in 3D: Empire State building from New York, etc.

13. Something made of amboyna wood.

14. Press cuttings about themselves from *Honey*, *L'Uomo Vogue*, *19*, *Ritz*, *Zoom*, *Cosmo*, *Barometer*.

15. Art history books, particularly Miro, Calder and Mondrian.

16. A Tretchikoff and/or Maxfield Parrish print.

17. A discarded Sex shop T-shirt.

18. Sci-fi props – tin robots etc. (specialized Them taste).

THEM FILMS

Beyond the Valley of the Dolls, *The Damned*, *Chelsea Girls* (seminal Them), *Les Enfants Terribles*, *Madame X*, *The Man Who Fell to Earth*, *The Night of the Living Dead*, *The Bride Wore Black*, *The Women*, *Blood for Dracula*, *Mean Streets*, *Scorpio Rising*, *A Bigger Splash* (about Thems), *Performance*, *Parrish*, Derek Jarman's *St Sebastian* (with a cost of hundreds of Thems), *Imitation of Life*, *Women in Revolt*, *The Bitter Tears of Petra von Kant*, Werner Shroeter's films, *Li'l Abner*, *Bad*.

THEM VENUES

Thems are not great restaurant people, but they retain a certain loyalty to Mr Chow's and San Lorenzo. They go to events at the R.C.A., I.C.A. (some), rock shows by Thems, certain fashion shows.

PEOPLE WHO UNDERSTAND THEMS

Miles Chapman, Judy Niland, Serena Shaffer, Joanna Jacobs, Lendal Scott-Ellis, Christina Berlin.

POSTSCRIPT

I showed the draft of this article to a Them for comment. 'Razor blades were last year,' he said. But generally they will like it. They like publicity. La publicité, they feel, is all good.

Thems were very important guides to the new Leisure Class that came up after them – the New Bohemia which was younger, rougher, but in a lot of ways more educated and less scared of politics and ideas, the Short-Haired Underground.

But the Thems pushed out the boat for the new sensibility, self-conscious, equivocal, eclectic, Post-Modern. And they were much more tied into Punk's beginnings than any of the punk apologists would admit for *years* afterwards.

Eyes right: Ranger-dom in Lower Sloane Street; scarf by Hermès, bag is the classic Gucci model

Johnny Rotten: *objets trouvés* including Eddie badge, psycho stare,
Seditionaries shirt, Iron Cross, and the pins

Above: The New Model gets a
paint job

Right: Machomania – in the
Clone Zone

Mayfair Merc: streak job, horizontally banded fox coat, Porsche, dog, lip-brush

Sloane Ranger Man: dogs, the eighteenth century, watch-chain, wa-wa

Right: Boys Own – new duds, new attitudes, old stuff

Below: Andrew Logan demonstrates one of life's quandaries

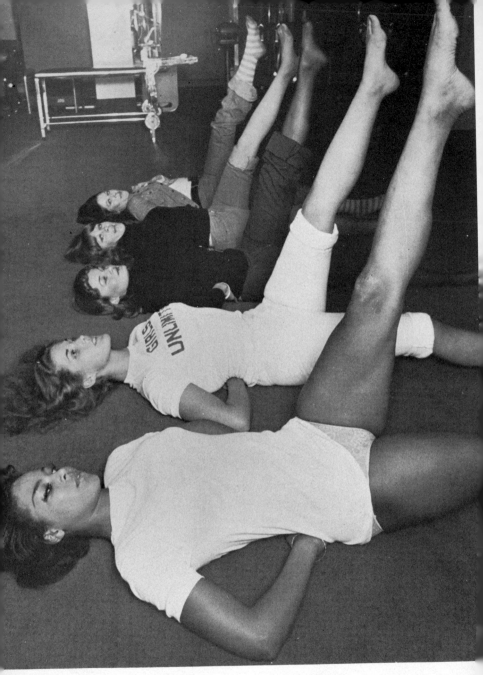

Me: onward and upward

One plants: a silver birch for the Silver Jubilee in Hyde Park

Recycling the sixties: Remember Marc?

Recycling the sixties: Remember skins?

No. 41 May 1980   Bailey and Litchfield's   Price 50p ($2.00 800/yr)

RITZ

Newspaper

Lord Hesketh   Laura Ashley   Meryl Streep   &   Clive Jame

Right: Little Magazines –
Seventh Avenue high society

Below: Kraftwerk – student
types take the trip to future past

Discontinued models: coalface shot

At home: Mr and Mrs Kenneth J. Lane, Murray Hill, 1975

New Mod: lads up against the cosmic wall

Punk (early): Johnny and Steve suggest haircut options at the 100 Club

That Tony Parsons. *That* Julie Burchill. Showing the *Sunday Times* readers
how in 1978

The
Post-Punk Mortem

Harpers & Queen, July 1977

Up the King's Road, round the bend into World's End, is the
little shop called Seditionaries, a.k.a. Sex, a.k.a. Too Fast To
Live, Too Young To Die, a.k.a. Let It Rock. ('a.k.a.' – 'also
known as' – is New Wave, or rock press, for 'formerly'. The
shop changes its identity every eighteen months or so.) The
assistants are now got up in a kind of comic-book manner,
spiky blonde hair, Cat-woman eyeblack. One has face painting
in precise diagonals. The clothes on sale are garage cum para-
military, surprisingly well made, with a great many zips. The
most popular style of trouser, for boys and girls, is in black
polished cotton, rather like Y.S.L. but with a strap between the
legs. This impedes running, but is O.K. for walking and posing.

The shop is neat; it has grey walls and an opaque glass front
with a brass nameplate like a High Street dentist. There are
Adeptus chairs, covered in orange nylon. Mid-sixties Modern.
Through an irregular hole in the ceiling thrust two spotlights.
New Wave conceptual art. Round the shop wander a number
of general girl customers, at once scared and expectant, puzz-
led at finding so little of the shock horror they've heard about.
They are half expecting Johnny Rotten to appear, to spit in
their eyes. This is where the Sex Pistols were invented.

Despite its low-key manner, the shop is oddly uncompromis-
ing. Strapped trousers, as their designer Vivienne Westwood
says, imply 'commitment'. (Commitment to *what* is less clear,

but Seditionaries is single-minded.) The stuff is quite expensive too, not quite the S.M. couture the wags call it, but almost up to, say, Jap prices. Seditionaries is a shop for the élite of Radical Displacement. To a remarkable degree, this élite and the sharp end of the people I have described as Them wear its clothes.

Further down towards Sloane Square (the King's Road is smart again) at No. 153 is Boy (a.k.a. Acme Attractions), the straight commercial take-up of the New Wave. Boy specializes in Early Sixties Revival and quasi-military quasi-S.M. clothing with redundant zips. Things are turning over nicely. On the walls are the yellowing front pages of popular newspapers with headlines describing boys in military or murderous situations. 'LONDON BOY MERCENARY FLIES HOME: I JUST WANT MY MUM.'

The shop's T-shirts, price £5.50, are printed with extracts from a biography of Dean Corll, the paedophiliac Bluebeard who murdered thirty or forty boys in Houston, Texas. Boy's P.R. poster shows a working-class affray, photographed in black and white. A boy lies unconscious, face bleeding, on the pavement, framed by two pairs of legs in shortish trousers and rubber-soled Doc Martens. *Skinhead*. The motto on the poster reads 'The strength of a nation lies in its youth' (Hitler). Boy is, says its owner John Krevine, all about style and style differentiation and nothing else. The kids are aiming to look good and to shock, but in that order.

The Rough Trade record shop in Kensington Park Road – 202, down the rough end, the Powis Square end, the Street Fighting Man *ghetto* end – seems a different proposition. It is awash with *messages;* from the band and record posters on the wall, in the Conflict Graphics style, to the scrawled Alternative top ten of hits by New Underground figures pinned to a notice-board, to various New Left posters at the back of the shop, and, above all, to the products of the New Wave press, the fanzine *Sniffin' Glue,* as mentioned in the *Sunday Times,* but countless others in the same manner, like *Negative Reaction* or a hand-written one called *Viva la Resistance* produced in Preston, Lancs.

Rough Trade has the look of a head shop – which indeed it once was. The more *oppositional* late sixties type, but a head shop nonetheless. You feel there could be discussions on élitism in the New Wave and how the groups should relate to the record companies: the whole issue of *selling out*. It is here you begin to think the *politics* could be for real.

In these little shops, little shops whose devotees used to enter like conspirators, as customers used to slip into Granny Takes A Trip or Hung On You or Back-ah-Yard, the black boy's place on Portobello Road, are illustrated all the underlying tensions and contradictions of the main style thrust of the last eighteen months: Radical Displacement, or what the rock press, searching for the cosmic, calls the New Wave (from Nouvelle Vague). The world outside calls it Punk Rock.

In the autumn of 1976, the Overground rock press – which incorporates much of what is left of the Underground press – that curious rag-bag of magazines from *Melody Maker* and *New Musical Express* to *Record Mirror* which produces some of the worst and the best of New Wave (i.e. not subbed) journalism in this country, started going bananas about punk rock.

They were not happy with the word; what they were looking for was a Movement, but punk rock more or less did until December, when Thames Television's *Today* programme made punk the most famous joke and Johnny Rotten the most famous person in the land, with the consequent spate of popular press nonsense about bin-liner fashion and safety-pinned ears. The rock press then decided to call it the New Wave and to talk about tower blocks, dole queue rock and disaffected youth. What was so exciting for the rock press – and exciting is the word – was that they were again the interpreters, the custodians of a music with social significance. Radical Displacement had put the key to the universe into their hands.

The older music paper writers had not been this excited since the late sixties, when music seemed to be carrying the standard, when it was legitimate to write pieces about Grosvenor Square and police brutality to blacks.

The younger writers liked it for more complicated reasons,

because in an eerie way it was both smart and significant, it was a put on and then again it wasn't. Punk grew partly from that inexplicable vocabulary of the pose and double-think called New York Nihilism which had nourished their favourites, Lou Reed, the New York Dolls, the Ramones, Patti Smith – even the thin white duke, David Bowie, had drawn from that source. These Young Turks of the rock press – there were six or seven, average age twenty-five, who started it off, who would actually bother to cover New Wave gigs – had an intellectual rationale for what was now chic (but they knew that 'chic' was a word to fight shy of now, like 'bisexual', 'camp', 'ambiguous' and all that). *All* the young dudes eventually followed this news. *Sounds*, perhaps the most hip of the three biggies (with *M.M.* and *N.M.E.*), even started an Alternative Chart in late 1976.

An alternative chart – what delicious echoes of 1966. Our secret. Issue after issue of *Sounds* and *Melody Maker* and the *New Musical Express* was devoted to punk/New Wave before a single record appeared and when almost the only band actually gigging was the Sex Pistols.

But sure enough, the music *was* exciting, almost hypnotic, and the verbal abuse of the performers more exciting yet for middle-class boys who liked to be told off by proles. The repertoire of the New Wave seemed at first pretty shaky, the words banal and the musicianship basic, but then, and here was the double-think again, *that was the point of it.* The point of it was that every street-corner kid could buy himself a cheap guitar and form a group and make something for himself. He could forget the geriatric quadrophonic superstars. It was at once both an idealistic and an extremely patronizing notion (which became, in its time, a cliché of interviews with New Wave bands). But it was true. The writers, and the kids themselves, had been waiting for the next style push for about six years. The big-selling stars and supergroups were basically multinational corporations. What had followed since 1970, with the exception of a few talented individuals like Ferry and Bowie, had been kiddypop on the one hand and bland formula on the other: capital-intensive studio music. The rock writers had worked their best to promote Neo-Decadence, but this had never amounted to much in the mass market – the mass market had gone for Glitter Thump like Gary Glitter and Slade – and as for significance, forget it.

But punk was music which was fast, aggressive, apparently working-class and full of menace, with nutty politics, peculiar sex. A music whose appeal the Turks hoped would leap over the hideous desert of M.O.R. (rock press for 'middle-of-the-road') and straight to the people of the abyss – the boot boys of the council estates, the urban white trash – the subjects of the rock press intelligentsia's transfixed imagination. The theory of punk rock, the New Wave, was the creation of the rock press.

In fact, although Johnny Rotten was, as far as the deepest digging could reveal, the genuine article from an Islington council flat, the first group of really dedicated New Wave *fans* were the Bromley Contingent.

Bromley was hardly the abyss. Bowie came from Bromley. It was in places like Bromley, Harrow and Ilford that you got that particular social mix of upper working-class and lower middle-class stylists that fourteen years ago produced . . . the original Mods.

The fans (the fans *were* the punks) were often boys and girls who were extraordinarily sophisticated in the vocabulary of clothes and pose (they knew the places, the dates, the faces), kids of fourteen to eighteen who recognized the style potential of their heroes very fast, and tended to go one further. Until the T.V. incident there were probably no more than a couple of hundred in the country. There were more commentators drawing various energy from the scene than punks.

These kids were works of art. Originals. They were there at the beginning. When punk had its own festival at the 100 Club in Oxford Street in September, they became celebrities. When *the* New Wave venue – the Roxy Club in Neal Street, Covent Garden – opened in December 1976, they became a kind of Alternative Society. They had *credibility*.

In the spring and summer of 1976, punk found its own places and developed its own ideology. This was, roughly speaking, for it was hardly a party manifesto (punks distrusted verbals) – Anarchy in the U.K., or, to be historical (1968), Smash the System. Babylon in flames. Or somefink.

The songs made it clear. The O.K. subjects now certainly weren't sex or love, for that was tedious and middlebrow, but the dole queue, boredom, urban violence and perversity, plus a lot of incestuous reference to New Wave and rock press characters. It was the Electric Apocalypse. It was Jean Genet and J.G. Ballard all in one. Goodness, it was strong stuff.

And then again it was a very sophisticated joke, a sixties nightmare of the future like Peter Watkins' movie *Privilege*, *Private Eye*'s Spiggy Topes and the Turds, a Warhol monster-mash. Nothing could really be *that* crude, no generation was that blank. Or was it?

The bright boys from the record companies came to watch the attendance figures, to clock the potential in what, even then, the brighter began to suspect was the *next leap forward*.

With record turnover down an alleged thirty per cent they were eager. And by Christmas, the signing up seemed to be going apace. Hundreds of untried, *cheap* groups seemed to be springing up everywhere. Those who remembered the first Underground and Middle Earth and after were inspired by the thought of Megahype. The music business, now almost the size of the military-industrial complex, had found its salvation.

Punk, early observers saw, had potential as a Movement. Back to the People. Authentic, raw meat, non-verbal politics. Relevance. Home-grown working-class heroes. The rock press now asked bands first what they felt about political issues – rather than about their favourite foods (1966), drugs (1967), bi-sexuality (1972) or tax exile (1975).

Despite the political stance, the bomb-site boys got themselves signed to record companies with alacrity. Clash, the most overtly political group of all, went to C.B.S.; the Sex Pistols to E.M.I.; and the Damned to Stiff Records.

Although the New Wave talked of anarchy – of a kind Proudhon wouldn't have recognized – their grass-roots appeal, worried social workers were heard to say earlier this year, could be to the alienated tinies, the twelve, thirteen and fourteen-year-olds, among whom there seem to be an extraordinary move to authoritarianism and a baby Nazi cult.

And again, although it was ostensibly anti-élitist and very much a Movement – 'What we want is more bands like us' the Pistols had said – the London élite of the New Wave bands, with its sartorial checking system, was fairly exclusive.

The seminal Pistols also said, in one of their best-known quotes – Johnny Rotten proved wonderful copy – that they weren't into music, they were into chaos. But Virgin Records, to whom they are now contracted, after being sacked from two other record companies, had presumably signed them to sell records. In the wings, happily for the record companies, was a boatload of competent musicians who had been around a while – particularly the New York bands – who could reasonably be sold under the punk banner, and a mass of kids who could be presented as Pepsi-punk, bubble-gum punk, and one day, groomed just so, would prove acceptable to *Top of the Pops*.

In fact the first New Wave group to grace T.O.T.P., in May, was the Jam – a neat, neat, neat group of apparent Mod-revivalists who wore sharp suits and two-tone winklepicker shoes and said they'd vote Conservative. But by April, most new bands that emerged cropped their hair and wore leather jackets and stovepipe trousers and Angry Shades. The Look.

New Wave was hokum in one sense; it meant the rediscovery of the Generation Gap. This wonderful market segmentation, first invented in the fifties, had been quiescent for seven years, during which, embarrassingly, young denim parents brought up in the wonderworld of Teen themselves understood what their kids liked. The class element aside, the New Wave really represents a revolt of the young against the youngish – against sophisticates especially. Punk was hard to take even for the most flexible parents. One middle-class son of the artigentsia described his get-up as 'a complex personal statement of alienation'. He meant his parents didn't like it.

Most punk fans were of an age and a class to live at home. The notion of a youth class appeals, so, within limits, does that of an underclass, brought into sharp though perhaps temporary relief by the number of unemployed school-leavers – and young graduates for that matter (unemployment isn't half as selective as they say).

But many of the hard core of original punks weren't unemployed. This led to some exquisite ironies, like the 'Butterfly Ball' in the Ladies at Andrew Czezowski's Roxy Club. In would go ordinary little girls, carrying bags containing make-up and safety pins; out would come Monsterettes, Street Vixens; crop-haired toughies apparently on parole from the remand home; Rocky Horrors in fishnet and stilettoes and black knickers. (Czezowski had to replace filched lavatory chains almost nightly.) The girls would then dance together, grapling, like baby psychopaths with epilepsy. Sometimes the innocent, supposing them to be fighting, tried to separate them. Then you got real fights.

The Roxy was a 35-year-old's vision of hell, beyond belief, the most grisly, the most sordid . . . Wayne County's coprophiliac lyrics, Charlie Manson's family's murders – all became elements in the style. It was, in fact, quite a cheerful and companionable place, but you could see what the *News of the World* would have made of it. There was no sense in which you could assimilate this style for suburban leisure-wear.

It seemed as if everyone who mattered in the New Wave – the Pistols, Bernard Rhodes the manager of Clash, Andrew Czezowski of the Roxy, had started off at World's End with Malcolm and Vivienne – Malcolm McLaren, owner of Seditionaries, manager of the Sex Pistols, and Vivienne Westwood. The one art-school trained, the other an ex-teacher. The influence of this pair cannot be overestimated. Malcolm, through the various incarnations of his shop, predicted major fashion movements – fifties/Rock Revival, fetishism, street punk – with extraordinary accuracy. Earlier he had managed one of the seminal New York groups, the New York Dolls (men); thus it was not surprising that he was to invent the Sex Pistols.

Vivienne, a pretty, energetic little woman with spiky bleached hair and royal blue eyeliner, has developed a talent for producing styles which feed into the fashion mainstream of youth culture, often by roundabout routes. It is now obligatory for young designers from Europe to check her out; inevitably the sharper ones copy her. Those who know point out parallels between her designs and those of Kenzo and Castelbajac.

Even the opposition, the roaming Teds, who, so it was said, beat up punks when they could find them and broke up their gigs, had ironically been in the shop as regulars when it was Let It Rock. 'The Teds,' said Malcolm and Vivienne 'are our friends.'

On 7 June, Malcolm and Vivienne, plus nine assorted Thems and punks, were scooped up by the police in an absurd mêlée after a promotional boat trip up the Thames for punks, friends and foreign filmers organized by Virgin Records. The police, clearly expecting intractable nastiness – they read their newspapers – had lined Charing Cross pier with Black Marias. The mornings next day duly reported Shock Horror. (In fact a quiet, cheerful time had been had by all on board.)

The New Wave look developed from a curious marriage of revivalist, fetishist and para-military imagery. The revival elements – often hotly denied – came from both the fifties and early sixties. The festishist was in the leather and the mutilation – the zips, the tearing. From New York cool came the shades – worn perpetually.

The fifties element was predominantly bikeboy; the sixties Mod, sharp, neat, pre-psychedelic. Indeed, notwithstanding the symbolic brutalities of the New Wave, it is immensely design-conscious, fundamentally a neat tight style. What it hates is the sloppy and the amorphous: the shapeless flared jeans and longish hair of bourgeois post-hippie.

Other key influences have been the mercenaries – the Angola boys' haircut, the I.R.A. from whom the collective unconscious absorbed berets, dark glasses and mackintoshes with turned-up collars. Another important source is the undergrowth of literature: pornography from the fetishist and S.M./bondage areas. The Sex shop, of course, had been a specialist outfitters selling rubbers and leathers.

In addition to these, punk was rock drawing on its own past. The recent past – Bowie and Ferry are there and the Rocky

Horror Show. Bowie had made the sartorial breakthrough of
the 1970s – short, spiky hair. At the same time, rock history
provided its own more naive input: early P.R. photos of Cliff
Richard in cuddly jumpers or photographs of forgotten mid-
sixties bands, X and the Ys, looking tough.

The New Wave has developed its own semiology. Take the
tie, which crops up in almost every group shot – the thin tie
spread in a hangman's knot from an unbuttoned collar. This
tie is, not to be fanciful, an atavistic – or pastiche – return to
formalism or sharp dressing as a reaction against the sloppiness
of the late sixties. But this tie, the tie no one else wears now,
also has to be pulled open, worn like a scarf, sometimes without
even a shirt. It comes, in fact, from a James Dean still. Youth
in revolt. School's out. The tie is thin, shiny, school or
regimental; not the well-hung jumbo knot of the late sixties.

Basically, hair must be short, trousers must be narrow.
These are ideological points of crucial significance. In a key interview in *Sniffin' Glue,* the Clash were asked whether clothes
were all that important, and said: 'Like trousers, like brain'.
(This was terrifyingly naive. One thing the sixties had shown
was that lifestyles are non-linear now – you don't necessarily
think like you look. How else can you account for those late
sixties entrepreneurs the breadheads?) Shoes were black, either
stylized winklepickers or so broad and ordinary as to be anti-
shoes.

The bits and pieces were less important. The safety-pins and
razor blades, for instance, were derived, it is said, from a
Warhol transvestite called Jackie Curtis via the Pistols. As a
serious phenomenon however they were finished when they
started to filter into mainstream fashion. More persistent are
the chains and spiked leather bracelets of fetishist drag. But
these too are making their way into the more outré shallows of
the mainstream. Chains in plastic can be bought from Mrs
Howie.

Much effort and, covertly, a fair bit of money go on achieving
this surreal Street-Corner Kid look. It is meant to be the antithesis of South Molton Street and of hairdresser kitsch. It is also,
implicitly, a reaction to gay overkill, particularly gay glitter.

It is also making a statement about class. The look, particularly the Clash look, is meant to be aggressively working-class, although, like the fashion for overalls, it is not something most ordinary working-class kids would wear. Looking, that weird is more the puberty rite of middle-class kids.

Underlying all is the increasingly important note of personal style as a work of art. Hence the do-it-yourself aspect. This notion, which had its recent origins with Them, became a point of faith with the punk fans. As one upper-class admirer said, 'It takes away the whole glamour of being rich' (horribly reminiscent of New York's Radical Chic reaction to the Black Panthers as described by Tom Wolfe). Takes away the glamour of . . . tell that to the groups signing the big record contracts.

Along with the music and the clothes there developed a distinct graphical style; no one could say quite where it started. It seemed like a collective unconscious memory of the old Underground, redacted (Warhol for 'transcribed') by a nine-year-old Cockney. Early examples were the press packs for the Sex Pistols.

From these developed a whole school of design, whose novel but limited repertoire turned up everywhere, including eventually, inevitably, the advertisements for New Wave records produced by big record companies, and this was indicative, because everything about the New Wave was full of wonderful contradictions. The closer you looked the more confusing it got.

The first fanzine was *Sniffin' Glue* (1976). The style is cheapo, spontaneous, letters cut from newspapers to make the headings (like blackmailers' letters), photo-montage for the illustrations, bad typing for the text. The text in the fanzines says 'fuck' quite a lot but little else; they are on Restricted Vocabulary, for there is a real terror of sounding interleckshul. Much of the content is sycophantic: *all* New Wave bands are good. In this sense *Sniffin' Glue* – and, to a far greater extent, its imitators – are like nothing so much as a cross between a naughty version of a conventional teeny fanzine of the Oh Boy variety and a youth club mag. But they are, so the party line runs, spontaneous, proletarian, irreverent, and Limited Editions. They are also, because of their Xeroxed production and lack of advertising, rather expensive – 30p for eight to sixteen pages, some printed on one side only.

Everything is – has to be – black and white, with headings in Magic Marker. The Magic Marker look they share, of course, with *Interview* and *Ritz,* as they share their transcribed tape-recorder interview technique.

A lot, however, is non-verbal, photo-montage combining shock headlines and pictures in bizarre juxtaposition. The total effect is disorienting – like propaganda. Certain motifs reappear constantly: graffiti, old film posters, packing-case stencils, official documents ('Anarchy in the U.K. – maximum penalty £5'), military subjects (plans of tank interiors, etc.) and cut-ups from *Marvel* and ultra-violence comix. It is all, in conventional terms, unremittingly ugly, like the product of some ancient Manifesto group which had set out to expunge prettiness and slickness. The point of this stylistic extremism is simple: it polarizes. Through alienation it creates a sense of community. Identity through Outrage.

To anyone observant who is past thirty much of the graphic style is extremely familiar; sixties aggressive, Generation X. One waits for the New Wave to discover grainy printing and fish-eye lenses, and, apprehensively, for fashion spreads set against tower blocks and trash cans. The bands themselves are often photographed in a 1965 manner for record covers. Jam look like Mods on theirs – mass Mods, scooter and parka Mods. Clash are set in perspective up an alley in a way reminiscent of Steve Marriot and the Small Faces.

At the same time, other style groups were zeroing in on the New Wave. The brighter Thems with an ear to the ground saw the potential first. After all, the Pistols had played at Andrew Logan's warehouse at a party in spring 1976. So despite the insistence on disowning the past – 'Today's music today' is a key tag – there was a fair bit of transmission of culture going on between the English punk bands and the Thems and the New York Nihilists who sprang from Warhol's Velvet Underground. Some New Wave bands have felt obliged to disown these roots, or are at best ambivalent about their predecessors' individualism and middle-class backgrounds. In fact the first New Wave bands were weaned on them.

This uptake of the New Wave by the Thems meant a transmission of ideas. Zandra Rhodes' collection shown in May had dresses in chiffon, strategically torn, held together with jewelled pins. Derek Jarman, director of *Sebastiane* – a Them film about rogering among Roman soldiers – has started work on a film about punk rock girls. Quick-off-the-mark Miles Chapman in this January's *Honey*, followed by *19* and in May by *Elle*, produced what were in effect *fashion spreads* on the new vocabulary. The hundred days of the Roxy were recorded for an E.M.I. album and a book is forthcoming.

In early 1977 clothes designers, retailers and record companies tooled up for a high summer of punk. Vivienne Westwood's designs from last year, de-specified by mass manufacturers, will be everywhere. Conflict graphics will filter through. By Christmas, ad agencies will be trying a few fliers . . . zips, Magic Marker artwork in Day-Glo. Look for working-class heroes, more T.V. documentaries on urban violence. Look for the emergence of a Tamla Motown of the New Wave record companies. Look for New Wave art; perhaps something like the atrocity window-dressing that hit New York last autumn. Watch Johnny Rotten's struggle not to be Mick Jagger. Wait for some spectacular recantations by New Wave performers and anxious back-tracking by the rock press as their own special music goes national – a C.B.S.-subsidized riot for every town. Watch for the development of a more sophisticated, musically competent Second Wave – an Avant-Garde New Wave for an older more sophisticated market.

The New Wave is a British invention and trade will follow the flag. For good or ill it will be photographed and reported round the world. No matter that it drew on American antecedents, the British style, British clothes, British music, however unpolished, are light-years ahead. American punk is more discreetly revivalist. It breaks little new style ground by comparison.

'It's only rock and roll': Mick Jagger. 'This isn't rock and roll, it's genocide': David Bowie, in *Diamond Dogs*.

No one really understands the politics of the New Wave. No one knows whether it has any, or whether radical politics have simply been liquidized in the style machine. Those who deny a political content, like those who emphasize it, sound a false note.

There *is* something there. There are of course elements which translate into the fashion mainstream and have no political content at all, just the imagery of violence. But real violence, truth to tell, is a commonplace of live rock music; the business employs a whole army of heavies and you can get some very nasty moments at the most innocuous performances of mainstream rock in Glasgow and Sheffield.

The most difficult question is whether in the last analysis the New Wave represents Terminal Decadence or a cure for it. Is it a sort of gladiatorial circus to go with the bread of economic stagnation, or is it, as its apologists claim, new and good and energetic like a gush of oil in the North Sea? Certainly on one level, that of pure style, it was inevitable, a fact of demographics; the style establishment was getting older, and richer, creating things that kids, and more particularly working-class kids, found unexciting and irrelevant. The radical input of the late sixties had become remarkably quiescent during the seventies. London, said the Clash, was burning with boredom. Could it be that somehow the radicalism has got displaced into style and music? For imaginative intellectuals, the putative 1984 aspects of the New Wave are all there. The *Clockwork Orange* imagery of violence (although the original punks were rather well behaved), the creation of unpersons – the vilification of older rock musicians in terms that go far beyond the boringness of their music – the renaming whereby the kids assumed identities (Billy Idol, Sid Vicious, Rat Scabies, Captain Sensible) to suit the ideology. This is Warhol Superstar (Viva, Cherry Vanilla, Holly Woodlawn, Ultra Violet) but also echoes the Underground, the Muslims and the Panthers.

There is some insistence on ideological purity. (One band, Generation X, even went so far as to issue a cod press release, stating they'd changed managers, for a kind of ideological refit.

This was a joke, but the rock press swallowed it.) And more double-think about origins.

The necessity for the bands to have authentic working-class backgrounds has led to some peculiar difficulties, because if the spirit was willing the facts were often weak. Thus band members would not only lie about age but about class as well. A couple of middle-class group members are famous for having been caught out. That there was a strong bourgeois strain among the groups, and, more to the point, a fair bit of higher education, was really nothing to be ashamed of, but the musicians had made class an issue, and were shy of being accused of intellectualizing.

The class point is important. The fact is, as surprisingly few commentators on the rock scene have seen fit to point out, the market for rock music is fragmented into class segments as well as age segments. In the late sixties and early seventies, however, the main input in rock music was taking place at an increasingly older and middle-class level. This left the kids out in the cold. The excitement had gone with the embourgeoisification of their heroes and the only alternative was commercial pop of the silliest kind.

Or of course raggae. Punk has affinities with Rasta, another kind of non-rational politics. Rastafarians in dreadlocks wake dread in their enemies. Punk is a sort of white dread.

In an alarmist piece this April, John Blake of the *Evening News* said that the National Front had been trying to recruit punk performers and fans, encouraged by the popularity of the swastika motif in punk get-ups. The suggestion was that the New Wave was ripe for exploitation by the Front. In the following issue of *Melody Maker*, there was a report of an angry Johnny Rotten telephoning their reporter Caroline Coon to say that the Front was wet and all his friends were black or gay or outcasts of one kind or another. The Front had simply failed to understand how punks used the Swastika, as they used pictures of Marx. It means something, but not what the National Front thought.

In fact, in so far as a few New Wave bands had politics susceptible to conventional analysis, their politics seemed a populist version of the New Left.

Most of the politics in the New Wave is non-verbal, consciousness-raising, according to the Clash. What do they want to do? They want the kids to think, to do things for themselves, they say. When they played at the I.C.A. in London once, the student audience, behaving as it felt it ought, started heaving glasses around. Singer Joe Strummer told them they'd be more dangerous at home sticking on stamps.

After this came out there was a response in the next issue of *Sniffin' Glue*. The writer, who was very good, went off into a very stylish harangue. It was obscene, he said, to have this kind of thing sandwiched between ads for Cartier and such like. It was those people making a fashion out of our lives. 'Fucking Harpers and fucking Queen come down our fucking place and get your fucking stole soiled.'

This really got me, because it was generally accurate and funny but also *wrong* – wrong in the sense that what I was doing was describing the inevitable fashionizing process then well under way, not *being* it.

The writer was Danny Baker. I met him at the *Sniffin' Glue* office – they really had one; a grace and favour room in Dryden Chambers, part of Miles Copeland's (now Manager of Police and very big time) little record company. Step forward – he harangued me too. I couldn't get a word in, and there didn't seem much to be said then. He had his act to follow. Most of it was the sharpest line of chat I'd heard in years and I thought D.B. – he was nineteen then – was going to move it; not only that, but he had obviously been quite a few places already. Later he started writing for the frightful *Zigzag* and I registered his name again because his stuff was so good and – this was the real point – he seemed to be picking up on all the little things I liked myself. Big mouth, but he couldn't be all bad. He'd say a record was good and I'd *know* it was worth buying, not just something to talk about. Later still he joined the *N.M.E.* Now he's on T.V. and everything.

Little Magazines

Harpers & Queen, August 1977

In 1976 a man could go to bed sane and wake up a magazine proprietor. The Alternative Media bug had crept out of the woodwork in High Energy Year, and was scuttling around. Young people wanted to do *little magazines* again. What they meant, of course, wasn't the little magazines of the Gutenberg age, the literary reviews and poetry magazines with delicious middles, or political numbers sold on Charing Cross Road. They weren't magazines for a world where Nicholas Bentley Drew The Pictures. Nor were they a mass newspaper of the Alternative lifestyle like *IT*. The beau ideal was something that looked like a cross between *Ritz* and *Sniffin' Glue* and had the logistics of the local bakery. A Personal Statement. Ecologists began to fear that there might soon be more magazines than people.

The last big burst of small-media frenzy had started in 1967 with the Summer of Love, had waxed huge – in its heyday *IT* was selling massively, and *Oz* – then fallen away as 1969 turned into 1970, and *Time Out* offered Agitprop listings.

The energy came back after 1970 in the form of overflow from Special Interest areas. Ecology for instance, in *Seed,* or sci-fi, in *White Dwarf*. (The sci-fi energy commanded its own book-and-magazine shop in St Anne's Court, Soho, called Dark They Were And Golden-Eyed – the title of a Ray Bradbury story.)

In 1975 and 76 the main specialist energy source was *music,* starting with the ethnic and specialist like *Zigzag* (now big) and *Pressure Drop,* a one-man publication for reggae freaks started by Nick Kimberley in 1976, and other alternatives to the radio playlist. Then in late 76 there was Punk. Punk begat a news-

stand full of little magazines, many of them written by incredibly young kids (one, *Moron,* is written by two North London schoolgirls), and financed on a hand-to-mouth basis with
the help of sympathetic outlets like Compendium or Rough
Trade.

While the content of many of these magazines is predictable,
the energy and resource and *potential* of their founders is impressive. It has begun to spill over in its turn in a second wave
of Youth Culture magazines, with their own wider mix of content – politics, fashion and gossip between the same covers; not
just music but Art and Ideas as well.

It seems as if we're in for one of those periods of adjustment
when the balance between energy and innovation and professionalism is re-set. Neophiliac words have risen again out of the
dust: 'vital', 'young', 'honest'. 'Polished', 'subtle', 'refined',
'sophisticated' are now suspect with the young. *The boys are back
in town.* The high-tone professionalism, the experiments in
technique, the *production values* that had begun to concern a
previous generation are also being rejected. The young are racing into the authenticity trap. Make it real, or, at least, make it
look real. There's that familiar line about plastic. 'Oh, he's
plastic,' etc. etc. And doubts about accepting advertisements.
The idea of a non-commercial magazine has, initially at least, a
tremendous draw; no pressures, compromises, discipline.

But the real underlying factor is that the multi-media person
has come home to roost. The kids of the post-McLuhan age
know that *the message is me* – screw the medium. The multi-
media person grasps the essentials of a medium in a week, uses
what's around. The lesson of all those Arts Labs has passed into the bloodstream. Express yourself by any means possible.
The Artist is the electricity that can go into anything. But film
is impossible, video expensive, radio already parcelled out,
access T.V. a future dream. It comes down to the format that's
most accessible, most familiar: the folded newspaper/magazine
of the late sixties, like *IT, Rolling Stone, Interview.* And for the
youngest, poorest kids, the Xeroxed page. Small, if not
beautiful, is valid.

The original underground press was based on two cheap accessible pieces of mid-sixties technology, I.B.M. typesetting (anyone who could type decently could lay out a magazine) and cheap small-run offset litho printing. This meant speedier, more flexible magazines, less vulnerable to the censorship of geriatric compositors: a devoluted unit. But many of the latest crop of kids aren't thinking in terms even of a print run of 2,000 (*Harpers & Queen* prints 86,000, *The New Statesman* 46,000). They are wondering if they can afford 200. (If they can't afford it, by 1976 everyone knew someone whose office had a Xerox 3600.) A lot of this little-broadsheet business had started with the community politics of the late sixties' residents' associations. Save Our Street, the Notting Hill Gate social experiment syndrome. Then, every pressure group, every Radical Feminist Collective had its own little magazine (and eventually a proper magazine grew out of that, too – *Spare Rib*). Come together, right now.

Implicit in all this is the idea of media access, fifteen minutes' stardom for anyone. So the new mags tend to follow an open-door policy – to offer space to the readers to say their piece. The irony of this all-comers policy, once outside the community newspapers proper, is that, like chat shows on T.V., it makes for cheap content.

A lot of today's little mags pay a lick and a promise to contributors when they start. The old literary magazines gave their authors £5 and a glass of sherry. The new mags get your name on the door and they get your name around.

The open-door policy persisted in the seventies. *New Style* solicits contributions from its readers, and Mark P of *Sniffin' Glue*, who says he's gone off writing, has turned his pages over to friends.

In 1977 the Second Wave of magazines is coming, you can feel it, people who have got the professionalism and energy nicely balanced, who know how to sell an ad and place it, who have learnt their lesson about distribution. Some of *these* little magazines, you feel, will grow big.

Bananas, Ritz, New Style and *Sniffin' Glue* all represent different but established positions among the little magazines of the last eighteen months.

Bananas calls itself literary: very Old Wave. But a literary *newspaper – IT* or *Village Voice* fold-over formula (design by Julian Rothenstein), a taste for the fantastical (*Encounter* knocked them for 'an abject love of the surreal'), very sharp political analyses by Tom Nairn, short stories by J.G. Ballard etc. make *Bananas* a mutant; it isn't sherry-party but it has a strong flavour of Upper Class Barmy, 1977 style. Its editor, Emma Tennant, aims to make it look 'as unacademic as possible – we wanted fiction that could read like news, we wanted to get away from the *London Magazine* image that's so depressing and unbuyable.'

Emma Tennant knew a bit about how magazines work; she was on *Vogue* before she married, on *Queen* after, has written two novels and been around. But she'd never edited anything. 'People attack you for being a silly lady – the magazine's been quite satisfactorily attacked. And of course there's much jubilation if you fail.'

Bananas pays a bit, but more important, it takes initiatives in *commissioning* fiction from writers Emma Tennant admires. *Bananas* started on £3,000 (half Tennant, half Rothenstein). Issue 1 (January 1975) sold about 3,000 through distributors Moore Harness. By issue 5 they were up to about 8,000. It is now typeset by Caroline McKechnie and distributed by Paperchain.

'They all say they hate it,' says David Litchfield of his and David Bailey's fashion newspaper, 'but they all buy it.' *Ritz*, started in November 1976, is a monthly fashion-plus-interviews-plus-send-up-gossip on a fold-over newsprint format – like *Bananas,* but heavily photographic. The most persistent criticism of *Ritz* is that it rips off Andy Warhol's *Interview,* but does it less well. Litchfield says this ignores the basic fact that *Ritz* is explicitly fashion while *Interview* isn't, but freely admits the debt on other points. 'If you're doing a magazine like this, of course you're going to end up looking a lot like *Interview* – logic dictates it!'

Litchfield, thirty-three, is, like Bailey, a 'pro'. After leaving a State Secondary Modern at fifteen, he worked in independent media – glamour mags, sex mags (the lamented *Curious*), the underground press, and a highly respected little journal for photographers and illustrators, *Image,* which he ran practically single-handed in the early seventies. Because of Bailey's name as a fashion photographer and Litchfield's connections, people are inclined to dismiss *Ritz* as a kind of alternative *Vogue* and suggest that there's massive backing somewhere, that it's too slick for a 'little' magazine, etc. etc. Not fair. In fact, *Ritz* shares the financial logistics of the other little magazines: Litchfield and Bailey's money, fifty fifty. '*No* backers,' says Litchfield. 'Whatever you may have heard, once you've got a backer, you're on a treadmill because he's always looking at the return on his assets – and comparing it with investing in Old Masters or tea.'

• Until this month, there was no office, no permanent staff. Like *Bananas* and several other little mags, it was a Caroline McKechnie/Paperchain effort. Litchfield did everything, commissioned, subbed, laid out, progress chased. Unlike most little mags, however, *Ritz* has got itself into Smith's, in London at least (from the July issue). 'Time and enthusiasm are the little magazines' alternatives to money, but the success motive is important – it's only by actual sales that you realize you're getting to people.' *Ritz*'s start – like that of *Sniffin' Glue* – was mythic. Litchfield's story is that Bailey rang him at 2.30 one night in August last year to say they had to do the paper they'd been on about. And Litchfield said yes to shut him up. Then Bailey told the *Express* and he had to do it.

He was determined to get the distribution right from the start. Most distributors, he says, don't care about little magazines, or about how many they print, since they're on 'sale or return'. A combination of over-optimistic print orders plus the complicated formula whereby the distributors pay the magazines a third of the net receipts for the first issue when they take the second – and so on – mean the hopeful proprietors can be bankrupt by issue one and not know it till issue three – with thousands of unsold issues in the warehouse. 'Returns kill,' says Litchfield. 'I learned that on *Image.*'

Who buys *Ritz*? He doesn't know, but he cites the headmistress of a heavily black school in South London telling how her sixth form girls read it.

He also says, 'Of course, there are 15,000 people in London who'll buy anything *once*. It's easy to start, it's keeping it going that's the problem.'

New Style has an *Oz* format: 11¾ by 8¼ inches, glossy cover, newsprint contents. Subtitles itself 'the review of contemporary mania'. Its editor, Mike von Joel, says this means the Arts, but it's as much Media as Arts mania. It's full of gossipy media stuff reminiscent of *Private Eye*'s revelations of the Street of Shame. Von Joel admits that the *Eye* is a source – it was his favourite sixties magazine – but thinks it's been boring recently. *New Style* echoes the *Eye*'s commonsensicality – 'I don't like sophistry; I like a bit of rationality' – but isn't philistine like the *Eye*.

Von Joel, twenty-seven, is Art School but Northern, non-fancy, a print-maker by training, with a strong entrepreneurial streak. In 1969 he'd become a loon pants (remember?) dealer at his art school, Winchester, and generated enough cash to buy a Cadillac with a T.V. in it.

Before *New Style* he ran a design studio doing small commissions for fashion shops – Chelsea Cobbler etc. – and writing occasional pieces for foreign magazines about what they imagined was London's youth culture.

New Styles (now in the singular) was started, he says, as an 'arts now' magazine, 'to capture the avant-garde of tomorrow; to tap that energy, to find those people now'. There were problems getting started. Though he knew how to lay out – sort of – and edit and had his own I.B.M. for setting, he was totally inarticulate in the vocabulary of commercial printing. The first issue was a disaster: black and white where it was meant to be coloured, the title obscured in the front page. They gave it away on London streets – all 2,000 copies – and lost £200. Thereafter it got more professional, though as von Joel says, little magazines that are more than self-indulgences are stuck in a curious Catch-22 – they can't catch good contributors and advertisers without a product, and vice versa. Also, he accepts only arts-based ads. He admits now that he almost 'fabricated' the content of issues two and three, which he distributed himself to big newsagents with lots of open display space like N.S.S. in Earl's Court Road. By issue four he was up to 4,000 and distributing through Paperchain. The secret is, he says, to get organized – 'not structured, organized'. 'And don't get greedy – that's what spoiled *Street Life*. They wanted full rates and expenses before they really got started. I don't need much – I don't spend much.' He doesn't class himself with the fanzines – 'We're New Wave I guess – there's a lot of similarity in approach, but we're not punk. Punk is doing it on a pad on your knee while you're watching the telly – we try to be professional.'

Mark P of *Sniffin' Glue* has already become a T.V. regular (interviewed by Janet Street-Porter), been subjected to massive publicity including snide remarks from the *Sunday People*, who said he was a dole scrounger, and become a kind of resident punk expert. You sense that he's already bored with it.

Sniffin' Glue too had a mythic start. Mark Perry, nineteen-year-old bank clerk from Deptford, bright, bored with job, long hair, flares, hears an album by the Ramones, the American punk band, then sees them, thinks it's so great he writes a review, copies eight pages on a Xerox at his girlfriend's office and dishes it out, cuts his hair, buys tight trousers and Day-Glo sox, leaves Williams & Glyn's and becomes Mark P.

This is the essence of the fanzine. 'It's-so-great-you'll-like-it too', with minimal layout, and logistics. Issue 1 of *Sniffin' Glue*, September 1976, had an authentic tone and a modest scale – print run 200, and it was interesting; nothing fantastic, but interesting. Then with the media overkill on the New Wave it GREW, and had to take on, by default, the role of spokes-magazine. This was a strain! and it showed. By issue ten it had a flavour almost of self-parody. They went the normal route – distribution through Compendium and the Bizarre Records shop at first. But by the fourth issue they were up to 1,000 and being backed by Rough Trade.

They now sell 8,000 *world-wide*, and although the format's the same it's printed by offset.

Mark P is in fact the classic multi-media person. He says he is bored with writing now and can't do it any longer, 'although I like doing the presentation – the layout.' He's formed his own band and become an A & R man (talent-finder) for a New Wave record label, Step Ahead. So he's giving over the pages of *Sniffin' Glue* to friends. 'The next issue, August, is about other people. I don't really like most of these New Wave magazines – but the best ones will last.'

And more is coming. Steven Lavers, twenty-three, ex Schoolkids' *Oz*, ex rock press, media obsessive, is working on a little mag divided between Ideas – the ideas section will be called 'No Future' (a line from a Pistols song) – and Style/Fun; called 'Tacky'. A mixture of Anarchism-Properly-Explained, photo-montage and New Wave fashion. He's got some experience and resources, plus a co-editor who can draw and lay out. But he hasn't got a bean. Somehow, he plans to get 1500 of *No Future* printed and distributed.

Caroline Baker, once fashion editor of *Nova*, now freelances for magazines like *Elle* and *Ritz*. Everyone admired her work but she was clearly avant-garde, not mass-market mainstream: problematic. So she's busy laying out a dummy for her own little magazine and going the round of potential backers. Will it be fashion? Not in the conventional sense, she says, not just stuff from the shops: things people have thought up for themselves. And there'll be *current* things, topical things. Like what? Like what it's like to be in prison. What's it going to be called? Possibly *Streets*, or *Off the Streets*.

One thing the new little magazines needed was some professional hand-holding – both to get them together and to get them around. Caroline McKechnie and Paperchain fill the gap. McKechnie is a typesetter. In her shabby little office up the rough end of Portobello Road, she thumps away at everything from *Ritz* to ecology on an I.B.M., swapping golfballs for different typefaces. She learned her trade with the old Underground press, on *IT*. When the original *IT* folded she went freelance.

Paperchain distribute smallish magazines – their biggest sellers are *Ritz* and Arabella Melville's *Libertine* – run by young people. Their great asset to the hopeful publisher is scale. They can pay attention to him, they can take the time to work out realistic projections for the print runs; his business is worth their while. Paperchain's catalogue embraces everything from *Resurgence* (ecological) to *Brainstorm Comix* (sci-fi).

Machomania

Harpers & Queen, February 1979

It's a group of . . . *Americans.* There's a cowboy who wears chaps and smiles a lot; a construction worker in hardhat and mirrored sunglasses; a black motorcycle cop; a black G.I., who looks like a Vietnam Vet – kind of hard-bitten – in fatigues; and a biker in black leather with the peaked cap, the chains and the eagle badges; and a Red Indian chief with the full headdress.

It isn't the Labor Day Parade. It's 7.45 and they're on *Top of the Pops*, these Americans. They sing, they dance, they wiggle their asses like mad. Their song's called 'Y.M.C.A.'. It's about men having fun. They're No. 13 with a bullet. If it weren't for the Christmas blockbuster, Boney M's 'Mary's Boy Child', they'd already be No. 1 in the middle of December. As it is they get to No. 1 in January.

They're very masculine, these Americans, they're called the Village People. According to the curiously worded press release from their record company, Phonogram, they generate something called 'unstoppable machomania'. What does it mean?

On *Top of the Pops* all is made plain.

They're very *macho,* these Americans.

They're very gay.

They're *macho gay.*

Perhaps the record company is hoping the *News of the World* will run it, that Mrs Whitehouse will descend and do what she did for the dance troupe Hot Gossip. Or perhaps they *really* feel it's a bit dodgy, that the B.B.C. might take it off the playlist. It's a mystery – and a joke in the industry – how, up until the

New Year, a record by six gay archetypes inviting young men
to meet new friends at the Y.M.C.A. goes unnoticed by the
national press. Maybe it's all just too American.

At one level the Village People are camp; they take straight
icons and up-end them; these men aren't cops and construction
workers, they're disco folk. It's very funny and they do it very
well. At another level, for camp is all about levels and am-
biguities, they are a very literal statement of the American Way
of Gay, or rather of the way it is going. Gay is a Big Deal in
America in a way that, Mr Thorpe's tribulations aside, it isn't
here. Gay is part of the debate over the American way of life:
sexual politics; self-realization; human potential; the whole Me
Generation shuffle. More particularly, gay is now a voice that
carries some political clout. In San Francisco, so they say,
twenty-eight per cent of the voters are gay. In most big
American cities there is something the local media call the 'gay
community' with its groups, its shops, its clubs, its local lob-
byists. A gay voice, a gay vote, gay business, some gay power.

Gays, like blacks and liberated women before them, are a
key element in the social mix of the new America. Gay has
reached the condition of ethnicity. In describing New York's
social geography sophisticated New Yorkers will tell you that
the Italians live there, the Puerto Ricans there, and the gays
there. Like any ethnic group, gays have a marching band, a
National Day – Gay Pride day in San Francisco in 1977 was
apparently the largest demonstration (125,000 marchers) the
city had seen – and a holiday resort (Fire Island). The implication of all this pride, togetherness, all these newly gentrified
gay homes in areas like San Francisco's Castro (once Haight-
Ashbury, *remember?*) is a very American one. No sooner had
gay found a voice than it became a growth industry, a *market*.

The fact that American capitalism can co-opt almost
anything, no matter how ostensibly subversive, is a truism so
bizarre, so fascinating in its implications as to give many sensitive souls perpetual culture shock: Black Pride, the Women's
Movement, Ecological Concern, all assimilated and registered,
all giving their names to new forms of – consumerism. The
process began early in the sixties, with the recognition that to

sustain the American Way in the age of leisure industries the U.S. positively *needed*, not Puritan Ethnic consumers but hedonists.

Left-wingers, inevitably, believe a conspiracy theory. They believe that somewhere sits a cabal drawn from the American Establishment, men with faces like David Rockefeller's. They plot, they plan, they buy off, divide and rule, offer the troublesome groups a share of the action, hose them down with greenbacks. The conspiracy theory fails to understand the real dynamic of America. Men with cigars certainly buy votes in darkened rooms, but the commercial assimilation of minorities tends to come from a more basic American process. America's minorities want to be the majority, billion-dollar babies like everyone else. The American drive to sell to minorities shows *real* respect.

And it works. These people sure as hell buy! A cornucopia pours forth new goods and services. Blacks get Ultrasheen hair care for the naturals, discofunk, Blaxploitation movies; women get Virginia Slims the female-oriented cigarettes, the Women's Bank of New York, movies like *Julia* and *Girl Friends;* gays get amyl nitrate and the Village People.

For some fifteen years a vision has shimmered before the eyes of American Marketing men. It is a vision of a very particular type of consumer. This consumer had not only a high income, but a high *disposable* income. He was without commitments. He was venturesome. He liked change, novelty, travel. He understood style and he would pay a premium for status, for design, for individualism. He was self-involved, went to a shrink and was into health and sex. No one consumer group quite fitted this picture, however: they all tended to drift out of focus, to take on commitments and to stop caring.

Then between 1974 and 1976 the market analysts, the publishers, the property developers, the record companies got homosexuals in their sights. Gays, they realized, were good Americans: they consumed and there were an awful lot of them – some estimates said there were as many gays as blacks – and they were rich. And what the gays bought today, the 'wise' straights would watch and copy and in a couple of

years there would be a mass market among the lumpen; look at
Brut, male jewellery, Art Deco. From Christopher Street to
Hackensack, New Jersey, in a few years. Let gays be your test
market. Gays have been the harbingers of all the growth stocks
in the culture industry.

At first, in the very early seventies, just after the gay political
breakthrough (Gay Lib etc.), what the business sold and the
gays bought was the traditional gay style, the *ghetto* style:
campy camp, divinely decadent Deco, glitter, old movies
(everything Susan Sontag had put her accurate finger on in her
1964 essay on camp; gay was out of the closet before there was
time to create a new style more relevant to life in the open)
mixed with post-hippie polymorphous perversity, with oddities
like the Cockettes, hairy gay hippies in glittery Frank'n'furter
costumes. Out of this hybrid transitional sensibility came the
first big Bowie incarnation and a lot of other early seventies
mass-market cultural phenomena. For the strange thing was,
the people who really responded to all this enjoyable sexy glittery nonsense were, above all, liberated straights, heterosexual
fellow-travellers and *women,* for whom gay liberation was an
automatic parallel to their own. All those little sprogs, those
bouncing little disco girls and boys, took to a spot of token
bisexuality like ducks to water, no sweat. At least, they took to
the appearance of it.

It was fun, everybody liked it. Gays were nice to have
around. Large numbers of quite ordinary young women learnt
about the sophisticated pleasures of a gay confidant from a raft
of magazine articles about faghaggery. From 1972 to 1976 you
could hardly turn on American television without seeing
transvestites (T.V.s on T.V.), transsexuals and even gay football stars with a book or a story to sell, telling all on daytime
chat shows for housewives. It all happened very quickly, the
transformation of gay from outcast to cultural commodity, so
quickly indeed that outside the sophisticated big cities there
was scope for considerable culture-shock and, potentially, reaction.

But something else was emerging. In New York, scarcely
had they swept the 1972 glitter dust off the sidewalks before the

boys were into a new costume – *Americana*. Divine decadence
gave way to reactionary chic in 1973/4. It started with
sophisticated gays who wore traditional iron-clad American
men's clothes in an *ironic* way, as a comment that these clothes
no longer had their coercive meaning. More to the point, if
suburban straights were camping it up, then these clothes,
these uptight blue-collar plain working man Archie Bunker get-
ups, had style. There was nothing new, in principle, about
gays taking up worker chic, they had been doing it for years, in
eclectic little ways – a funny reference to an icon, the straight
working man. But what was different this time was the way
they went about it – it was so complete, such a uniform, that
you might almost think these people wanted to be construction
workers, footballers, lumberjacks.

One of the tightest dress-codes in the world was evolving,
and with the costume – for these things can work from the outside in – a new attitude and a new/old language, the mythology
of the hard man, *macho*.

The costume was Basic Street Gay (or 'Lumberjack'):
straight jeans, cheap plaid shirt, construction workers' yellow
lace-up boots, short cropped hair – and the moustache, always
the moustache. That gay men took to the moustache in droves
from 1973 on is one of the Great Gadarene Mysteries of all
time. But there are clues. Reactionary macho had made a
cultural reappearance – in movies primarily – from the late sixties on: movies built around a theme of male bravery; male
pair-bonding movies, from which women appeared excluded,
relegated to minor roles. The conventional interpretation of
these movies – and it seems reasonable enough – was that they
provided nostalgic escapism for unliberated heterosexual men
who were in shock at the way their womenfolk were acting
now. But often these movies had a good quotient of sadism,
and the characters wore moustaches.

Then there was the Marlboro Man, one of America's most
eerily pervasive cultural icons, and one of its most successful
advertising campaigns. The Marlboro Man had been around
for ages, inviting smokers to Marlboro country, but the company were always reshooting him, using new models, subtly

updating the timeless. Somehow the focus shifted in the early
seventies and the Marlboro Man changed from an old cowpoke
like Randolph Scott into . . . *macho man,* a moustached person
not unlike the actor Burt Reynolds. And the people who really
picked up on this imagery were gays. They didn't just groove
on it, they became it. At a time when straights and women
were moving even further from the sex-role stereotypes that the
women's movement was always on about, when the Ultraman,
oppressor of gays, appeared to be in retreat, the gays replaced
him by *internalizing* him, his clothes, his hardman values, his
contempt for sissies.

An English girl tells me about a night out in Los Angeles
with her boyfriend. They are being shown the town by Gary,
an English friend. In The Spike they squeeze into a room packed, heaving with Marlboro men in plaid shirts, with heavies in
leathers, with college boys in button-downs. She is the only *girl*
there, her boyfriend the only *straight.* The hard men give them
hard, disapproving looks. Gary wears: white satin shorts; pink
blouson; knee socks; pink Kickers. The disapproval is mainly
directed at Gary. Gary is the only *sissy.*

Mass macho had started for a variety of motives (camp
irony, defensiveness – the world got harder in 1975 and reaction set in in 1976/7) but set solid by the late seventies into the
most archaic possible stereotype: the gay as Ultraman. The
new gays rejected the old neurotic over-identification with
women – the Judy Garland, Bette Davis, Marlene Dietrich
syndrome – as a kind of Uncle Tommery. In a couple of years,
gay culture went from a slavish adoration of a kind of
womanhood that never was to a kind of manhood that never
would be.

The macho image of the hyper-sexual gay seemed to answer,
to saturate all the real problems of self-definition in a changing
world. Like Superfly for young blacks, Macho Man was a rein-
forcing fantasy that took gays precisely nowhere. Indeed, it
seemed likely to impose massive psychic strains.

Perhaps a map of the development of minority/pressure
groups would show the point at which their vanguards seemed
to become chauvinistic, erratic, at which they floated off on

separatist fantasies – radical feminist collectives, S.C.U.M. (Society for Cutting Up Men), black studies – that fragmented the thrust of the one-dimensional campaigns behind them. The original movements had demanded the right of their members to be different but ordinary; the transitional movements, the splinter groups, that emerged between breakthrough and assimilation were so hysterical, tempted providence and the man in the street so sorely, that you couldn't but suspect they were looking for a cure for freedom, a reaction, a *punishment*.

The theme of punishment is not coincidental. Sado-masochistic imagery has crept into the American aesthetic and the media sensibility to a disturbing degree. From *Playboy* to fashion magazines, the leather/constriction, slave/master references recur. Disturbing since (although the original intention was often aesthetic, ironic distancing, raising the ante of outrage because the old postures had lost their potency) the reader and the viewer tended to take the messages straight. Irony, as Robert Christgau had once said of punk, 'is lost on pinheads'. Nowhere was this sado-masochistic imagery more evident than among American gays. If macho meant Joy through Strength for some, it certainly meant humiliation for others.

By 1976, reaction had already set in. Homosexuality, American right-wingers had found, was an effective 'red button' issue – like abortion and the bussing of black children into white neighbourhood schools – on which to raise the irrational vote, using approaches developed, ironically enough, from the techniques of the sixties political counter-culture. Gays were presented as a threat to the sanctity of the family and to the stability of the country – like liberated women, only worse. The story of Anita Bryant, ex-beauty queen and then television presenter of Florida Orange Juice, versus the gays of America is a bizarre mixture of red-neck morality, pressure-group politics and financial calculation.

Ms Bryant's little lobby, Save Our Children, sought to prevent Dade County, Florida, passing an ordinance banning discrimination against gays. Bryant presented, among other things, the spectre of gay school teachers. The gays replied by·

organizing boycotts of Florida Orange Juice. The Florida
Orange Juice board, eager to please, supplemented Ms Bryant
with other, less controversial presenters, and did research to
see if Bryant could still shift juice. Then gays and liberals put
pressure on the First Federal Savings and Loan Association of
Miami, which Bryant also presented, withdrawing deposits of
around two million dollars. And it isn't over yet. It was
Americana of the most lurid kind, and, to English eyes, very
funny. By 1978, however, Californians found themselves
actually voting on something called Proposition 6, an extraordinary right-wing measure that would bar homosexuals from
holding any kind of public-sector teaching job – and bar any
heterosexuals that supported them. Proposition 6 was
defeated – after a maximum publicity campaign against it
featuring liberal movie stars like Paul Newman and
others – but it was close.

And, by 1978, the uneasy alliance between women and gays
seemed in danger of breaking down in America.

If swishy camp was unsettling for many heterosexual men,
then gay separatism, macho, was distinctly threatening to
women; it seemed to suggest a whole new and quite unforeseen
phase in the war between men and women.

Women's potential hostility to gays is aroused at the notion
of gays not as comforters but as competition, and by the
misogyny apparent like a mean streak in so much of the hardman mythology, healthy minds in healthy bodies. ('Keep away
from the girls, sonny, they'll make you too weak for the big
fight.')

Where will it all end? Are the boys going through a phase?
Will they come out the other side content to be just ordinary
Americans? Or will gays live increasingly in the new
Boystown, a ghetto of their own making, realizing themselves
through bodybuilding and leather accessories and parodying
the confusion, the neo-conservative styles of America herself?

Increasingly in the West high style and fashion are so divorced from their old functional and expressive roots that any
costume can mean anything, meanings are redifined by the
month. Everything is available so anything can become *leisure*.

Thus in a period when, to the great annoyance of hardliners, relationships between men and women are being redefined in irreversible ways, and when many have taken on board the new, confusing but biologically correct notion that men and women are mixed from the same elements (different proportions), gays can no longer define themselves in relation to the norms (tragedy queens, strong and silent closet cases etc.). The norms in society itself are shifting too fast. Macho, therefore, had a surface appeal; it was a chance for the gays to redefine themselves in an extreme way by leading with their sexuality, but forfeiting along the way their right simply to be ordinary. Macho gays had opted for an extraordinary, an almost frightening uniformity that stood American commercial hedonism, the *Playboy* culture, on its head. On the principle that the extreme illuminates the mean (and macho is only an extreme) and that gays always have been a sensitive indicator of what will happen at other levels of society, macho *could* be a portent of the new hardness, like body culture, and the pornography of violence in general. All very American.

But America is America and costume is costume. Americans, we know, go over the top. The following little story going the rounds in London may be nearer the mark.

An English interior decorator is in New York's Studio 54 seeking new friends. He sees a cowboy in the most wonderful, the most *authentic* kit he's ever seen. He strikes up a conversation.

'Where're you from?'

'Phoenix, Arizona.'

'Where did you get those spurs?'

'*Elsa Peretti.*'

The cowboy, it transpires, does hair at Bloomingdale's.

When I telephoned *Gay News* for information, the man I talked to (very helpful) had a conspiracy theory. The media *exploit* gays, he says, especially the glossies. They use the work of, say, gay fashion designers but don't acknowledge the existence of gays or, worse still, they're snide about them. *Ritz* is guilty he says, and *Vogue* and *H & Q* for that matter (he's wrong there).

Gays, he says, want to see positive gay stereotypes in the media – something different from Stepin Fetchits like Larry Grayson. I've heard this theme before, in 1969 or 70, when academics researching black people's amour propre came to the conclusion that blacks were disadvantaged because they hadn't enough black role models to identify with. Hence, at first, the lurid Blaxploitation movies that followed *Shaft* and *Superfly*, but, later, black *middle-class* stereotypes popping up everywhere, as news presenters and the like, as the new black middle-class began to make it in American society. (American television news shows seem to function as a kind of air-lock to introduce the disadvantaged to mass-cultural authority – most shows have a woman, a black and an Hispanic presenter.)

This raises the question of *gay newscasters*, and the problem of what visual signalling devices to use to show the public that this is the newsroom's new and fashionable token.

The German Connection

Harpers & Queen, December 1977

Written with Steven Lavers

In July 1977, Brian Eno, the thinking aesthete's rock person – ex-Roxy Music, Bowie collaborator – is standing in line in a record shop when he hears what sounds like a quite revolutionary record. To a background of an unusually regular, fast, tight, and tinny beat – an almost mechanical sound – a black girl is singing breathy disco lyrics of the usual banality, 'I feel love, aaah', in the simulated orgasm style. Interspersing the vocals is an electronic whiplash. When he reaches the head of the queue, Eno asks to buy it. What he'd heard had been 'I feel love', a track from an album by Donna Summer, a black girl with a large following in what the music industry calls the 'disco' market. The track, issued as a single, went to No. 1 in July 1977 and stayed in the charts for eleven weeks.

Now, Summer is an attractive girl with a flexible, light but unremarkable and certainly unfunky voice, and disco is a kind of genre music that appears the antithesis of the music business's current preoccupation – punk. Disco singles regularly make the charts. So why was Eno zeroing in on it?

The fact is, as Eno recognized at once, the real star wasn't Summer but the record producer who engineered that extraordinary mechanical pulsing, for the whole thing is done by machines – beat, whiplashes and all are produced on programmed synthesizers by Giorgio Moroder, an Italian producer working in Munich.

This kind of stuff had never been covered by the rock press. Disco, in their view, is conveyor-belt trash. The rock intelligentsia was busy continuing its curious sado-masochistic affair with punk.

Punk was a reaction against the boring pretentions of 'progressive' rock, a return to minimal technology. Musical Ludditism. But the real revolution was not the personally *authentic committed* musician but the punk event itself. The lyrics, the social comment, were redundant. This created a paradox. In a technological age, a formalized primitivism is an avant-garde stance. This was a central problem of punk, though the punks wouldn't thank you for articulating it.

The fact was that many of the original punks weren't blank at all – they had too many ideas rather than too few, hence the anti-Art, Manifesto aspect of the thing. Thus punk is becoming as alienating as hippiedom to the average punter – weird, freaky all that. (Anyone who believes punk isn't avant-garde should take in the surrealist kitsch of the Buzzcocks album cover and the experimental sounds within – and the Buzzcocks have immaculate punk credentials.)

The only logical counterpart of modern Ludditism is the cult of the machine. The only counterpart of intellectual primitivism is intellectual futurism. They are, of course, intimately linked.

On the principle of equal and opposite reactions, something else was happening, in the very vortex of the music industry.

'Give me steel, give me steel, give me pulses unreal' – *Diamond Dogs* by David Bowie.

The story develops when myth-person David Bowie was sighted recording in Berlin. Bowie went there partly because of British tax problems and the famous fear of flying; it was conveniently close to his home in Switzerland. But also, as Bowie had sensed, Berlin was on the wires and the brain again. This isn't surprising. Berlin is the symbol of the West German economic excess ('consumer terror', the Baader-Meinhof people called it) locked in the middle of the world's bleakest communist state. Typecast for a starring part in the Third World War. Perhaps predictably, it has become a centre of what are called the avant-garde arts.

In September 1976, Bowie had predicted the future of rock in one of his cosmic declarations: 'It will return to the sensitivities of the working-class. That excites me.'

If he'd cut it there, he'd have achieved credibility with the New Wave orthodox. But he diverged. 'Sound as texture rather than sound as music. Producing noise records seems pretty logical to me. My favourite group is a band called Kraftwerk – it plays noise to increase productivity. I like that idea, if you have to play music.' The Kraftwerk band Bowie was on about were examples of what the music press called Krautrock, the generic name for the work of the rather highbrow German pop bands who developed after 1967, playing synthesized electronic music. And in September 1976 that kind of thing sounded, well, posey.

What Bowie hadn't taken account of was the random factor. Who could have predicted Malcolm McLaren, creator of the Sex Pistols (search your heart). When punk emerged in mid-1976, Krautrock, which some of the press had quite fancied, was immediately relegated to the back burners. The media spotlight moved over.

But something was cooking at the back. By autumn 1977 – take the British singles charts for any week in October, for example – this kind of thing was showing up all over the place. On 1 October, for instance, the official B.B.C./B.M.R.B. chart numbers 3 and 4, 'Magic Fly' by Space, 'Oxygene' by Jean-Michel Jarré, were both electronic, while at No. 30 and shooting up was another pulsing synthetic disco number by Summer's producer Giorgio Moroder, 'From here to Eternity'. And bleeping away, pretending to be electronic, was the orchestral theme from *Star Wars*. In the album charts the 'Oxygene' album stood at 2, the 'Magic Fly' album at 11 and Summer's own album at 16. 'Oxygene' and 'Magic Fly' were instrumentals – the first a sort of 'Tubular Bells' rendered in a pretty, vapid Club Méditerranée style, while 'Magic Fly' was Telstar and Nut Rocker synthesized. Electronic music was quietly taking over.

The electronic music had grown up in discos.

Discotheques are hardly new. The Scene, in Ham Yard,

brought the idea to London pre-Mods in 1962. But the sheer number of new discos (10,000 in the U.S.A. alone), the development and the sophistication of the hardware, were what distinguished the seventies. And the development of a special kind of music just for discotheques was entirely new.

'Disco' has its roots in 'soul' music – urban black American sounds styled up for white consumption. This kind of sound, in one or other of its incarnations – Tamla Mowtown ('the sound of Young America'), girlie groups, Otis Redding or whatever – has *always* been the number one music for sharp urban teens, black and white, because it is always danceable. Even the last track off a Motown sampler of unknowns usually had more life in it than the most progressive band going. Soul was the real alternative to the tedium of hippie music.

But by the early seventies, 'soul' was changing its form, with input from increasingly sophisticated producers and musicians, like those at Philadelphia's Sigma Sound Studios, making an even smoother more seamless product with more inclusive appeal – older and whiter.

By 1973 the studios were extruding a kind of soul sound which could not be performed live. Barry White, for instance, orchestrated soul to its robotic extreme – one guitarist playing one note repeatedly for twenty minutes.

What was being developed was essentially a formula for ways of making you dance. If nobody could quite put the finger on how and when it happened, what was certain was that by 1973/4 the generic disco form existed, and had taken over from the charismatic star system, working invisibly through a network up and down the country.

In 1974 discos brought the Brave New World of the feelies to every High Street: 1974/5 saw an unprecedented number of discotheques opening across the world. Kids Hustled, Bumped and Phillied to – funky Muzak.

It was in those years that the rock intelligentsia began to ask where all the excitement had gone – it was shaking in the synthetic dance palaces of the new Disco.

Disco music had effectively made the transition from its black roots, and, rather like Hollywood going European in the sixties, its production started to fan out into Europe.

The people who turned out to be the best at producing the new sound were the Germans. Out of what you could call the Funk Factory in Munich came a succession of production-line sounds by people like Silver Convention, Bony M, Donna Summer and Roberta Kelly which made the world's disco charts. From 1974, the most effective way of manipulating a single's success was to get it played in the right discos. Snaking down the right disco grapevines, production companies even pressed special 12-inch singles specially for disco turntables. The highbrow music papers never really cottoned on to this – it was left to *Record Mirror* and the real kid's papers to chart the progress of disco, who was getting what down where.

Disco evolved a discipline of its own, like early sixties American pop music trash in its day (now held sacred by writers who actually disliked it at the time). Disco is equally simple. Giorgio Moroder, Donna Summer's Italian transEuropean-style record-producer/arranger/songwriter, explains: 'There are a few little rules for making disco records – one is that most of the people who go to a discotheque are not really dancers. If the music is too funky they are not able to dance like the black people in the States can. So we make the rhythm extremely straight and hard. That's the basic rule. Also, the lyrics aren't that important; they should be repetitive. We found that a short chorus is best.' All very logical.

And this logic had liberated disco from the constraints of blackness, ethnicity, roots, whatever, it had created what food manufacturers call a base. Infinitely plastic in its most literal sense. Sound that could be spiced and shaped and served up in any flavour of the month you wish – like soya beans. Thus there was classical disco, Latinized disco, which became popular when New York's gay groups decided that Spic Chic was it in 1975, party disco, nostalgic disco. Disco, like technology, could be anything you wanted; as long as you wanted to dance.

It all looks like the application of Teutonic logic, but German Funk, like all real commercial art breakthroughs, was a product of accidents and constraints, no logic or ideology. According to Giorgio Moroder, 'There are just two producers that made the disco sound – Michael Kunze, who produced "Silver Convention", and Michael Balotti and me.

'Kunze was just recording a few tracks when something went wrong with the singer, so he put three girls singing la la la to a little melody. That was the start of "Silver Convention". I was starting with Donna and I made a very different sound from what they make in the States, simply because I had fewer resources, particularly the strings. In the States, they'd use fifty violins with a lot of echo. We haven't got fifty violins, we used eight at most and we multi-tracked them, so they all have to play well and the result is very good.'

The German producers were aiming at the same sounds as Philadelphia but on smaller budgets and with fewer skilled black musicians; necessity threw them back on using the resources of the studio to maximum effect.

Donna's sci-fi disco success was also simply accident. 'I was planning an album for her,' says Moroder, 'with six different sounds, one for the thirties, the forties, the fifties, the sixties, one for now, and then we thought we should do something futuristic. That was "I feel Love".' Futurismo.

The disco itself as a controlled technological environment developed in parallel with the music. Those who fondly imagine that the disco age is over in Britain should realize that it *hasn't even started*. There is nothing here that remotely parallels America's amazing disco boom. In places like Studio 54, Infinity, and dozens of lower-grade people's palaces, New York makes love to the modern world in discos with smoke bombs and laser beams and computerized light shows – a total environment. And assimilated into all this technology, giving flavour to the musical plastic, is the Superfly funk of ghetto sounds and the space age funk of hybrid black groups like Parliament.

All human life is there. There are black discos and white ones, gay and straight ones (gays had kept the disco going through the late sixties – it fitted their needs). Discos are also curiously democratic.

A reflection of this, without the beautiful people, the high technology, the Latin American sounds, or the heavy investment, is in Britain already, but not only have the music writers ignored it as far as they are able, rock's own highbrow musicians tend to avoid it. Disco makes the guitar hero feel redundant.

'I could play the wild mutation as a rock and roll star': Ziggy Stardust by David Bowie.

Mutation had always been a recurrent theme in Bowie's early lyrics – it came from his heady dip into science fiction; the notion of new kinds of people produced by cosmic accidents. This sort of nonsense sent the rock press wild in 1972 and 1973, when basically all Bowie was doing was talking; my, how he talked and how they lapped it up. The music magazines were awash with the metaphysic of Bowie's poses. In 1975, Bowie actually went and did it – with an album called *Young Americans* he created avant-garde disco, perhaps the most remarkable musical mutation of the seventies – ultra-white Bowie took the black soul disco source and added his own levels of meaning and irony.

That was when the rock press went off him. Bowie honed his image to absolute simplicity at the same point. The borrowings from mime and bisexual chic which had served to launch him were gradually dropped and along with it the long interviews, the apocalyptic social comment and sexual outrage. *Young Americans* sold more copies and made Bowie more money than anything he had done before. All the early cult stuff came nowhere near this album in terms both of its effect and its earnings, and, of course, in terms of Bowie's acceptance at street level. Bowie became the first white to appear on the American black music T.V. show *Soul Train*. He had made disco into Art. This was unforgivable.

In a recent retrospective on Bowie in *Record Mirror*, the Clash's Joe Strummer said, 'What he makes is decadent disco music, it sure ain't rock and roll.' And here is revealed at a stroke the critical problem of punk gone ideological; that an idea made flesh develops its own orthodoxies.

Bowie stayed in the critical shadows in this country for 1975, 76, but 'Low' was high in 77. In 76 he could not have seemed more wrong; he was, after all, a self-confessed plagiarist, the rock press thought of him as a 'media-manipulator', he was certainly a self-mythologizer, and all this ran counter to the current themes of commitment and personal authenticity.

Personal authenticity is a possible ingredient, but rock and pop are inescapably about technology. The hit singles industry is built around transistor radios and the music itself is produced in studios that make *Star Trek* look positively homey. In fact, you can relate many of the basic stages of rock revolution directly to stages in the development of the technology. Point one is amplification; then electric guitars – instruments purpose-built for electronics; thereafter an increasing change in recording itself from a passive to an interventionist process as the studios learnt how to double-track, to piece together and build up sounds and generally make a record in bits, like a movie.

The very height of the hippie dream was also the height of the technical augmentation phase, rock using new technological devices to produce an essentially bogus and old-fashioned sound – a sort of kitsch classicism, which while dependent on technology used the technology merely to tart up the music. The stage became a mass of trailing wires, boxes and foot pedals; groups became so laden with technology on tours that they needed articulated trucks to move from gig to gig.

At the same time, the economics of the business were changing. Tours in the late sixties began no longer to cover their costs, they were used mainly as massive devices for promoting equally massive album sales. Tours lost money and the records made it.

Neo-classicism reached its apotheosis with the strange spectacle of a classically trained pianist called Rick Wakeman, who took to wearing a full-length silver cloak. The peak of Wakeman's solo career was the presentation of his 'Myths and Legends of King Arthur' performed by a 45-piece orchestra and a 48-piece choir, to a musical pageant on ice at the Empire Pool at Wembley in 1975. The problem with all this pro-

gressive virtuoso music was that without a chemically expanded consciousness, it was boring. Its appeal was to the
acidheads, showering dandruff on to army surplus greatcoats,
banging their heads on the bass speakers.

Meanwhile, in Germany, groups had developed who refused
to play the old instruments and sat in the dark with their backs
to the audience playing knobs and keyboards. Synthetic boys.

The electronic sound synthesizer was invented in 1928. In
1955 R.C.A. built the first real music synthesizer, the Mark 2.
The thing cost $175,000 to make, it was 17 feet long and 7 feet
high and filled a room. It created one note at a time which was
then recorded on tape to build up a piece of music. This series
of bleeps and tones was called musique concrète and was the
quite legitimate butt of every casual joke about avant-garde
music for the next ten years.

But in 1969 an American electronics engineer called Robert
Moog linked a keyboard to a compact transistorized unit. In
other words, he had turned the synthesizer into a playable instrument.

For a couple of years, predictably, the Moog was used in an
entirely conventional way – as an extra instrument for
dinosaur progressive groups or, in the context of modern
classical music, by people like Sebotnic, John Eaton and
Walter Carlos, a former recording engineer. In 1968, Carlos
released an album called Switched On Bach – synthesized
classicism, a theme that was to recur for the next seven years. It
was and remains the biggest-selling classical record of all time.
By 1971 they had refined the thing even more – to make the
mini Moog, a portable synthesizer about the size of an electric
typewriter, which took its place among the keyboards of many
rock groups. This was the basic technology of a new genre of
the sound circus called space rock.

Back to the front burners.

After the British music industry had thought about it, they
decided punk looked like the Second Coming. Life became exciting again. The record companies' first instinct was to sign
anything that spat or made more or less the right noises. And

A. & R. men were terrified to miss even the most obscure gigs in case something quite quintessentially punk happened. Every major record label wanted a name punk band of its own.

But punk didn't work quite as they'd supposed, and by the autumn of 1977, they were confused again. The punk product – the hard-edge punk products that is – was not shifting as fast as they had expected. This, of course, was because the most important part of the punk experience disappeared on vinyl. Anyway, by the autumn of 77, the original punks were visibly moving in new directions.

At the same time the rock press, working as always on the principle of artificial controversy – build 'em up, smash 'em down – had decided implicitly that punk was over, and it began to show in their reviews. Not that they wrote about anything else, for the moment, but they started increasingly to bitch – to pull apart the orthodoxies that they had largely created and wished on the kids. If the build-up had been fatuous it looked as if the pull-down was going to be downright cruel.

Whatever its shortcomings, punk had done a grand job – it had opened the way for new talents of all kinds, although it had been a Pyrrhic victory. It had also had an extraordinary effect on the musicians themselves – they had become deinsulated. What was so exciting about 1977 was that all kinds of lively and innovative music was cropping up all over the place. Punks had broken down the walls, others had rushed in. Now record companies started combing pubs and clubs for new young acts.

On the back burner of most major record companies' repertoire one or other example of Krautrock was still quietly simmering.

Krautrock had once been quite an intellectual fad but when the prevailing tone in 76 became anti-intellectual, Krautrock, notionally tarred with the same brush, was seen as a no go. In fact, the German thing, for all sorts of cultural reasons, was quite different from English or American 'progressive'. It was, to begin with, less well-funded, more anonymous, more rigorous serious stuff. It was quite literally avant-garde. A succession of humourless German experimental groups with names like Can and Tangerine Dream produced a succession of odd and undanceable records that sold mainly to highbrow hippie dippy whites in America. It wasn't surprising that Krautrock got fed through the same old system, but in fact it had no star network, no charisma and no corruption. It did not rely on live performance. It was recorded music of the most experimental kind. Perhaps the most extraordinary – even lugubrious – Krautrock group was the one Bowie praised, Kraftwerk, German for power plant (Kraftwerk is based in Düsseldorf in a studio in the middle of an oil refinery complex).

Kraftwerk's music seems a curious blend of futuristic revue and artiness. Their own training was classical but, unlike the British rock/classical crossovers, they do not attempt to produce synthetically hyped neo-classical music: instead they work in a stricter avant-garde fashion. This means they have abandoned conventional instrumentation and gone over to machines.

They call it total music, mechanical music with mechanical voices to go with it: their own voices are recorded like robots. They differ from their predecessors, however, in that they make a commercial sound. They did it by moving – whether consciously or not – in the direction of music based on a simple repetitive mechanical beat; disco. In 1975 Kraftwerk had a massive American hit with an album called *Autobahn,* a futuristic celebration of speed and machinery. Today's speed and machinery, however, cars and roads – for Kraftwerk were no more into outer than inner space. They were, so it turned out, in love with the modern world. At the beginning of 1977 in all sorts of places, one began to hear a thing called 'Trans-Europe Express'. 'Trans-Europe Express' was synthesized avant-garde disco, triple fusion. It became a grapevine and disco hit by working through the fashion world – it was regular background music in the younger collections of spring 1977 – to the discos and then across America, ending up, fascinatingly, with – black Americans. In 1977 Kraftwerk won a disco award in New York.

In a recent issue of *The Village Voice,* hidden behind a portentous twenty-page supplement on punk, is an interesting interview with a salesman in a Manhattan late-night record shop, who explained that while the market for the German bands had once been what he called hippie dippy white college kids – it ain't any more. 'Typically, I'll sell Kraftwerk's "Trans-Europe Express" to a fourteen-year-old black kid carrying a stick and a giant radio.'

In Chicago, meanwhile, they have spotted another mutant form – disco punk.

A curious pivot to this dialogue between trash and art was Brian Eno. Eno was that difficult thing, an intellectual – though he lacked the pretensions that usually go with it in the rock world, and added the intellectual rigour that was usually missing. Eno could really talk, and it held up when transcribed cold. He was very very clever. Eno left Roxy, an avant-garde band, to work on his own as a kind of guru, a link between electronic avant-garde and avant-punk – particularly in America. He also helped fuse Bowie's frankly inspirational, fitful working style to the service of some of the most advanced synthesized avant-garde disco ever, that on 'Low' and 'Heroes'. The point about what happened in 1976/7, says Eno, was that it allowed naives loose inside the machine – like the extraordinary transition of reggae from a 'primitive' to an avant-garde sound, 'dub'. The possibilities of playing around with the improbable, the informational part of music, against the rock-steady beat, the anchorage – this, he says, is why he finds disco so interesting.

He draws the beat on graph paper, square and regular. The information fizzles across the page like a heart monitor.

Eno thinks that art is for disorientation, a rehearsal ground for new situations, thus rock and roll is the democratic art, the one which answers the eternal wrangles about Taking It To The People, because the people are buying it already. It doesn't need subsidizing, and records as art objects are intrinsically valueless. Rock matters, says Eno. Thus his new album studies a world 'Before and After Science'.

'It is easier to blame someone else (society, one's mother, whatever comes easiest) and turn anti-intellectual than face the problem and try to take part in the inevitable change by doing

something about it. Thus we have the New Wave refusing to
do anything but scream for help because they can't cope with
the world in which they are living. This is, of course, significant
and even interesting as a sign of the sickness of our times but I
think we have had a little too much of it in the last years.'

This is not a passage from one of the twenty-five forthcoming
books on punk, it is from *Science Fiction: What It's All About* by
Sam J. Landwell (Ace, 1971). In the book, Landwell accuses
the science fiction new wave of being a 'vociferous minority'
with what he calls a 'Tourette's syndrome', an obsessive need
to employ obscenities. Science fiction pre-figured and il-
luminated the underlying debate of the seventies: would
technology – machines – cure us or kill us? (In fact they would
do both, it depended what you told them to do.)

This was an issue on which a previous generation of artists
and writers had taken extreme stances.

By 1967, the machine age had gone badly wrong, as those
who liked playing with historical parallels loved pointing out.
The fact that, in late 77, there were those who remained dog-
gedly, shamelessly in love with the modern world, to the point
that one could discern a *new* cult of the Machine and of the
Future – returning to the recurrent themes of sci-fi and robots
and cybernetics – seemed downright worrying to them.
Futurism seemed extreme Right, whatever that meant, to the
parallels men. Were we booked into the same show? In fact, it
wasn't at all clear who was Left or Right or, in the continuing
context of pop culture, whether that kind of chat meant
anything at all. Revivals, after all, are never quite the same.
What these historical parallels miss is that we are living in a
world where the real conflicts of yesterday are being relived as
today's . . . leisure – through the media.

Certainly, there are economic parallels to be drawn. The
simplest is that in Depressions the environment looks hostile
and in booms friendly, thus popular art forms which reflect the
popular spending, like rock and roll records and movies,
display attitudes to the future very quickly.

S.F. is a mutation in itself which lumps together strands as
distinct as pulp and speculative fiction, but the best S.F. harps

on themes which later surface in society. The energy crisis was prefigured by all those books about invaders from alien planets whose food or energy supplies had run out.

In the 1950s and the early 1970s, movies reflected a state of increasing funk about technology, bigness and its implications. Disaster movies showed aeroplanes falling down, tower blocks turning into infernos and youth increasingly as dangerous.

In 1976 and 1977 things arguably reached bottom. Punks were showing up the scabrous backside of big city life. By the end of the year, rightly or wrongly, there was a feeling that things were starting to go up again, and indeed the indicators suggested at the very least a consumer boomlet for 1978. The future looked tastier, hence a rush of love for the modern world. This was at one and the same time escapist and realistic. Escapist in that the future is a bolthole from the horrors of the present. Realistic in that it involves accepting the modern world and trying to shape it. In other words, it all depends on the kind of futurizing you went in for. The brief surge of primitivism had come and gone.

Star Wars is bunk, escapist, upbeat: very enjoyable bunk, but the clearest focus is on the robot. Robots have cropped up everywhere – particularly on the covers of records. One indeed was called *I Robot,* after an Asimov story.

At the same time, the arts mafia is looking into Futurism. The Russian Futurist Malevich show packed them in at the Tate in 1976. The most aware people are carrying around monographs on streamlining and Fritz Lang and Thames & Hudson have a Tisdall work on Futurism in the pipeline. But the pre-war Futurism was about bigness, and the seventies Futurists, whatever the imagery, seem to be more involved with small-scale technology, intimate symbiotic electronic machines. Devoluted machinery like the computer terminals that are predicted for every home by the 1980s. 2001 seems closer than 1984.

Steven Lavers, whose big obsession the German Avant-Garde originally was (he's all for synthesizers and home computers and suchlike – the Bionic Boy) had the idea that this new Second Wave would *leapfrog* everything, it was the music of the Future. I was always simply gaga for disco because I like to jig. The idea that you could put the two together seemed pretty clever, although I think you can see the joins between his enthusiam and mine. After it came out we kept on thinking *when's it going to happen.* Then, of course, it did – jointly and severally.

The Krauts themselves never made it big except with the Art School crowd, but the *ideas* were around and a bit later – the autumn of the following year – there was Steve Strange and 'Bowie night' at Billy's in Meard Street, where you got the whole stylized Neon poser aesthetic full tilt, not very lively but quite something to look at. It was photographed everywhere from *Ritz* to Paris *Vogue,* and that was the point at which Steve Strange, who had been busking in a small way ever since 76 – I remember him asking me if I wanted to back a band called Moors Murderers – really started *to make it socially.* Now there's a career.

The music made it too – mass overground disco really happened in this country in early 78 – *Saturday Night Fever* and the Embassy and all that and I loved it. Good new disco singles came in a flood for the next year or so.

And in 79, of course, there was Gary Numan who took the Kraut influences and the Billy's/Bowie aesthetic and made it work as pop. There were also a couple of really important Avant-Disco singles, which seemed to show the way, like Blondie's 'Heart of Glass' and M's 'Pop Music'. By 1980, there was real kids' stuff like the Buggles, a couple of session musicians, who did numbers like 'Living in the Plastic Age' and other antique modern fun, and the whole aesthetic was pretty and much played out.

Recycling the Sixties

Harpers & Queen, January 1978

Voice over (V.O.): 'You've lost that loving feeling.' A girl in a crochet mini-dress bends over. Cheeky! A white E-type, shot through a fish-eye lens, drives round a Chelsea square. In the passenger seat is a straight-haired blonde. You know how it hangs even though it's flying back – she's that type (Samantha Juste? Patti Boyd?). A dolly-bird.

This is 'Echoes of the sixties', a thirty-second television commercial made by McCann-Erickson for a Polydor album of greatest hits by Phil Spector, Tom Wolfe's First Tycoon of Teen in *The Kandy-Kolored Tangerine Flake Streamline Baby* (1963). It was all shot in 1977 – a reassemblage put together with the help of location-finders, props companies (Cars for Films and the others), stylists, make-up artists – the morticians of the nostalgia trade. Pastiche, because David Lindsay and Stewart Winning, the art director/copywriter team at McCann's, found the past curiously elusive when they looked for original sixties footage.

The real stuff didn't measure up. 'We wanted Mods and Rockers, but there was nothing usable. Just a blur from a hand-held camera on Margate beach.' Or people wouldn't release the past. With Ike and Tina Turner, for instance, who are currently divorcing acrimoniously, the lawyer wouldn't allow any film showing them together. And the most obvious sixties images – the Beatles, hippies – were out.

Lindsay is thirty-five and Winning thirty-six. The Spector compilation album is 'the record for people like us, people our age, people who had one or other of his records but never quite had the lot'.

The sixties have a name now, all the contradictory tensions neatly resolved in a few Golden Age images (as the Jazz Age is flappers, Wall Street, cocktail shakers). And now that it is officially *period* the stuff is waiting, stockpiled for this spring. Already on Broadway you can see *Beatlemania* one night ('something to show the kids' says a young mother earnestly in the T.V. ad.), and the revival production of *Hair* the next. Books, movies and revival fashions are all waiting. My memories of the sixties, your memories of the sixties, the lid off the sixties. There must be a publisher's generic for it by now.

But nostalgia is not the whole of it – there's another strain, which might be called re-evaluation.

Thus Jerry Rubin, in *Growing (Up) at 37* (1976): 'In the sixties' I stressed one part of my being – the traditionally "masculine" part – the achieving "doer" – while underemphasizing the other part – the "feminine", accepting "beer". My vision of the model human being was a totally committed person fighting against oppression, willing to sacrifice his life and freedom for the people.

'In the consciousness movement of the seventies I have a new vision: a loving person, without expectations, who lives in his senses and in the moment.'

What's it all about, Abbie?

Or Sara Davidson's *Loose Change* (1977), subtitled 'Three Women of the Sixties'. The dust jacket asks, 'What became of Tasha, Susie and Sara – and people like them?'

There is a third, more hostile, theme in all this pondering on the sixties. 'No more Elvis, Beatles or Rolling Stones in 1977,' sang the Clash. The Clash's manager, Bernard Rhodes, was so enthused by Elvis's passing on in August that he is said to have sent telegrams to the rock press predicting that the Stones and Beatles would be next. And there is a serious argument behind all this, a belief Mr Rhodes would share with some very disparate bedfellows, that the sixties were a time of unparalleled wickedness and self-deception, when causes and decencies were betrayed, the future sold out, etc., etc. Mrs Whitehouse would be with him on this, though for a different reason.

And if the sixties are now period, so too, so the line goes, are

the sixties people, darling dodos, blinking against the light.
Like the pop singer whose style – hippie meets Lord Fauntleroy
– now looks oh so very Kensington Market 1969.

I remember taking a nineteen-year-old to a King's Road
café in 1973. Looking around at a lot of familiar faces, a lot of
denim jackets, she said, without any particular malice, 'I call
them the sixties people – the grey-haired blue-jean boys.' The
average age, I calculated, looking around, was thirty-five.
None was over forty.

Why all this re-examination? One view says we have
awakened from 'the dream state' into grim reality. Thus a concern to trace the events of the fantasy, interpret them, take cau-
tion, etc., rather like the exegesis at the end of a classically constructed detective novel: everything is explained.

My own view is that it is all about the changing sensibilities
of a generation of people who, if not wiser – some are – are certainly older. It must be difficult for the jeunesse doreé of the
sixties to negotiate the prospect of ageing and dying, and worse
still *the certainty of boredom and constraint.* For what is quite clear
from the prevailing sixties fantasies is that the young did not *expect* to get old. When the Who sang 'Hope I die before I get old'
it was merely flip – it wouldn't happen.

The resulting traumas and adjustments, plus the prospect of
a new generation upping the romantic ante, has spurred more
lookback than any previous growing up struggles. Time presses
harder on their heels: the average age of sixties reassessors is
just thirty-five to forty-five. There is also the technology of
nostalgia itself. About two years ago I wrote, in a piece on canned T.V., that nostalgia was becoming more systematic. Most
record companies now have a selective re-release policy. At the
same time a new and obvious market-place has appeared – the
just-too-young. After a ten-year gap a record will be *new.* (Sha-
Na-Na at the Round House 1972 – we talk to some fifteen-
year-old hippies who have *never heard of the Everly Brothers.*)

So too with clothes and other ephemera – they will be subtly
re-presented, nothing is ever *quite* the same.

After twenty or so years this technology can be applied to
ideas. Thus extreme and absurd fantasies of Right and Left,

totally discredited twenty years ago, and monumentally irrelevant to today's or any other reality, can be dusted off and taken down. They look startlingly new to the kids. In this context, against what is constantly described as 'the bleak grim reality of the seventies' (itself a ludicrous overreaction expressed in a thirties vocabulary – the seventies are sheer fantasy, though of a different kind), the sixties assume the character of a Golden Age; a time of infinite possibilities. A good time was had by some – and an awful lot of people have heard about it.

This all raises, as they used to say on the more serious kind of chat show, some very interesting questions. And a lot of those questions are about Media.

The first radical reassessment of the sixties, Christopher Booker's *The Neophiliacs,* is now eight years old. The burden of the book, unpopular and unfashionable at the time, was that in the sixties the world in general and Britain in particular fell into a collective fantasy (at other points he calls it a psychosis) of novelty and change, dérèglement for all. Thus, according to Booker, the best and brightest of the sixties people – the media, pop, fashion, politicians, the City – were engaged in a kind of unconscious conspiracy to elevate the new above the established, the disorderly above the orderly, fantasy above reality. Britain was obsessed with change, sex, drugs and violence; it had gone mad. A lot of this Booker attributed to the workings of the avant-garde and the trendy intelligentsia and their fatal conjunction with the media – the sort of media phenomenon that Fleet Street later came to describe as posh pop.

I found *The Neophiliacs* fascinating reading at the time – although I couldn't agree with what seemed simplistic conclusions – and have re-read it constantly. It is easy to fail Booker on points – an occasional Blimpishness of style, surprising in a writer then only thirty-two, the tendency to force unlikely events and personalities into his theory of rampant psychosis, and above all, the final chapters, where the answer appears to be God and the irrefragable verities, balance, organic order, etc. etc.

I remain suspicious of the organic balance argument, because it is so elusive, potentially a rationalization for massive complacency. But I get his drift.

The other contemporary turn-of-the-decade memoirs came nowhere near grasping anything so grand as a theory of sixties culture. Bernard Levin's *The Pendulum Years* (1970) is witty and observant in the Levin manner, covers much of the same material, ostensibly from a similar standpoint – there is some overlap between the Levin and Booker milieux – but fails to follow so strong a line. 'It was a credulous age,' he starts, and he ends with the dream of King Arthur. Neat.

The other source-book of 1970, David Bailey's *Goodbye Baby and Amen,* has no theory at all; its scanty introduction is written by Peter Evans. It is a series of snapshots of The Way We Were, last week's fantastic party, written in the totally showbiz expectation that we *will* see its like again. In 1970 the party was nowhere near over.

What actually happened in the sixties to make them, for Booker, a period of collective psychosis, for very large numbers of people the best years of their lives, and for the Ultras the sell-out of Olde England or of working-class solidarity (depending on position)? What is certain is that eye-witness accounts differ radically, not only as to what mattered in the sixties, but about what actually happened.

There is a whole social anthropology tradition of eye-witness accounts, the Remembered History of individuals, that concerns itself with what happened to people in their childhood – or what happened to them ten years ago. Usually the answers come back easily – they were rich or poor, had friends or had none, fell in love, married or did not.

But when asked about the sixties, there seems to be a qualitative difference in people's responses – they seem to be confused about what really happened (to them) and what the media had said was happening. This kind of conceptualizing seems true across the social board. Most people under forty, in describing the sixties, at least defer to the media sixties.

My own main sixties memories, however, seem to be about *things* – having them and wanting them. Early on my parents acquire a kind of washing machine called the Hoover Keymatic, which claims to be programmed. I am fascinated because of the allusion to computers. A bit later I get a gramophone (pre-stereo) called Bush, which has won a kind of design prize. It looks slick. On it I play my favourites, Blue Beat and Soul, Sam the Sham, Dusty Springfield, Dionne Warwick and the Motowners. I hate Rhythm and Blues, Dylan, folk rock and anything indicating thought. I like what the music papers then used to call 'up-tempo beaty numbers'. I know a girl who looks like Carol White. I save up for a black John Michael jacket with a tartan lining. Twenty-five quid. At no time do I: take L.S.D., protest (I hardly know or care about Vietnam), join a pop group, meet a Beatle. I like *Hair* for the same reason I like the Archies – good tunes.

The reality of the sixties was new money, new technology, *things* – and the choices they implied. There is a theory – well argued – that says America's prosperity in the sixties was substantially based on the massive Vietnam war-chest tax, raised primarily by L.B.J. What irony then if one could attribute to the new money of 64–65 the class of 68 – Abbie and Jerry and Rudi (Hoffman, Rubin, Dutschke – you can't have forgotten) – which ran in the streets of Paris and Chicago. The 'revolution in English life in the sixties' (Booker) had more to do with getting things for the first time than with barricades. Revolution was the name of a nightclub, and, later Che Guevara that of a boutique. Tom Wolfe, in his latest collection, *Mauve Gloves and Madmen, Clutter and Vine* (1977), describes going to a university seminar in the late sixties. He is preceded on the platform by grimly chic revolutionaries, who point to struggle, exploitation, decadence and despair. We have hit bottom, they say. He isn't sure what he will say. As the speeches go on he realizes there is only one thing to be said. 'You are living,' he tells a disbelieving audience, 'in the middle of a happiness explosion.'

For student protest and hippies, substitute Engelbert Humperdinck, a first taste of prawn cocktails at the Batley Variety Club, holidays in Spain, real cream, not having to have an Army-issue haircut. Wrighton Californian kitchens. A cornucopia of consumer goodies – only contemptible to those who'd got them already – and small miraculous important freedoms. And, in the beginning at least, a feeling of convergence, the famous classlessness, which though constantly demolished in angry articles in *New Society,* was there, at least in the head. The new aristocracy of photographers, designers et al was indeed recruited from a wider social catchment – all sucked into the imperative of the new. Things *did* change (but not enough).

Did these people matter? To professional Zeitgeisters, unconsciously part of the process themselves, they mattered inordinately, while to a host of older critics the 'trendies' (© 1961) showed a fatal preoccupation with trivia. Hence Paul Johnson's rantings about the Beatles' fans. The 'Youthquake' of 1963, as opposed to the counterculture of the late sixties, which was downright puzzling, appalled serious folk to Right and Left. Yet it expressed, in terms that cut right across traditional class and ideological lines, things that were really happening, at least from 1963 to 1966/7. There was a sort of consensus liberalization starting to operate. There were kinds of shared experience that made old categories irrelevant. And, Zeitgeist aside, the products of the Butler Education Act of 1944 were getting jobs – moving into the Civil Service and the burgeoning bureaucracies of large companies. One orthodoxy has it that the working-class proportion of, for instance, higher education has not changed since the twenties, ergo no social mobility. This interpretation depends on an amazingly flexible interpretation of 'middle class' and ignores the vast expansion of higher education in the sixties.

This ostensible convergence was a feature of the early and mid-sixties. Wilson's white hot days undeniably caught the mood – a reflection of Kennedy's Camelot. This mood seemed to herald a softening of cultural absolutes – of any absolutes. 'Flexibility' was the key word. It led in the end to the chat show syndrome, the media relativization of absolutely everything – 'It depends on your point of view.'

That peculiarly sixties phenomenon the chat show, with its manic juxtaposition, so easy to send up now, put dissimilar and unlikely people together because the contrast *looked* so good; black and white, young and old, brain and brawn, united in uneasy complicity in the cathedral of the media. Photographers put beauty in exotic slums. David Bailey's box of pin-ups featured the Kray Brothers as celebrities.

This approach, along with a number of other sixties notions, went manifestly over the top at the end of the decade. It is now unfashionable – in seventies eyes it is cynical and exploitative. But this applies seventies hindsight. The people who did it were caught up in it; it seemed a good idea at the time, like David Frost's infatuation with money and the City Game.

In the sixties media, if nowhere else, we could come together – right now.

Because the visible youth culture has pre-empted the popular image of the sixties it is easy to forget the host of new modes and 'lifestyles' (itself a sixties word implying choice) that emerged. The Corporation executive life – the Organization Man on speed and colour supplements. The New Civil Service of planners and social work administrators. The 'cool classless young professionals', 'the caring professions' and the New City – secondary banks, property companies – the Power Game men (remember Wilder/Wymark on television). The pension funds – anonymous investors of millions.

Two professional groups in particular represent the Light that Failed: Physical Planning and Social Work. Physical Planning – the notion of redevelopment – planned spanking new total environments ably managed by the brightest and the best. It was a Utopia created by a euphoria on the part of architects and planners, many of whom had been raised against a background of the Depression, slums, tight money, constraints, but who had the guiding light of Le Corbusier and his machines for living in. Sweep it away, build a rational future. This euphoria, rather than Poulsonism, explains the faith in physical planning.

When a Birmingham mother recently committed suicide by throwing herself off the eleventh floor of her high-rise council block, the press avidly seized on it as an example of the hideous inhumanity of building high. So far had the conventional wisdom moved from 1966, when the *Queen* set fashion photographs against a New Brutalist council tower block with a

commendation of its 'stark elegance'. The shots merged jumping girls, mini-skirt fashion and tower block in the convergent
imperative of the New. Both interpretations miss reality by a
mile. The inquest on Mrs Hibberd, the Birmingham suicide,
suggested strongly that she suffered from intractable personal
problems rather than architecture. The fact is, whatever is said
against council flats by people who have no idea what their interiors look like, that a lot of council flats work very well, that
high-rise suits some people and others not at all. What was
wrong was not the principle of public housing, nor building
high, but the technology of total order called redevelopment
that imposed the Plan on vast inner city tracts in such a way as
to sterilize any spontaneous development till 2001. Urban
defoliation.

This type of development, so it was becoming apparent by
1970, tended to have extraordinary effects on the social
'ecology' (early seventies key word) of the inner city, destroy-
ing small businesses and shops and often actually hastening the
practical decline of the twilight zones it was meant to revive.

By now, in 1978, there has been almost a complete turn
round on the planning ideal, in part due to writers like Booker
and Conrad Jameson, who put the overweening vanities of architects and planners up for merciless scrutiny, and the ac-
tivities of all those vocal P.R.-conscious little pressure groups,
from the Friends of the Earth to the Georgian Society.

In fact, what actually stopped 'Planning' was not its
wrongness but that the money ran out. The collapse of the
housing finance market in the early seventies scuppered many
more projects than any official changes of heart. An incidental
benefit of this otherwise disastrous boom-bust was that
'rehabilitation' – making sound houses inhabitable again –
became not merely fashionable but necessary, and in fact
urgent.

The other light that failed was social science. In the new
plate-glass universities of the sixties – Sussex, Essex, East
Anglia – Sociology was the vogue discipline for new admissions,
while there were often problems in filling places in Applied
Sciences. The appeal of a hybrid discipline like Sociology was

obvious. It appeared to explain the mysteries of the universe in a 'relevant' (© 1968) way, to combine concern – an eventual career in social work or some branch of the 'caring' professions – with calibration, statistics and science. It had the omniscience of religion without the problems of faith (though it invented and named social forces at least as mysterious and arbitrary as Good and Evil). It appealed to the cool (© 1962) urge to relativize everything, and this underpinned the kind of cheeky iconoclasm that disturbed a previous generation raised against more black and white issues: Hitler/Allies, Franco/International Brigade.

The new 1970s backlash sees Sociology as liquid Marxism, although sociology has probably done as much to confuse and disabuse Marxists as anything else. But now it is out of fashion – or rather the first flush is over. It turned out not to have a monopoly of explanation. Fashions and schools of interpretation came and went rather fast in the years 1968-72.

This October *The Times* reported a marked fall in applications for sociology courses: the first drop since the early sixties, paralleled by a rise in the 'vocationally oriented' (© 1965) applied sciences, civil and electrical engineering etc. The back to work mood, already so evident in American campuses, was making itself felt. Once again, the money had run out – the old worry, so unthinkable in the sixties, about getting a job weighed heavy. The Civil Service, the growth industry of the sixties, had been a victim of The Cutback and it was unclear whether a sociology degree was negotiable.

But the sixties were certainly a Golden Age of Service Industries, of Media and Advertising ('The "hot shop" boom – you could jack in your job every other week and get a thousand raise in the bargain,' remembers a copywriter), of Leisure, Whiz Kids and Asset-strippers and Trouble Shooters.

By the turn of the decade it became clear that Britain had a remarkable, *real* difference from other Western countries: fewer of its people made things than in, say, France or Germany, while more of them sold, advised on or fixed them; offered insurance, relief massage in saunas, merchant banking services, or were notionally 'white' as against 'blue' collar. This was seen by some as evidence of Britain's unstoppable decline; by others as the prototype of the Just Post-Industrial state. If we were no longer the workshop of the world, we certainly had what Brian Ferry called Stylepower, and this too was an invisible export.

After it was finished, after the whole thing had boiled over the top, with the O.P.E.C. oil price hike, the miners' strike, the property market and secondary bank collapse, there was a period of stunned quiescence during which a large number of people felt that Mrs Thatcher was probably right in suggesting that the answer lay in hoarding tins. A neo-Conservatism, always waiting in the wings, became more evident. An articulate backlash from the new hard men, (the Amises and Braines), the Black Paper on education, the Responsible Society, the Gould Report, which found Marxists in Higher Education, the rightward moves of Paul Johnson and Reg Prentice, the National Association for Freedom, and the increasing sales of Karl Popper, suggested a change in the centre of gravity.

Mary Kenny in the London *Evening Standard* recently gave an insight into what was going on. Miss Kenny said that it upset her to read the papers now – random rapes and murders, madness and mayhem. Ten years ago she had been for the liberalization of practically everything – at one with signatories of *The Times'* advertisement pleading for the legalization of marijuana. She had believed that family, State, and institutions were all a sham, a conspiracy of vested interests to imprison the inner man. She had felt safe to espouse all this from an upbringing of certainties – the 'Enid Blyton' security and *structure* of a fifties childhood. Now she felt it was time to call a halt, looking at the search for certainties among the disoriented young and the conservatism of the early twenty-year-olds. Her generation, she felt, would probably maintain its early sixties liberalism but she wasn't sure about the rest.

Indeed, the sixties produced more compassionate, socially-conscientious people than any previous decade (it also produced more cynical opportunists) for the simple reason that it produced more educated people who had a chance to raise their eyes from the trough. A larger group of little liberals the world had never seen. While it is true that much of this was mass-market Bohemianism, there were certain levels of belief, certain ideas of personal and political freedom, which, while troublesome for the orderly running of a democracy, would prove quite disastrous to anyone with totalitarianism in mind.

Of course, some things went over the top. I remember in the mid- sixties visiting a schizophrenic friend in an experimental commune for young male schizophrenics, 'Villa 21', at Shenley Hospital. This was run by a young psychiatrist called Dr David Cooper, an associate of R.D. Laing, who was then beginning to make a name for his radical approach to patients.

I had been sold on the place before I went there; I was predisposed to think it a brave experiment. In fact, I was horrified by it. There seemed to me to be a quite fatal ambiguity about the deliberate non-roles played by the staff. In the late sixties I kept meeting people who paraphrased R.D. Laing and Cooper's work to make it read *the mad are saner than the sane*; no more or less than a reflection of society's pressures. In the late sixties, craziness was esteemed and every sub-Bohemia had its quota of *crazies* and madmen. It seemed to me, however, that this lack of discrimination was every bit as bad as total order and, following Booker's principle, seemed to encourage the world's natural authoritarians and *heavies*. Charlie Manson gave pause to those who believed that a total dérèglement of all the senses, a constant revolution within the revolution was the only way to live. It was during this period that the backlash started.

On the other hand, it was after the grand design had been abandoned, and 'working within the system' taken up again, that it all started to have some concrete effect. 'Smash the system' was so apocalyptic as to be meaningless. The environmentalists, saying technocracy should serve people and not people the Machine, began to look distinctly less cranky when the energy crisis became a reality.

In the late sixties, I found myself feeling unsympathetic to the idea of spontaneity to order, to American notions of the occult, to the 'natural' kick, to clever people making themselves sound stupid on purpose. I found many hippies arrogant and

lugubrious and out of touch. But then, to be honest, it was
partly aesthetic – I didn't like the style or the language. And at
the end of the day, in the Heavy Metal, post-hippie thing of the
early seventies, I thought that the built-in contradictions were
all set to produce some real Frankensteins.

But there was always a certain hand-me-down quality about
the British end of the sixties scene. They never had to lay
themselves on the line.

The real beneficiaries were not the large minority who went
over the top, but those great chunks of the mainstream, many
of them now middle-aged, who started to think for the first time
about immediate issues and improved their own and other people's lives in doing it. The women's movement appears to have
been one of that small collection of lower-profile causes that has
survived. It is not a joke, if it ever was.

There is a theory called 'one step forward, two steps back',
which supposes that we are now in the fifties, with the Cold
War, Free Enterprise, Self-Reliance, and a spell of National
Service perhaps doing no harm.

Another faction thinks that the Ice Age will melt, and things
will take up from where they left off in 1971/2. North Sea Oil in
the tank, a touch on the throttle. Let 'er rip.

Another group, swollen by unfortunates with sadomasochis-
tic tendencies, pre-war hardliners of Right and Left and their
tiny recruits, and people of unsound mind generally, like to
think we're doing a re-run of the thirties and coming up for the
crunch fairly soon.

All these perspectives are fantasies of a particularly seventies
kind – divergent, fragmented. In the sixties most of the prevailing fantasies converged – remember the alleged similarity of
the Labour and Conservative parties. This homogenization
was called the 'end of ideology'. In the seventies we cast about
for principles and came up with Jimmy Carter.

But if consensus has slipped away, fundamentalism doesn't
really do the trick either. The real keynotes of the seventies are
fragmentation, devolution, fantasy and *paranoia* – impossible
new situations like Stagflation, the Arabs, oil money and
political power. Fragmentation and devolution are inevitable.

The continuing boom, by increasing choices, simply meant things became differentiated, and divergent. There were elective lifestyles: see *Westworld*, a movie about a kind of 1980s Butlins where you act out your fantasies in a range of settings, from Western to Medieval. Your companions are robots.

The sixties will continue to erupt into the eighties. In 1980 kids born in the Summer of Love will become teenagers. In the early eighties the graduates of the movements, the pressure groups, all those voluntary organizations ('working for change within the system' © 1969, 1970) will emerge. The children of the revolution who couldn't be fooled will be running things.

We continue, however, to live in a perpetual time-warp. All the cycles are foreshortened. This kind of weirdness is peculiarly seventies. We have to live with instant replay. Movies on T.V. mean a wraparound past. But there is something odd in the way the media doppelgänger presses on our heels, moving from the twenties (early sixties) to the forties (early seventies), to the fifties (74/5) to the early sixties (76/7). It's getting close.

Presley's death was a news item for me. Marc Bolan (né Feld) slammed against a tree in a car accident at twenty-nine actually got me.

Now *there* was a child of our time – I remember the Stoke Newington Stylist in the *Town* article in 1962. The Wizard nonsense of 67, the sub-teen hysteria in 1971. This September, about a week before he died, I saw him enter a club with David Bowie. Bolan looked totally, touchingly absurd and anachronistic in a leopard jump-suit and green cummerbund. I'd seen him around quite a lot last summer, and I felt that, having stuck it out, he was going to be very *right* for Spring 78.

On the street *now*, there are tiny Teds, new skinheads, punks, disco kids, clones of every youth culture group of the last twenty-five years – all out and running *at the same time* – and there is an upcoming wave of new Flower Children in the pipeline; fifteen-year-old bubble-headed freaklets – not your laid-back Frye booted early-thirties Eagles fan, but the Real Thing. A friend tells me he's setting his dial for Radio Invicta.

Just after this came out, the whole thing got into overdrive among the Leisure Class, the New Bohemia and the art students and so on. They started working up the *early seventies* – glam rock re-done, Roxy re-interpreted – which all came in very handy as an aesthetic for the neon-disco punk period in early 1978, Lycra, Lurex (again), Day-Glo primaries (again). The sixties themselves were taken up in the Mod Revival, then just a little sub-theme in punk, but, come 1980 . . . *Two-Tone.*

Grey Hopes

Harpers & Queen, September 1978

I'm watching *Revolver,* the pilot for Mickie Most's new T.V. pop series, and thinking, 'I *almost* like this; it's *almost* like *Ready Steady'.* Then they actually run a clip from *Ready Steady* and all is plain.

A few weeks later there's the first Kenny Everett Video show (T.V. is sending feelers back into the music market), and after some very mixed stuff, there's a clip of Dickie Pride from *Six-Five Special.* Then, in the break, there are all these Fonz-style ads starting with 'Lip smackin' Pepsi . . .'

On *Revolver* I note Billy Idol and Tony James from Generation X, first-wave . . . *Punks* . . . in the hand-picked crowd, grinning sarcastic Jagger-grins. Gered Mankowitz, the photographer who did the Stones' classic cover portraits, tells me a little story about Generation X. Apparently they sought him out to do their album cover. 'They said, "We really liked your Rolling Stones covers, we can remember them as kids, can you do something like that for us?" It was weird – but sort of flattering.'

By this time I am multitracking; Generation X's best-known song is 'Ready Steady Go', a little number whose perspective on Cathy McGowan and all that is, to say the least, ambiguous. I remember Billy and Co. on the first night at the Roxy, in Pop Art T-shirts; Billy explaining to me how he felt you had to promote Right-Wing Repression, Red Brigade style, in order to hasten the apocalypse.

The paradox of rock is that at precisely the time that a new rock sensibility *is* starting to invade the commercial heartland (the new/old pop T.V. shows represent the end of a two- or three-year cycle in musical terms), the whole rock thing is, un-comfortably, coming of age. Rock, whether it wishes it or not, now has a history, and that history weighs heavy.

The *Hollywood Reporter* recently ran a story on some research carried out by Warner Communications Inc. – an entertain-ment conglomerate that owns three major record labels, Warner Reprise, Elektra and Atlantic, among its other in-terests – showing that 25-to-44-year-olds, and not teenagers, are the largest single group of record buyers, and predicting that changing demographic patterns would swell this group's commercial importance still further. Meanwhile, a new set of letters had filtered into the rock business language: A.O.R., adult-orientated rock – the 'product' for the post-hippie generation. This new slice of rock life is in fact something rather different from traditional M.O.R. music – good old middle-of-the-road Andy Williams, James Last – which was music built around performers who might perhaps borrow from the rock idiom but had been raised in a different, showbiz world. A.O.R., however, means something more eclectic, more rock-based. Many A.O.R. artistes once had some rock credibility, if not strictly roots.

And why not, since large numbers of the Woodstock genera-tion ('We are stardust, we are golden') still have music as their main leisure interest, have disposable incomes (smaller families, the self-involved lifestyle) and several thousand dollars-worth of hi-fi? Why indeed should they graduate to Tony Bennett when they can have Linda Ronstadt, the Eagles or Carly Simon; feel funky with Stevie Wonder or chic with Manhattan Transfer? Some kind of shrink-wrapped rock ex-perience will be theirs till they die.

Rock and roll is the hamburger that ate the world. Electric rock music creeps, like chemical seasoning, into everything. Rock and roll is mother's little helper on the housewife radio, plays across film sound-tracks and sells packaged goods. Rock has won.

The totalness of the victory must have stunned rock's pro-tagonists. The latent effect took longer to recognize; namely, that rock lost its real potency as a tribal music for adolescents in general and adolescent sub-groups in particular when almost all rock, one way or another, entered the public domain. The old race – between the sharp kids and mainstream assimilation – now speeded up to a frantic pace; once a style of music was taken up by the system it was discarded by the kids and the ranks regrouped around the wound, perhaps eventually wondering if music itself was salient.

But then, of course, 'youth' itself, in the sense of a *consensus* market, was over. Kids simply don't matter that much any more, and they know it.

Rock is now weighed down by a body of political theory. There is a corpus of perhaps a hundred writers making a regular living from rock commentary at one or another level in this country (and more like 500 in the U.S.A.). And a nice publishing side-line in rock books, from hagiography to emergent blockbusters like Simon Frith's *Sociology of Rock,* and coming in November from Pluto Press, *The Boy Looked at Johnny: the obituary of rock and roll* by Tony Parsons and Julie Burchill. This all raises rock to an unprecedented level of self-consciousness, and helps to pull it apart. Each man kills the thing he loves.

Rock ideologues are looking for a transfiguring experience – rock made new – but have an uncomfortable awareness that it won't be like that ever again. Hence the desperation that attends the sanctified memory of, say, the Roxy club (Dec 1976 – April 1977). And then there is the deadly weight of Art. It was popularly supposed that punk, being generally sold as 'raw/vital/young/proletarian' meant the end of all that poncy pretension – that high sixties analysis stuff. In fact, punk ushered in an era of more self-conscious simplicity, more elaborate Emperor's New Clothes than ever. The Gamesmanship of rock this time was beginning to draw, whether consciously or not, on the most perplexing set of precedents possible – *critical theory from the visual arts.*

From 1967 on, with the discovery of a middle-class rock market, rock started to become both stratified and conspicuously 'arty', though in retrospect the art seems about as relevant to developments in the fine arts as a Peter Max poster.

The rock art was a petit-bourgeois notion of nineteenth-century classical music with added sex. Still, there was an *intent*.

By the early 1970s, however, there *was* real art rock. Rock which drew on recent – if not current – developments in the visual arts; rock which was sophisticated, allusive, and never sweaty. Art rock involved pulling apart the old sounds and re-assembling them as holograms, so you weren't sure if the substance was there or not. This kind of art rock coincided with the beginning of the Golden Oldie boom, with tongue-in-cheek popular acts like Gary Glitter and Sha-Na-Na who derived at least *some* of their appeal from being, ultimately, a joke.

Art rock was important in a number of ways: first, it created a precedent for a new type of entrant to rock and roll, one who consciously saw the music as a *medium* like any other and used it to create certain effects that he could create equally happily elsewhere. Such people quite openly avoided paying their dues, in the form of five unsuccessful years on the road in a mini-van. More people like this came into rock after 1971. There had, in any case, always been a strong art-school contingent in the upper ranks of British rock and roll music.

But the new art rockers maintained links with the visual arts in a way that, say, the Who – despite Pete Townsend's art-school background and the colour supplements' basically inaccurate labelling of the Who as Pop Art – had never done. The art rockers weren't just *like* Art – they were Art. Roxy music was Hockney music.

Once the cahiers du rock were established, once the real links to the fine arts had been forged (even though they were invisible to the average fan in 1971), a series of processes, inevitable but ultimately deadly, started rolling. Rock, in coming of age, began to parody, sometimes unknowingly, the sacred conflicts of the fine arts; those between the two wars in particular. Rock started to generate its own Modern Movement, and, later, to be seen as a medium for political commitment and political education.

And all the while, the creatures down below were growing up in a most peculiar way. Perhaps it was the chemicals, simply that rock had been introduced into their mothers' milk, but

as far as music went the kids were really wise. This was not surprising, for the archives of rock were the most accessible kind of
wisdom to a kid from any background, anywhere. At the same
time, the past was beginning to be mapped in new Wisdens
and Bradshaws like the *N.M.E.* rockbooks and *Rock Files*. Rock
was becoming a known world.

The gilt was rubbing off music in other ways too, as kids,
young musicians, a whole generation became more knowledge-
able about the *business*. Not the least interesting part of the Sex
Pistols' story in the years from mid-1976 was the attention it
focussed on their contracts. And on their manager Malcolm
McLaren's remarkable trick of making money from record
companies simply by getting sacked. It was like the discovery of
industrial muscle; scales fell from kids' eyes.

By the early seventies the business had itself changed, con-
solidating the extraordinary spurt of the sixties into ever larger
multinational companies and conglomerates, with a corporate
imperative to 'stabilize' the product-mix, to bring music into
the grasp of common sense and accountancy. To sell it like
baked beans. Behind the ostensible anarchy of a host of
'labels', a drift of independent producer specialists, the real
commanding heights of the business – the manufacturing,
distribution and marketing, the *rights* – were controlled by a
small number of very large companies with a spread of non-
music interests; E.M.I., C.B.S., Warner Communications,
R.C.A., Philips-Siemens (Polydor), etc.

A recent report on the U.K. music business from
stockbrokers Vickers da Costa came to the view that it now
merited a serious look from the sober investor, since it was increasingly being run on sensible lines by serious folk. Two
developments in particular brought the business into the
baked-bean world. First, the way high-street retail giants, most
importantly Smith's and Boots, annexed a massive share of the
trade by offering cut prices and limited selection, thus forcing
the record companies to think in less hit-and-miss terms: fewer
products, more push behind them. Second, early in the seventies, a lively little Canadian outfit called K-Tel, operating from
right outside the biz, started flogging mass-market records,

advertising them on T.V. in a style that made detergent commercials look subtle. They thought music *was* baked beans and
didn't care who knew it. Since then, slowly and painfully, the
record companies have reorganized themselves to become
marketing companies. This meant that many of the little bolt-
holes and safety nets in businesses originally built, like fashion
houses, by high-profile entrepreneurs – just disappeared.

The business was Big Business – and a hip accountant wearing Levi straights was still an accountant. At the same time, on
the 'creative' side, rock's rapprochement with mainstream
showbiz – so unthinkable in the late sixties – became a reality.
Rock did not merely merge with showbiz, it *took it over.* The
progress of Robert Stigwood, producer of *Saturday Night Fever,
Grease* and *Evita* is a paradigm. Stigwood started in rock
management.

Meanwhile, glaring uneasily across the barricades, crouched
the rock press. When I started reading the *New Musical Express*
in my early teens it was cobbled together from what I now
realize were crude press-releases – this group would tour,
another would make a movie (they never did); groups'
favourite food; they love their Mums – and it suited me fine. In
a series of cultural spurts from 1967 on, the rock press became
increasingly hip, in parallel with the fans' own development.
In three definable periods (Class of 68, Class of 72, Class of
76), they hired successive waves of young journalists from the
avant-garde margins – the underground press, the fanzines
etc. – who were anything but hacks. These personality writers
became celebrities within their milieu, and major reputation
brokers. Their first duty, just like a real critic, was to the
reader, to Art, to their political commitment. These new
writers wished to shape the world, the biz merely wished them
to interview the 'products' favourably and spell their names
right. Thus by the mid-seventies you had something nearing
open war between the commercial departments and the
editorial bloods. Many old-style business hands were empurpl-
ed at reviews that described their artists as 'Tory rockers',
cretins and bozos and the product – product advertised in
those very pages – as dross. The rock press went increasingly

below the belt, aiming for the artiste's privates – his sexual/social/intellectual credibility, especially the last. There was more action to be seen on the pages of *N.M.E.* than at most gigs, more layout talent at *Sounds* than in most record company art departments.

The writers regarded the Business balefully. Depending on their perspective, they hated it for its growing philistinism, for its mega-capitalism, or both. A number indeed chose to think the business a sort of commercial equivalent of the C.I.A., infinitely conspiratorial and devious. In so doing they felt braver in jousting it. The real fact was that it was just a business like any other, with a normal quota of meatheads and bureaucrats. A lot of it was plain bor-ing.

The rock press itself, particularly *N.M.E.* under Nick Logan's editorship, was *not* boring. Running off at the mouth, it was self-important, bigoted, self-indulgent; it gave a lurid perspective on the whole world. It was irresistible, the liveliest writing going. And a great deal more exciting than the 'art' it served. The classier reaches of rock were better at setting the mind going than the unreachable parts moving.

Ultimately, however, both the rock writers and the business had an uneasy complicity. They shared a common imperative: the need to discover the Next Big Thing. The writers wished for a transfiguring experience, a reaffirmation of the faith (oh Cavern, oh Woodstock, oh Roxy). The commercial departments wished for some shock horror to raise the readership and boost the advertising. And the biz wished to lift itself out of the mid-seventies' doldrums (and, to be fair, to convince itself that it was about something more than baked beans).

No one could admit that it was over, there would be no Next Big Thing – mega-money would be made, a good time would be had, but ultimately everyone would know in their secret hearts that it was only rock and roll. *In the future there will be Rollerball.*

A recent piece of research conducted for the Recording Industry Association of America compared the attitudes and expectations of the business and the punters. They were significantly out of line; the record companies were looking for

'a Beatles-type shot in the arm'. The punters, however, believed that there was quite enough of everything to be going on
with; they merely wished it was better.

The two really important new developments in *sound* between 1974 and 78, punk and disco, weren't 'rock' at all. They
were each, in their separate ways, a different kind of *experience*.

But the cahiers du rock went on, throughout 1977 and 1978,
launching new isms – new ideas about how rock should
be – like there was no tomorrow. The Akron School, the Strictly Roots college of Rasta believers, Rockabilly ('Gene Vincent
is risen!'), Power pop ('The Searchers live!'), Politically
Committed Relevant Rock. But if 1976 hadn't actually been
the year the music died, it certainly would never be the same
again; there were other things for people to do. During the
remission there was a lot to enjoy, particularly the re-
emergence of soul, i.e. vocal feeling, in black disco music.
However, as Julie Burchill of *N.M.E.*, the best, rudest, most
observant reviewer on the rock press, was forever saying, 'I
wish . . .'

(. . . *I didn't know what I do?*)

(. . . *I liked it more?*)

She's nineteen.

In 1979, Johnny Rotten, who came out of the whole thing with
at least a measure of dignity and started his own band called
Public Image – the sound was beyond me – said, 'We're
against rock 'n' roll, rock 'n' roll is quite disgusting.'

Mods:
The Second Coming

Harpers & Queen, September 1979

This February, Jim, sixteen, from the nicer part of Clapham, wearing his Ramones ripped-knee jeans and Clash T-shirt plus badges, the uniform he's worn for the past eighteen months, say, is diverted from a U.K. Subs gig (an approved, never-made-it-big punk group) to The Chords at the Wellington in Waterloo. His friends drag him there. He hasn't seen them for a while, because he has this evening job, and now – just like that! – they've got parkas with targets and Fred Perry shirts and Who badges, and he can't believe it, because the last time he saw them they were true believers of the provincial, late-punk faith and aesthetic.

Jim goes along. And there are a whole load more parkas and *some* punks, sneering, but more than a bit defensive, because, as he can feel, it's all on the edge of a change. For one thing, people are dancing side-to-side jerky movements instead of up-down pogo or shoulder-barging. For another, the music, though it's basically what he's used to, thrash speedy, has a happy little edge to it, and The Chords are dressed sharpish. People are quite clearly enjoying themselves. It's something of a release this feeling, because the aggression part of punk weighs heavy on Jim. The sneer has never come naturally.

Within a week Jim is in the new uniform – fairly basic, but he's learning. In May he's in Soho at the Marquee on Mod Nite for Secret Affair, and the Mods out-number the punks massively. The little knot of punks are giving out all the stuff – some really major sneers and spitting and so on. No one reacts for a while, but eventually they do and the punks are done over, and hereafter Mod Nite is Mod night and there's very little trouble ever.

This incident, the trouncing of punks in what Jim feels is a *fair* way, completes Jim's release, although he feels a bit guilty.

He feels more at home in Mod. It's matier, boys check each other out without risking the 'poser' accusation for talking clothes talk. Judging a group is more on style and whether it gets you going than whether it's approved ideologically.

So by midsummer, Jim is fully equipped with the essential components of a new-old youth subculture, namely a) a recognizable clothing style, b) a defined musical taste, and c) an attractive ideology (of which more later).

It was the other two, Michael Jones and Steve Grocott, whom I'd met hanging around Carnaby Street, who were *surprising*. The things they said were extraordinary because they were so spot-on. They were cool, cynical, cowardly, clothes-obsessed, very honest and very funny. They were just like the original Faces, the early leaders of Mod style. They said things just like Marc Bolan said when he was Mark Feld, fifteen, from Stamford Hill, being interviewed by *About Town* for that 'Faces without Shadows' piece in 1962, and I wondered if they'd read it.

Besides, they were doing something so risky it was barely thinkable. They were got up as Faces/Individualists/Stylists of about 1966/7, and they had *Nehru jackets* and *little gold-wire-framed specs* like Jim McQuinn of The Byrds, and talked a lot about the late-Mod early-psychedelic overlap period, which they'd read up on. In other words they were right up against the cosmic wall called hippie.

I remember a conversation in mid-76 with a group of people from the new Covent Garden fashion establishment. It was in a flat in Notting Hill (cream walls, Deco ceramics, a bit of Hyper-Realism – that style) belonging to Chris Trill, who's big in women's bags. There were Paul Howie and Lynne Franks who get their clothes in the papers a lot, and Mark Tarbard, who designed for Jeff Banks, who's married to Sandie Shaw, and so on. And we talked about Mod, which, as it turned out, was preying on all our minds. The true definition of a Mod: surburban, white-collar working-class, cowardly, clothes-obsessed, etc., etc. And who'd been a Mod and who hadn't; for instance, how people then used to laugh at Rod (Stewart) the Mod, because he was a *bit* tacky and wore too much make-up.

A little later, late summer 1976, it happened – the Mod revival. What convinced me was doing a vox pop in the King's Road. The youngsters we talked to and photographed came from Stoke Newington and Ilford and Newcastle, and looked better and said more interesting things than for years. A lot of them were going to Acme Attractions to buy the sixties warehouse-clearance stuff (before Acme went tourist punk as Boy). They simply looked good. There were spikes and bristly haircuts and the word was out about punk; but punk, so it seemed then, was simply a part of a larger thing, a good new mood. A group called The Jam looked like sharp mass-Mods – French crops, suits and two-tone pointed shoes – and played like early Who.

But by the end of 1976, punk had taken centre stage, while the ideas that were projected into the punk ideology – a strange mixture of Dada/Situationist Art and more conventional radical resurgence and Brutality Chic – sent many of the best minds around into a flat spin. Things were never the same again. And little, ordinary things, like The Jam's two-tone shoes, which were being worn by real people who liked to look a bit sharp, didn't rate too much comment.

Well, it's happened now. There *is* a Mod revival going on, and kids are turning over to the style – an easy uniform of parkas and Fred Perrys and Hush Puppies that freezes five years of subtle change into one big Brighton Beach frame. It has been working through for a year and *Quadrophenia* has brought more. It's so far gone that the Mod Revival firsties came to really dread *Quadrophenia* and the tinies getting into ins-tant Mod, and started trying to avoid the word itself (no Mod Stylist would have used it in the sixties, it would have been *ob-vious*, and that was what the originals avoided most). And the rock press, of course, have done it to death, to the point where they now think that it's been and gone on their own pages, that being their world-view.

New Mod works, as they say, on three levels. First there are the kids who are getting into it for the simplest of reasons, because they like it and it is the first post-1976 alternative to punk that appears to present the basis of a real group identity.

Then there are the sophisticates, who are still working through it as an exercise for Thems (some, ironically, because they were ex-original Mods before they caught Visual fever).

And then there's the business level, particularly the money invested in The Who's films and the Polydor Records money that's riding on Mod. Polydor, whether by luck or planning, have carved a major slice in New Mod. They have The Who and The Jam, and, through a subsidiary arrangement, the outfit Jim heard, The Chords. Other record-business money, burned by overinvestment in unsaleable punk, is more wary, knowing that the real money will probably go to whoever owns the rights to the great Soul and Motown catalogues and those little pop-y pre-reggae black sounds from Harlesden, 1969.

There is, however, a fourth, different group of people with a most intense interest in the Mod revival: the Mods who've never stopped. All over the country, long after the whole hippie progressive thing was supposed to have buried Mod entirely, the Mod aesthetic kept going, sometimes explicitly as in the scooter clubs and sometimes just in a line of indirect descent. Northern Soul – which was a dance-based life – and skinhead, which has never really gone away, both came from Mod.

This means that New Mods can find people their own age doing it a different way. The tiny Teds of the mid-seventies revival were relating to people – often their dads – who were pushing forty, but to revive Mod was to revive what was barely history at all. Hence a little attendant *weirdness*.

The big problem, however, for this steadily growing scene, is that Janet has done it, blown it wide open. Janet Street-Porter, presenter of *The London Weekend Show,* had a programme out on 20 May which was a while *before schedule.* And T.V. is a whole lot different from the rock press, it brings a thing right out where you can't keep it a little insider's number any more. Nor was Janet's approach easy to dismiss, although a lot of people tried, saying she'd featured the wrong bands and asked some pretty crass questions. The fact is, Janet Street-Porter is the only person on T.V. who has the remotest idea about these things, and who's ever known what it is to be Suburban Chic herself, and she got it right. It's barely started and she's asking 'Where will it all end?' and 'Who's pushing it?' and '*Is* it all a con, an invention of publicists?' and '*Why aren't you authentic?*' because she remembers what it was like. And then she comes to the key question, the most revealing note of all.

J.S.P.: 'O.K., but why become a Mod, because the word Mod is going back twelve, fourteen years, right? It is a kind of backward thing. Why not choose something entirely different?'

Now here speaks the Modern Movement (J.S.P. studied architecture) which has crept into rock criticism. One of the central ideas of the Modern Movement is the avoidance of historical reference, which means, in youth-culture terms, that *revivals are wrong.* Q.E.D. Anything that looks like a revival is politically reactionary and artistically *inauthentic.* None of this hits the kids who liked Fonzie and The Darts, and it won't actually cut any ice with the New Mods either, but it weighs heavy with intellectual punks like The Clash, whose Joe Strummer says he thinks the Mod revival is *a bad sign.*

But the answer to Janet's question, from a very articulate group of people who run this New Mod fanzine *Maximum Speed,* shows both how things can never be the same *and* how the Mod thing has some real continuity in it. This kid said that Mod today is a totally different thing yet it all comes down to a tradition – dressing smartly, Soul music – that's worked right through and come back to where it belongs (and, presumably, although he didn't say it, it is alive enough to develop its own new stuff).

But the difference is that kids know a lot of things now and will never unknow them, since the recent past is so accessible. The sensibility is Post-Modern. A punk retread has been through a whole load of rhetoric which he won't forget, though he'll have a new perspective on it. Hippies hadn't been invented in 1962, nor O-level sociology, or Gary Glitter, Roxy and Bowie, disco, or video discs. A Mod revival, to be *correct*, would have to revive some impossible attitudes – a whole sensibility of realism (Mods avoided the fantastic), gradualism, subtlety; the opposite of the apocalyptic/fantastical elements that made flower-child hippie and high punk two sides of the same coin.

Where punk went wrong was in getting *so* fantastical, and so arty and so extreme. And the most fantastical part of punk, the most irritating part of it, was the altogether lurid ideas it put about about what it was to be working-class in the mid-seventies. For punk ideologues – and more explicitly political bandwagoners – it was a particularly Grim Slide view, all high-rise, unemployment and inner urban decay. The eagerness with which this imagery was taken up made it clear that there *had* to be a lot of class tourism going on. The reality, of course, of the mid-seventies was that 'working-class' was an inadequate way to describe a range of life-styles stretching from problem families on truly hideous estates to prosperous working-class owner-occupied suburbia in the South-East.

In other words, the punk idea of working-class authenticity, in a time of social mobility when 'middle-class' was expanding and changing before your eyes, was a *period* fantasy, a narrow focus. The reality was that 'working-class' and 'lower middle-class' were so confused – basically a matter of generations – you could play it any way you wanted. In Croydon or Ilford the taxi-driver's daughter works in Barclay's and the plumber's son lectures in computer technology at a Poly. And high-rise alienation is pretty remote to kids from there, since nothing can convey adequately the sheer pleasantness of their kind of background. It produces kids who've had things nice pretty much from birth – it was their parents who'd been through it before they'd got the mortgage and left Kilburn or Camden Town.

This sort of suburbia produced the original Mods – white-collar working-class suburbanites who rejected the factory wage-slave thing for a cooler job as an office boy in the City or – really prized – in an advertising agency, but never came within a mile of the tweed-jacket leather-elbow style of the traditional middle-class, which was still going strong then. These kids were always totally into style, and when their seventies successors got into punk it was as a style thing. They were into it fast and out again when it became no fun. One of the most ironic things about punk was that it had instant appeal to bored *rich* kids because it was so extreme, hence 'punk art', the S. and M. elements and all that, which was a bit much unless you were that way.

The other no-fun aspect of punk was the 'committed' politics that developed as punk was politicized in 1977. While commitment was a key word, commitment to what was never clear. The idea of 'militant entertainment', which developed out of something originally brave and admirable (the punk opposition to creeping racialism and the National Front revival), institutionalized the free-floating aggression in punk and turned a lot of kids off, finally. In any case, commitment sounded pretty odd to kids who knew, even at third hand, about Watergate *and* Gulag.

All the New Mods I've met have said they were glad to lose their weight without having to unlearn the lessons of 1976, and glad too to stop pretending not to be a real person.

In particular the idea of 'commitment' ran against all the central realities of life in the seventies – that was part of its initial appeal – not just social mobility but individual change and development. If punk's idea of class was doctrinaire, its attitude to other groups was equally extreme. In particular the attitude to hippies – punks had hippies on the brain. Hippies, so they said, were self-indulgent decadent middle-class wankers. Teds and greasers generally were reactionary, but it was O.K. to admire the Mods (ironically enough, a new upside-down story is developing which says punks were all middle-class posers and the original Mods the real thing; but in 1979 no one can claim to be the real thing).

This implies that people never change. But the embarrassing reality, the wall of death that Michael Jones is approaching is precisely this: that in 1966/7 most of the top Mods, the originals, the Faces, whatever their backgrounds, went some kind of psychedelic. *Mods became hippies*. And the only writer I've come across to bring this out explicitly is a man called Penny Reel, on the *New Musical Express*, in a brilliant piece in April based on his own memories.

Now this hippie thing is the wall of death, the last inhibition, the terminal worry for two reasons. The first is that the detritus of the hippie culture and aesthetic have recently been *the* most degraded, discredited and generally unfashionable set of ideas and artefacts around, to anyone under thirty with eyes and ears. They couldn't go any lower. And while that lends it a certain perverse fascination for firsties, and documentary-makers, any serious uptake of hippie, is *absolutely* forbidden, so the new Faces who've been working up to 1967 in their revivals of styles know they've *got* to make a big . . . detour, a big change soon. And second, I personally believe that a psychedelic revival would, quite simply, mark *the end of the world,* a schlock-horror, vanish-up-the-black-hole movie, an *Airport 77* in which the stewardess doesn't get the jumbo safely down to earth. Manson time.

Which brings us to Bernard Schofield. A couple of months ago he sent us the manuscript of an obsessive, detailed history of Mod called *Neat.* It's all there, from the post-war modernists and the Wardour Street boys through to skinhead. And particularly the clothes, mainly the boys' clothes, because that was what it was about. The placement of buttons, the pursuit of excellence within a tight framework, nothing fantastic (to the Faces the uniform styles were obvious). And the thing is, Bernard Schofield's been writing this book on and off since 1964.

Bernard Schofield's own life is a paradigm. He's thirty-three, slight, sharp-faced, neat, born in 'working-class' suburbia (Welling, Kent). He started off as tea boy in a commercial art studio, graduated to illustrating a bit himself, was sacked and spent three years doing summer casual jobs on the coast. Then, late, and under his own steam, he went to art school, became a style hippie, produced an underground/ecological magazine called *Country Bizarre* and has ended up as an author and compiler of books on quirky subjects.

In his head, as he says, he still feels nineteen, and he's felt at home with most of the youth cults since Mod. He likes disco, he loves to dance, he's been to the Embassy and all that but he feels more at home in the working-class discos, and the dancing's better. Punk hit him hard. 'It kind of pre-empted everything. For a while everything else looked positively uninteresting.'

Bernard and I talk in the vinyl gentility of the Army & Navy's self-service tearoom, laying out photographs, comparing originals with stills from *Quadrophenia*. We have an audience of three kids who are clearing tables. 'Are those Mods?' – they want to see. Their friend, Jim, sixteen, has just turned Mod, he's got a parka with 'Mods' on the back and targets and everything.

Things moved very fast after that. The Nouveau Mod scene was of course *transitional*. It wasn't phoney, although things can never be the same again, but it wasn't *quite* satisfactory, not quite gelled, either. The big thing *did* come out of a hybrid of 'those little pop-y pre-reggae black sounds from Harlesden 1969', i.e. 'Two-Tone', the first real big teeny bopper craze since the early seventies. A totally different kind of teeny bop however; Post Punk. Come spring 1980 millions of little boys, eleven up, wanted to shave their heads and be Rude Boys or Skins and beat up any punks or anyone left with a Parka.

Post Modern

Harpers & Queen, January 1980

Earlier this year, at a show of Duggie Fields' at the Kyle Gallery off Regent Street (or Bond Street, as you prefer), Maggie Norden, daughter of Denis and presenter of Capital Radio's adolescent fun show *Hullabaloo,* was roaming with her Uher, looking for nifty comments. I thought she would ask me about Fields' famous get-ups or the little gang of arty weirdos he hangs out with, Andrew Logan and Kevin and Luciana – Them. In other words, social stuff. She didn't, she got straight down to it, she asked me about Post-Modernism: what *is* it?

The honest answer was, of course, 'Search me, lady,' or 'You've got me there, Guvnor,' or something. In fact I rabbited on, making it up as I went. I don't know what I said.

It is a big question, this Post-Modernism, the key indeed to the true seventies style. You can see the seventies style now, you can distinguish it from the sixties follow-through (which went on till 74/5) in both popular culture – a sixties sociologese word – and the finer arts which respond to them: popular music, fashion, commercial product design, graphics/ advertising on the one hand and architecture, painting and the big stuff on the other. And the point of differentiation is the Post-Modernism attitude.

Post-Modern has always been a little joke for me, part of the Art way of describing things, which, like Art itself, I find funny, so I lifted the language in the early seventies. 'Very Post-Modern!', much as Kenneth Williams makes people laugh on the radio when he shouts 'Deviation!' That kind of language, I thought, Art chat, *if taken seriously,* makes you an ill person. Besides which I vaguely apprehended that, somewhat in the

way people say of textual analysis of Marx, it was all a bit irrelevant and out of date. But the fact is that long before I'd
tried to work out what Post-Modernism was, I and most of my
friends were living it. The fashionable Post-Modern life – Trash
with Flash – of the early seventies.

Before we grasp for the theory, let us zero in on some crucial
early seventies words, words of approbation, opinion-leading
journalistic buzz-words that by the late seventies became a
regular drone, staples of down-market magazine writing.

'Glamour', for instance (the New Glamour – high heels and
gold lamé – moved from sharp end to mass market between 72
and 78); 'eclectic' – there was a lot of that about, commending
designers, decorators and *Art*ists themselves; 'retro', a Paris
post-Underground coinage of the early seventies, used in relation to almost anything and ending up – like Che Guevara in
the sixties – as the name of a clothes shop. Or such expressions
as 'ironic references', of some use as a period motif. But, above
all, *'style'* and *'stylish'* and what is it and who has it (always,
Noel Coward). And again, 'class' and 'classy', used in a way
that made them somehow synonymous with style (but for
ideologues class was synonymous with revisionism, back to the
bad old ways; in *Animal Farm* terms, pigs becoming men). And
whatever it was, it was 'ambivalent' or 'ambiguous' (in terms
of meaning, of sexuality – whatever).

In sum, the emerging art criteria of the early seventies were
that a work, an entertainment, should be stylish, ambivalent,
ironic, eclectic, a touch retro, a bit classy (but that classiness
distinctly ironic: *post-classless*, you understand).

And so you have Bryan Ferry, in a tuxedo, in 1974, singing
'Smoke gets in your eyes' – a song which was kitsch in the
sense of forties 'cocktail' classiness from the word go. It proved
his hyper-sensibility – using cod 'classy' materials and sentiments from lower-middle-brow popular culture (it is a self-
consciously literate song) – and his voice even vibrated so am-
biguously you couldn't tell whether he was laughing or crying.
Bliss.

These early seventies experiments in music foreshadowed
the Art Attitude that is beginning to take over the thinking of

young groups – the more so if they tell journalists they reject the Art Attitude.

The basis of all Post-Modernism lies in a particular attitude towards the acknowledged twentieth-century Great Time, the *breakthrough*, the quantum leap and the New Masters – and, more important, in attitudes to the critical ideology and rhetoric that sustained them. After the revolution – any revolution – comes the implementation ('Let's get on with it'); then second thoughts or covert revisionism, in which the original ideas are compromized, fragmented or otherwise changed, in practice – though no one owns up; and then the Post-Modern period, when the original notions are so thoroughly assimilated that everyone asks where they've gone – what did you do in the Art War, Daddy? – and sometimes consciously rejects them. This carry-on, as Tom Wolfe has pointed out, does not go on in the sciences – critical fashion does not reject electricity.

Each major art, the big stuff, has had its twentieth-century revolutions, with all the implications of new vested interests, ageing revolutionaries and rhetoric. The process is at its clearest in architecture – over the last ten years the most embattled and demoralized of arts. Architecture is expensive, it has a long gestation period, and impacts more significantly on people's lives than the other arts. Architectural movements are therefore easier to trace and identify.

Architecture's Modern Movement was conveniently called the Modern Movement from its turn-of-the-century beginnings; had its seminal or 'white hot' period immediately after the First World War; spread transatlantic in the inter-war years; had its greatest flush of implementation as the International Style (basically the tall, steel-framed, curtain-walled box-of-boxes rectangular building without traditional decoration) in the fifties (the early sixties, in Britain). By the late sixties, the style was fragmented, discredited and blamed for an extraordinary variety of social problems. Thus it was architectural criticism, and Charles Jencks in particular, that came up with the first well articulated notion of Post-Modernism.

The job of Post-Modernism is to unravel the rhetoric from the real advances. With architecture, this had to do with the

simplest of issues, the language of *ornament*. The ideologues of
the modern Movement, from Adolf Loos to Le Corbusier to. . . .
well, till very recently, had rejected the use of traditional ornament, wood and plaster mouldings, covering devices, elaborate
gilding and colouring – everything they associated with the
sham and hypocrisy of nineteenth-century bourgeois art and
design. They did this in a rhetoric that linked the anti-
ornament theory to the 'for real' advances of the Movement in
such a way that ornament – along with other traditional notions of street layout and entrances – was barely mentioned in
enlightened architectural circles until well into the 1960s. The
traditional *language* was uncool. The Modern Movement in
architecture had sustained itself with a hypnotic set of key
phrases like 'honesty to function' (you can see the sewage
pipes), 'pure form' (see the *form* of the sewage pipes) and other
things of the kind. But much of what they described as 'rational'
was in fact *expressive*. Ideological.

Once the Modern Movement had won, was established, and
its grand designs were built – large schemes, not just in-
fill – certain problems began to show up. A series of books from
the early sixties on describe what went wrong, but most deal
with *effects*. Only in the seventies did you find the critical debate
finally allowing a hatchet job on the Modern Movement itself.
David Watkin's *Morality and Architecture* (1977) nailed the central fallacies of the Modern Movement (the book was widely
described as 'reactionary') and Charles Jencks' *The Language of
Post-Modern Architecture* (1977) described what might be on the
way. Post-Modern, as Jencks saw it.

Jencks described a situation which had been developing over
the last twenty years and is 'now in the process of focussing
very quickly into a new style and approach'. A Post-Modern
building for Jencks is *ambiguous*, i.e. it 'speaks on at least two
levels at once', the traditional outsider's language of symbols
plus something for the Boys. The buildings most characteristic
of Post-Modernism show 'a marked duality . . . conscious
schizophrenia'. It is simplistic to regard Post-Modern buildings just as those which appear to gainsay orthodox
Modernism – i.e. are squiggly or bizarre as against rec-

tangular. Post-Modernism *acknowledges* Modernism, in that sense it isn't a conventional Revolution. Indeed Post-Modernism *incorporates* Modernism and uses it as a style like any other, when it is appropriate. Post-Modern architects have, many of them, been trained in Modernism, but have moved beyond it, and acknowledged a wide range of apparently irreconcilable influences – Renaissance architecture and popular culture forms (Route 66 and hamburger stands) on an equal footing. And crucially, Post-Modern allows for revivals of the recent past, on the criteria of *plausibility* alone.

And here Jencks is touching on the fundamental of *all* Post-Modernism, of the seventies style itself – this curious relationship with the past. If you had said, for instance, that the main form of seventies style was period pastiche it would be unfair, but it makes a central point. There was an immense range of borrowing from the very *recent* past, not only in architecture and painting, but particularly in the applied arts. There were constant accusations of 'revivalism' and 'sterility' about early seventies fashion (that systematically re-worked the twenties, thirties and forties as 'looks'), the ziggurat 'Gospel Oak Deco' furniture, the music that re-worked early sixties music in an odd way (Bryan Ferry again, singing a *girl's* sixties song: 'It's my party and I'll cry if I want to').

This relationship to the past made a lot of people very angry indeed – both committed Modernists, the Clean Break men who believed in an absolute *commitment* to . . . well, to the Tradition of the New (no mucking about, onward and upward) and traditionalists of another kind: those who were fighting a rear-guard action for 'authentic', 'roots', traditional values (the original vitality of 'real' rock and roll; four-square Portland stone low-rise office blocks or anything else *unreconstructed*). Neither group liked Post-Modernism. The traditionalists recognized the ambiguity of the Post-Modernists' approach to the things they loved. They knew that Post-Modernism was very rarely 'revivalist', it just used period styles and references as the whim took it: it killed the things they loved. Modernists, on the other hand, thought it *was* revivalism when the old stuff was used like this: and therefore was 'reactionary', 'not relevant', 'inward-looking', 'empty stylization', etc., etc.

Both camps ignored the fact that the original notions of The Future, Definitive Modern, etc., were all themselves rather quaint and period in a time when, as Duggie Fields has said, 'nobody knows exactly what the past is'. When all the immediate past – like computerized information – can be easily retrieved on film and tape, with video discs in production by mid -1980 and hologram movies-in-the-round on the way, *the past looks different.*

In London, in youth culture particularly, the time frames are utterly scrambled, the past is all around: in that world the notions of either rejecting or embracing the past look irrelevant. Post-Modernism, which deals with the past like one huge antique supermarket, looks very relevant indeed. Pastiche and parody is just an uncomfortable transition to a time when period references will be used without any self-consciousness.

Similarly the popular/high-culture problem. The sixties relationship between the two was forced and uncomfortable – one knew those nice middle-class *Sunday Times* writers had self-conscious mixed feelings about Ken Dodd and football, that Pop artists were hedging their bets when they used popular imagery (itself a little 'period' and back-dated by the time they used it) – showing by their theories that they were *superior to their material*, theories about 'iconography' or 'repetition' or some such, while the viewers liked it mostly for itself. 'Tongue-in-cheek' and 'camp' were therefore crucial to the sixties approach to posh/pop culture hybrids. The art chaps bridging the gap had grown up in a different world, and they didn't really know how to take popular culture straight: they needed a little *theory* about it before they felt at home.

Similarly, over-educated Post-Modern American architects like Venturi and Rauch, in their funny little book *Learning from Las Vegas* (1972), show that when they try to apply what they've learnt from all that vibrant, vital, vulgar, oozy neon and hamburger world, they produce really stiff-jointed, pedantic little buildings.

A lot of 'early' Post-Modernism has this terrible self-consciousness ('You thought I liked this garbage . . . c'mon, I was joking!') in the use of ornament, references etc., which gives the impression that Post-Modern is a bit lifeless. It's because the transitional men, the ones who've got the theory but gag at the practice – who *can't dance* – are simply too old.

There is, however, a younger group of artists who are Post-Modern without knowing it, people who've taken in popular culture the normal way, by sitting in front of the T.V. since they were so high. Some of these people can incorporate popular culture, like they use the recent past, in a less self-conscious way. They don't believe they're smart for being able to cross the borderlines, because they know those borderlines barely exist. They hang out at the sharp end of 'Business/Art, Art/Business' (Warhol).

All this eclecticism means the true Post-Modernist needs a steady hand and a sound traditional technique if he's not going to turn out sequined mush. (Glitter cakes and ice-cream, one hears, have been presented as food art.) Much art in 'new' media – the Xerox/Neon/Polaroid set – seems to me infinitely more banal than the commercial material and imagery it uses. The most exciting kind of Post-Modernism eventually arrives factory-fresh from straight commercial sources – zipped up, *wised up* by the Art Laboratory. Playing back in fact, the advances that the Post Modernists have made by playing about with popular culture forms. Which brings us to the structural supports of Post-Modernism – the new network of arty-little-businesses/businessy-little-arts that has developed in the Covent Gardens and SoHos of the world in the last ten years. These one-or-two-people businesses are the medium of exchange between the commercial mainstream and art about art. They work on the right scale – these consultants and style brokers – to help the whole process go full circle. If Post-Modernists are using popular culture then it's using them too. In the little outfits that design record covers for independent record labels, or with fashion entrepreneurs like the Howies of Covent Garden, who patronize a lot of young artists in their business, this exchange is going on all the time.

With these cosy commercial linkages set up, the traditional

lines become extremely blurred. Crafts and Fashion become Artified, hence the crafts revival of the early seventies and the reverence for hand-made furniture like John Makepeace's, which was really Art Object Investment Cult. Hence too the American terminology 'fiber artist' for weavers and suchlike.

And around and about it all, the culture of Silly Art statements; the leopardskin fabric-covered car, the Andrew Logan pageant, and the Miss General Idea group of the Toronto artists. These were Performance Art (people did things) *and* Conceptual Art (they stopped doing them; it wasn't an art object for posterity) and Craft Art (people made funny clothes) and Fashion Art (they wore them) and multi-media (music! lights!) all in one go. What more could you ask – every commercial and avant-garde sixties notion at one swoop and as much Silly Food as you could eat.

Up until 1976, you could see the Post-Modern attitude spreading, straining at the leash. One thought it would take over the world. In 1976, however, a curious complex of things happened – or rather were thought to have happened – in London, which marked both the consumation and the end of Transitional Post-Modern. It was punk. Punk, and the initial effects it had on sharp-end youth culture and all the little arts parasitic upon it, was quite devastating. Punk clothing and terminology were *so* Post-Modern it hurt. The clothes were literal 'cut-ups' which pulled together bits of previous youth cultures and Art references in a way that suggested history was a trashcan – Ted's creepers with bondage strides or *Jackson Pollock trousers*. Dada for tinies. And they said it, just like that: 'NO FUTURE' – what the more genteel Post-Mods had been pussyfooting around. It made cocktail kitsch look very . . . transitional.

Along with all this the language appeared to change in a most remarkable way. Punks used words like 'committed', 'modern' (meant straight), 'moral' (as approbation) and 'decadent' (as a hate word). They made a full-frontal attack on art – songs like 'I didn't go to no art school', attacks on art students as poseurs. They had art on the brain.

In context, these attitudes now look like the ultimate art

statement (indeed, they came directly from art politics), but they had strange effects on the world. By 1978 the crucial style was 'uncompromizingly modern' – and you could hardly talk to a young person of sensibility without hearing how they hated anything retro, that we must look to the future, to technology, for our salvation, and how they liked modern materials like plastic, neon and aluminium. The ultimate expression of this funny mood was the Neon Night culture that developed round an odd little chap called Steve Strange – ex-punk and Generation X roadie, who started 'Bowie night', a portable event at various London clubs in 1978. This scene was very modern – futuristic indeed. Look closer however and it was . . . *moderne,* a rehash of a period idea of the future – Bauhaus and sci-fi trash, *Star Trek* and Thunderbirds, art and 'Low' all mixed up. Sweet, a bit feeble and silly, dated from the word go, post-punk and, intractably, hopelessly, Post-Modern.

Tom, Tom, the Farmer's Son

Harpers & Queen, October 1979

Tom Wolfe *married?* ('This is my wife, Sheila.') I hadn't allowed for Tom Wolfe being married, or having his parents-in-law around, or for conversion work being done on the brownstone. I don't mean I thought he was the other, or that I'd had no curiosity about his domestic arrangements – quite the opposite – but I hadn't been able to get my mind around the idea of him being *set up.* My picture of the man in the white suit was that he *glides free.*

Things don't appear to have gone quite so mommy-hubby far as children, but even this is on the cards, given that Tom Wolfe and Sheila *are* married and Sheila looks to be in her early thirties (Tom is now forty-nine). They married last year – I checked it – but they've known each other about twelve years. Sheila Berger Wolfe is art director of *Harper's* magazine, the New York intellectual monthly (no relation to *Harpers & Queen*), which publishes Wolfe's cartoons and some pieces. She has straight dark hair with specs pushed back on it and looks like a combination of Barbara Parkin and Stephanie Powers – those promising girls who were wiped out when Hollywood did away with women in the seventies. Her parents look like the kind of Jewish professional people who used to contribute to the National Association for the Advancement of Colored People. But I don't get to talk to Sheila or her parents, so I'm running on spec, some of it probably coming from certain passages in *Radical Chic.*

Tom Wolfe isn't expecting me, which is to say he hasn't put it in his diary and has forgotten I'm coming. It's a *bit* awkward, since there are clearly domestic plans for the evening. But he is

---

'I was in the Hamptons last weekend in a kind of a trick outfit – four-button seersucker, sort of Adolf Loos 1907 – and this man became quietly furious, like a fire in a sofa: What is this rig?' TOM WOLFE

---

tremendously courteous and apologetic. We go upstairs and then down again, to the first floor, while things continue upstairs. There are four floors, which appear to be organized – or to have been organized – as separate flats, although Wolfe owns the house. It's a brownstone in the East Sixties, between Second and Third, which means it's on the edge of the Golden Square that runs from the East Sixties to the low Nineties and across from Fifth Avenue to First, but has a view on the world, being near the bridge and a bit of life.

I *think* the style is Chelsea, London, England, mid-sixties New Boy. It reminds me of rooms in sixties magazines. However, the people in Chelsea, London, who would've gone in for this style have the place redone every four or five years, and are most of them now still in the hairdresser cream and L.A. palms number that took root in 1975.

The room we're in has ochre walls and a remarkable Hicks carpet with a yellow ground and multicoloured blobs, and mainly sixties modern furniture. Wolfe says they're having it done over – I say they'd better keep the carpet.

When he opened the front door to me and took a while to register (which he does on a number of other things), I had time to see exactly what he looks like in the light. The main change from the sixties photographs – he wears broadly the same clothes – is in his face, which is much thinner, plus specs, which means that he could at a pinch be cast as an Anglican clergyman. In *those* photographs he looked far chunkier, more combative. Although his lower lip still looks a bit subversive, jutty.

And the outfit. He actually wears it. He isn't expecting me, it's a domestic evening, and still he's wearing it. To be specific; white giraffe-collar shirt with collar pin; narrowish black-white spotted tie; black-and-white striped seersucker jacket; white trousers slightly high-rise, slightly Spic in the cut, two buttons on the waistband; white buck brogues; and those shiny black evening socks with the thick/thin stripes where the thin is like nylons – you can see the hairs on your legs.

Socks are an area of interest to Wolfe, possibly the last, since Jerry Rubin and Abbie Hoffman wore body paint on the Dick Cavett show in February 1974 and made further experiment in clothes irrelevant. Socks he will still experiment with, for instance the hot pastel nylon jobs from Ian's, the semi-punk boutique on Second Avenue.

I have a friend from Virginia (Wolfe's home town is Richmond, Va.) who feels the Wolfe style – which is generally understood as a kind of sixties Pop Revival-time Dandy hybrid of his own invention – owes quite a lot to certain Southern stereotypes, in particular the dress code of his university, Washington and Lee in Lexington, which retains some of the Southern aristo style. But I can't believe there are whole squads of men in the South done up quite so. Wolfe agrees: Washington and Lee had quite a strict dress code – jackets and ties at all times; but it didn't extend to white bucks and collar pins. Washington and Lee also had a rule that you spoke to everyone you passed – 'which was not bad at all. I'm a great believer in false courtesy'.

Virginia *must* be important in the making of Wolfe, Virginia and Carolina being practically the only states with a for real, *unreconstructed* fetish about the past and the eighteenth century. Richmond is very much an F.F.V. – First Families Virginia – town, with a social style coming nearer the English sense of class than practically anywhere in America.

Wolfe's own background is a 'Virginia family: my father was from the Shenandoah Valley and mother was from Amelia County'. Long-settled, of English stock. W.A.S.P., but 'I don't remember any talk about F.F.V.s'. His father was a farmer and professor of agronomy at the Virginia experimental station and edited the *Southern Planter*. 'That's where I got my idea of writing – he'd write and there it'd be, later.' When his father died in 1952 he left a hundred monographs on agriculture, and the first standard work on field crops.

Small-town/agricultural/professional/hierarchical traditional – a more romantically *solid* background could not be conceived as a perspective on Fifth Avenue/Seventh Avenue/Haight-Ashbury/Venice Beach and every other variety of lurid passing-show Americana that Wolfe has written about: every *fluid* social scene, where Americans could express and define themselves any which way they wanted, standing under the money pump. Virginia, when Wolfe was growing up there, was poor, meaning stagnant: no statuspheres; fixed positions.

On 27 September something like 185,000 members of America's Book of the Month Club have Wolfe's latest book *The Right Stuff,* about the astronauts, thud through their doors and into their mail boxes (no exaggeration, it is 436 pages) at the same time as ordinary readers could buy the Farrar, Straus & Giroux edition from their bookshops. *The Right Stuff* is the B.O.M.C. main selection for September, meaning that members get the book unless they say no by post or choose an alternative, a technique known to the trade as negative option. Farrar, Straus & Giroux's own first printing is 103,500, their largest on a Wolfe book to date. (The first, *The Kandy-Kolored Tangerine-Flake Streamline Baby,* came out in 1965.) In other words, this is Wolfe's bid for the mainstream.

The Right Stuff is a major enterprise, a really ambitious book in two ways. First, it is a big shot at getting down on paper exactly what the absolute essence, the juice of manly courage really is ('Has he got what it takes, let's see what you're made of'), right up to The Point, the Gulp, where for instance a military pilot is choosing whether to be *sliced* by his ejector seat or *fried* on the ground.

Second, it is a broad history of the most glaringly public scientific programme ever, the first part of the desperate American manned space programme, Project Mercury. It's packed with detail, surprisingly different detail for those who remember Wolfe for *that* book (or the other one, the hippie thing . . . *The Electric Kool-Aid Acid Test*). Detail you'd expect from *Flight* magazine; pounds of rocket thrust, G forces, retro-rockets and heat-shields. It is the story of the first seven US astronauts and of the post-war fighter-pilot morality and mystique they emerged from, in particular the world of Edward's Air base at Muroc Field in Southern California, 'Fighter Jock Heaven'.

Now the *Saturday Evening Post* has gone and *Life* is . . . reconstructed, the Book of the Month Club must be the unchallenged demographic dead centre of middle-brow America, the heartland of family-centred Great Books to

---

'There's very little uniquely American serious art or music – it's all down to this sense of awe about Europe. You would think that by now, after the U.S. has become the most powerful country, the richest country, in many ways the most exuberant country, that this would find expression. The only place you find all this energy bursting forth is in popular culture. The whole rest of the world loves American junk – the U.S. might have stood a better chance in Vietnam if they'd sent down rock singers, records and blue-jeans by parachute.' TOM WOLFE

Cherish, that enrich the home. Self-improvement the traditional way.

And *The Right Stuff* is ideally suited to B.O.M.C., as an improving book, with History, the Miracle of Flight and the persistence of the Right Stuff, the air-ace fighter-jock individual *jousting* thing in the face of the tightest political and scientific constraints. Strapped flat, literally, the astronauts *assert* themselves on every page. And, of course, there is the question of patriotism, The astronauts, the fighter jocks, clearly have the Right Feelings in the best possible low-key lay-it-on-the-line way (except for John Glenn, who was T.V. High Key throughout, but meant it).

But, *hold on*, as Tom Wolfe would say (it's all coming back; the surfers, the noonday underground, the Bernsteins, the Sculls, Andy, Baby Jane – that *style*, interrupting the narrative, extraordinary devices, repetitive dots, dashes, exclamation marks, continuous use of the historical present, *that style*, got it, know who you mean). Hold on. *Is* there a middle America any

more? It's heart-warming, it's almost Norman Rockwell to imagine the family waiting for a book that makes you feel good for
a change, a book about *bravery,* but we know from Tom Wolfe
himself that middle America is into *a whole different thing.* Me!
The Third Great Awakening is where America's head is at.
Psychobabbling, Marin County, *The Serial, Self* magazine, personal growth, assertion therapy, and quite certainly wife-
shucking and moving home. And kids getting into *really* weird
things at college, weirder than the hippies ever did, this blank
generation who've already signed on for I.B.M. Little affectless Neo-Conservatives. That's where middle America is at.

   And there is a grimmer view of the Me Decade than Wolfe's:
Christopher Lasch's *The Culture of Narcissism,* 1979, 'American
Life in An Age of Diminishing Expectations', which is *the*
popular malaise book now, especially since Jimmy Carter, it is
said, took it up on the mountain with him while he decided
what to say to America about the Energy Crisis. Carter was
impressed, which is like hearing that Jack Kennedy was
inspired by . . . Vance Packard. This psycho/sociopan-
technicon reports psychiatrists all over America suddenly
sighting the Narcissistic Personality (Of Our Time). The New
Man. Like the super-rats and the virus proof against an-
tibiotics, these patients 'do not fit current diagnostic
categories'. The scientists are baffled ('So you've seen it
too?'). But certainly the wrong stuff.

   One would have thought to judge by U.S. bookshops, that
the Wrong Stuff was everywhere. I mean, is there really a
market for a book about the Right Stuff when Disney apparently has problems with the under-tens now? Even the tinies think
there isn't enough of the Wrong Stuff in the product.

   And is Tom Wolfe the man to write it in any case, the man
who gave us the most shameful pleasure possible by talking
about the central concerns of the sharp young everywhere in
the mid-sixties, namely, precisely how people looked and carried on and jockeyed for the *statuspheres,* and all described in the
terms you and your friends used; brand-names and song lines
and Culture Mash and T.V. soap references.

   Shameless himself, Wolfe went on as late as 1973 to erect all this into a case for – or rather a monument to – a new literary form called the New Journalism, which, he said, threatened to displace the novel from the pinnacle of literary achievement in favour of an art form concerned with the placing of buttons and the celebration of the most worthless people imaginable.

The case against Wolfe has been building up from the word go – worthless subjects/trivia, a meretricious style, and irresponsible, amoral approach (you couldn't see where he was coming from). It was a *trick*, like using a throat mike. The Wolfe-haters were legion among traditional littérateurs, especially what have been unkindly called knee-jerk liberals. Some simply couldn't control themselves, they frothed at the typewriter, and at parties. After *Radical Chic,* 1970, friends remember that he was always being cut at parties. But the most enraging thing had been his earlier description of the *New Yorkers'*s superannuated star contributors as 'Tiny mummies . . . the walking dead of 43rd Street.' He once worked on the *New Yorker.*

By the early seventies, however, a more effective Wolfe put-down had been devised, 'a small talent to amuse, but so dated, so Sixties, so minor-league, neophiliac'. The suggestion was that Wolfe was discredited with his subjects. Christopher Booker, author of *The Neophiliacs,* said in *Encounter* that he'd O.D.'ed on Wolfe but had woken to realize that some of his

---

'I used to solve writer's blocks by going out and getting clothes made, you could use up a lot of time that way.'   TOM WOLFE

---

comparisons – custom cars and Venetian architecture for instance – were frankly ludicrous, illiterate. Now, free at last from the mad rhythms of Wolfe's prose, he could see it plain; what a fool he'd been!

Is this the man to write about the Right Stuff, to address the last remaining three of four unreconstructed middle-brow American *families* in Kansas or Ohio, without laughing himself sick at the whole thing? Or rather, sniggering, at the reader's mommy-hubby taste in drapes, knitwear, hairstyles,

books, bookshelves and sentiments; such men make fun of ordinary people.

Wolfe's timing is, of course, perfect for the *Time/Newsweek*
cycle of 'Where are the Heroes?' (except that he told Anthony
Haden-Guest in *1970* – in *Harper's Bazaar,* January 1970:
'Right now I'm just going to Houston . . . I have a
little . . . *fantasy* . . . about the astronauts. That will need a
different style.') I am not implying any kind of low P.R. band-
wagoning market sense here, simply that Wolfe's *instincts* are
absolutely right, so right that he's often been The Man Who
Peaks Too Soon. The astronaut book is right in the way *The
Deerhunter* was right, hitting the right collective nerve at the
right time – although, unlike *The Deerhunter,* not a pack of lies.
America needs assurances.

And, of course, Wolfe is *the* man to write it, being an essentially conservative *rational* cultivated man who has nonetheless
all the Right Instincts, *and always has had.* But especially in the
case of the astronauts.

In *The Right Stuff,* Wolfe describes the astronauts' surprise at
finding how men of real achievement and power who have
nonetheless never been stretched, tested in the Right Stuff
sense, i.e. direct single-combat, test-flight bravery – Captains
of Industry and so on – are painfully eager just to get *near* the
astronauts, for the glow of the Right Stuff. This is a theme he
has explored before, directly and indirectly in 'The Commercial', a story about a Negro ball player, in his last collection,
Mauve Gloves & Madmen, Clutter & Vine, 1976, and in the
tremendous Vietnam pilot piece 'The Truest Sport: Jousting
with Sam and Charlie' from the same collection, which seems
to be a trailer for *The Right Stuff.* Well, something of the kind
seems to have happened to Wolfe himself. One way and
another, the astronauts appear to have *got to him* in a way that
his previous subjects haven't.

Their morality, for instance. Notwithstanding their 'massive
Papal egos'. Wolfe 'found virtues in U.S. military officers I
never dreamed were there, idealism, a really pure patriotism.
You don't find it in the business world or the media world now.
You find it in some artists, I suppose.' One knows the response

he is risking, even courting, going around saying that kind of thing. 'Any show of sympathy to military people tends to strike people as chauvinistic.' To say the least . . . and they will say more. He *knows* what they will say. 'But then it's so easy to shock people in our world.' He means the New York world of The Word, and in particular the liberal intelligentsia that dug itself in in the sixties, and against whom the last fourteen years have been a continuous skirmish. Wolfe is *exactly* the man for the job, and for the job he adopts a different tone, a far more plain-speaking, hickory-hollow, even slightly button-down tone that changes less often. In his other writing, the styles and rhythms skid and change pace from one interior monologue (the subject's voice and style) to another (other actors in the piece) to Wolfe's own (the quietest). *The Right Stuff* seems more of a piece, more of a straight read.

We don't know much about Wolfe in Britain. Journalists know about him and readers of the *Telegraph Sunday Magazine* and *Harper's & Queen*, and suppose that everybody else does, but in practice Wolfe is a minority taste satisfied mainly by imports. Until I started checking I hadn't realized quite how minority – the P.R. departments of two hardback houses who'd published previous Wolfe books asking me to spell his name while they looked him up. They wouldn't have asked that of a one-shot novelist like Elizabeth Smart. Anyway, most of the Wolfe market is in London, serviced by Corgi or imported Bantam paperbacks. And his last collection, *Mauve Gloves . . .* wasn't published here in hardback: a fraction of the Farrar, Straus & Giroux edition was brought over. With the exception of the *Electric Kool-Aid Acid Test,* 1968, Wolfe and his books are an import speciality. *Kool-Aid,* the hippie/drugs one about Ken Kesey, sells, year in and year out, as a kind of *primer* to a particular market in England and America. Hard, as I say, for a journalist to grasp, but Wolfe doesn't have the resonance here that he has in New York, and in America as a whole he's hardly a Safeway check-out impulse buy.

English journalists are hyper-aware of Wolfe. First because he was a particularly liberating influence on a whole crop of them in the early/mid sixties, at the time when the colour supplements were getting into their stride and specialist magazines like *New Society* were encouraging a more visually-orientated pop/sociological kind of writing. (I remember being very struck by Reyner Banham in *New Society*). And it goes without saying that Wolfe has affected the rock press for all time. Subject-matter, style – sometimes a malign influence until a writer worked his way through it; Wolfe's style was hard to handle unless you understood the underlying structure, unless you knew all the things Wolfe knew – just the confidence to let go the 'pale beige tone' of received journalism, all came from Wolfe.

That was one thing, but the other reason English journalists know all about Wolfe is because he, alone among journalists, was regularly written up in the sixties as if he was just as interesting, more interesting indeed, than the people he wrote about. They heard about his dandified, period-cut three-piece suits (often white), longish hair in what Haden-Guest calls a prep-school cut (parted on the left), and they heard what everybody thought of him – to use a popular word of the time, his image. And this was well before featured regulars on the *Express* or *Mail* had their names in subheads and small photographs of themselves attached to their work. And ten years before Nigel Dempster was to come right out and say how interesting *he* was.

Wolfe was a celebrity to journalists all right. And he had done more even than set an example in subject-matter and style and celebrification, he was providing the building blocks of a rationale that said journalists – journalists on the low-brow papers and slick magazines and the specialist press – could be in the *fast lane of Modern Culture*, pushing deadbeat novelists off the road. This was the general idea he was to articulate in his introduction to *The New Journalism* anthology in 1973. Wolfe had developed a talent to annoy that delighted many other journalists outside the 'literary' areas. He made the most arrogant possible remarks in the most courteous Southern-gent voice. He was famous without regular appearances on T.V., or, after 1965, having to hack it in any way he didn't really want. *Choosing his own subject matter* while making a good living.

Not surprisingly, Wolfe has a tremendous literary conceit which is presumably why he identifies with the fighter jocks' Papal egos . . . and their dream of appearing on the balcony before the waiting millions, wordlessly, for a few moments . . .

'A certain amount of attitude change was inevitable in the Sixties. If you met a totally new kind of people they would alter the way you looked at things. I remember when I was writing The Electric Kool-Aid Acid Test, and after one of those all-night-long sessions with Ken Kesey – like being with a primary religious group – I would drive out and have that feeling that I knew something that all these poor creatures, all these poor slaves on the freeway, didn't know. This feeling would last until I had my first human encounter, like buying a newspaper.'   TOM WOLFE

'My overriding interest,' as he says, 'is a vain one; to hear the reader applaud. All other interests are separate . . . and this is true in the case of all good writers.' And he is not having it when I bring up Norman Rockwell in reference to the astronauts, since he thinks I'm comparing his work to Rockwell's – a commercial artist who painted clichés to order from photographs. I hadn't meant a comparison, just that some cosy feelings of Forgotten America and down-home virtues are going to be aroused by the astronauts rediscovered.

No, Wolfe's chosen reference group is the great novelists, especially the nineteenth-century French ones; Balzac and Zola in particular. And the criticism of his early subjects he parallels with contemporary criticism of Fielding as obsessively interested in Low people like ostlers and provincial doctors.

Tom Wolfe's critics take risks. Not to say he bears grudges, but his three house-raids on the New York intelligentsia – the *New Yorker* piece, *Radical Chic* and *The Painted Word*, 1975, a short book on recent fashion in art criticism, have left a hefty body-count. Wolfe has a wipe-out kit, a 'Roach Motel' ('Roaches check in, they don't check out') for pointy heads. They talk to him and are lured, disarmed by the most utterly reasonable soft-spoken Southern gent imaginable. Then they read what he thought. This eighteenth-century rational gent attacks Nonsenses, Ideologies, and Emperors' New Clothes of all kinds. This is what Lewis Lapham, editor of the American *Harper's* magazine, who publishes a monthly cartoon by Wolfe and any writing he can get, so likes about Wolfe. 'He has a view of U.S. society not shrouded by cant, he sees it in terms of money, sex and class, he's free from ideological arguments. It's a real problem now getting good writing that hasn't gone through a . . . screen of abstract opinion. Wolfe's instincts are conservative – in the best sense.'

Wolfe wrote afterwards, he said he liked it but if it was going in a book, there were some . . . little points he'd like to put right. First, he hadn't lived with Sheila for twelve years, he'd *known* her twelve years. (I'd read him quoted elsewhere saying living together was getting kind of Low Rent now.) Second, his father wasn't a *farmer* in that sense . . . he *owned farms*.

I'd asked Wolfe if he didn't think he'd been a big influence on young writers, establishing that kind of – now clichéd – popular culture repertoire for them to work on and those stylistic tricks. He wasn't having that either. He said he'd read a lot of stuff that'd been influenced by him and usually it was pretty good. And he told me how, when he just wanted to get the juices going, he'd sit down and have a quick read of *Henry Miller*.

Wolfe knows his own worth, he knows he's important and that his analysis of post-war America, far from being super-ficial, was about the most fundamental thing of all – what money was doing to people. If you re-read his old stuff, par-ticularly the series of pieces he did in England in the mid-sixties, like the 'Noonday Underground' piece about the first Mods, you can see that he got it right about the social and stylistic dynamic of Mod-dom, and almost all the detail is cor-rect too. I've only ever picked up on one or two mistakes – the origins of Edward Heath's accent for instance – which means that beneath all that, there must be a pretty careful process of researching and cross-checking, whatever Booker says.

Sontag Times

Harpers & Queen, March 1979

*'Look at all this stuff I've got in my head: rockets and Venetian churches,
David Bowie and Diderot, nuoc mam and Big Macs, sunglasses and
orgasms.'*   I, ETCETERA

Susan Sontag is going up alone in the Warhol Factory lift, a
real good lift with a heavy trellis gate. At the top she opens
the gate and tells the cowlicked youth 'We've come to see Andy'. 'Oh,' says the boy in that flat New York androgyne voice,
'Andy isn't here.' Discomfiture, end of film. It was the
B.B.C.'s arts programme, *Monitor*, around 1964, commanded
by Dr Jonathan Miller, and Susan Sontag – a great enthusiasm
of Miller's – was showing the British all about Andy with the
aid of this new technique called 'cinema verité'. It was very
funny, especially since I didn't actually know what it was
about. Here's this big intellectual-type woman, who takes
herself very seriously (I'd never heard of her), saying we're
going to visit Andy, we'll just drop in, and this Andy Warhol
person – I don't know who he is either, except I've read that
he's a Pop Artist which I take to mean he's something like a
Pop Star – isn't there. A man who can be out for the T.V.
cameras, I feel, has a lot of style. I interpret it as a *style*, like the
growing convention of Pop Star Interviews where the kids fool
around, send up the interviewer – who isn't cool – and talk
direct to the other kids in the audience. One learned later that
Warhol simply was out – you can read too much into
things – and that those pop stars' interviews were carefully
choreographed.

My impression of Susan Sontag then was of the intellectual

type sent up. It was her manner that put me off; I liked her looks. She was about thirty.

Susan Sontag is America's best-known culture woman. The book jackets describe her as 'critic, novelist, film-maker'. She has worked on the New York culture-magazine circuit, turning in essays on all the newest things, from the very early sixties. Before that she was an academic prodigy: Berkeley, Chicago, teaching at the University of Connecticut, Harvard, Oxford. Her essays and reviews were irritating, trendy, exciting and original. She wrote on literature, on criticism, on the theatre, on modern sensibility and, above all, on avant-garde Euro-movies. She followed pop artists and English rockers. She was the very model of a new intelligentsia – except there was no one really like her. Tall, handsome, Europhile, liberated before the term was coined, she proselytized boldly for the New, for pornography as Art, for a recognition that Form and Content are one, for things French, for a new sensibility that bypasses the simplistic 'Two Culture' argument, and more equivocally for Camp, which, she says, both fascinates and repels her.

The 'Notes on Camp' essay in *Partisan Review* made her into a famous person; she had hit on what's really going on, and what was going on wasn't all these French ponces, all that hand-held camera stuff, but a New Way of Looking at Things. She was made into a cultural commodity with dazzling speed; there was even a *Time Magazine* piece on Camp. She didn't like it, or is quoted later as saying so; she turned down the plum job of writing the movie reviews for *Esquire*. She wished to write fiction, and, later, to make movies. And she writes fiction, *The Benefactor* (Eyre & Spottiswoode 1964), and *Death Kit* (Secker & Warburg 1968), and she makes movies, three of them – two in Sweden and one in Israel. I've read the script of one and it sounds pretty boring, and the novels are hard going.

In the early seventies her reputation declined, along with that of the generation of artists she'd espoused. The real new sensibility was coming of age.

Then, in 1977, she produced a quite wonderful book, *On Photography* – again a collection of essays, but on one theme, the implications of the universal spread of photographed images. It isn't about photography – it's about everything: aesthetics, morality, all her preoccupations, I doubt that she's done photography justice but she's put up an excellent case for the Life of the Mind. There are two or three good things on every page. Photography is the new Surreal for instance. 'Surrealism,' she says, 'lies at the very heart of the photographic enterprise.' Photography of horrors reduces our capacity to react, raises the ante of outrage; photography has promoted the value of appearances. She argues finally for an ecology of images.

Unlike her earlier work I understand almost all of it, it's more accessible. It also sells (more than 70,000 in hardback), it makes the lists. She's on T.V.; profiled in *People*; American *Vogue* describes her as 'the most interesting American woman of her generation.' And the coincidence of critical with 'popular' success is entirely justified; it is her most readable book and her best one.

Then in 1978 she produces *Illness as Metaphor*, just published over here. Literary title, but some substance: it is about ways of perceiving illness, and two illnesses in particular – T.B. and cancer. In 1975, as *People* tells you, but *Vogue* doesn't, she'd got cancer, and had a mastectomy and various other operations. She is still having chemotherapy. The burden of *Illness as Metaphor* is that literary and 'psychological' ways of perceiving T.B. and cancer perpetuate a cruel mythology, in particular she condemns the condescension that sees the 'cancer personality' as one of life's losers. These two books resolve, almost, the problem I have with her writing. Formerly, I've found many of her reviews inaccessible – too many references, too much I've never heard of; her tone solemn, slightly wooden. She hasn't a light touch with anything. It's a matter of style. The *titles* of her books – *Styles of Radical Will* (Secker & Warburg 1969), *Duet for Cannibals* (Allen Lane 1974), *I, Etcetera* (published in America by Farrar, Straus & Giroux, and in Britain by Gollancz, 1979) – irritate me at a level I'd be hard put to explain. Then there's her almost rabid romanticism about the intellectual life. The covers of her books – even the layouts – have this irritating quality. She is aware of it too;

much of her writing is really about resolving the contradictions between educated ways of seeing and experiencing reality. She often says that being an intellectual isn't cerebral – that intellectual life is about feelings. She's right, but she doesn't always sound sure. Off her books comes a smell of – Grove Press, American Europhile female graduate scholar. This is all unfair, but, as she's said herself, sensibility/taste is everything. I admire terrifically but my taste rebels.

I call to fix the interview. She's got that very direct, low voice. No, I can't bring a photographer, she won't be photographed.

The photographer, crestfallen, and I take bets on how the interview will go. I have this feeling that it will be hard going, that she'll accuse me of being crass, journalistic, of asking idiotic questions.

Precisely. Within the first twenty minutes we are off at cross-purposes. She has said, by turns, all these things, but added 'English' and 'offensive'. Only English journalists ask about the 'Monitor' appearance, she says, presumably because that's all they know about her. And why do I associate her books with the whitewashed shelves of female graduate scholars, why female? It's an offensive use of language.

She is very handsome, in a certain style. All in black, very tall, strong face, olive skin, amazing black hair that's incredibly thick, like a different breed of animal. She's well-dressed too, Rive Gauche precision cut, with black jodhpur boots. A touch of the Francoise Hardys. The apartment, too, is Europhile. It's a duplex, the top two floors of a lower East Side brownstone. It's big, open architectural, in that mid-sixties high-class monastery style, wood floors, oak trestle table, austere dining chairs, the Charles Eames leather chair and a tweed sofa. No Camp. No jokes. No Park Avenue. Just yards of bookshelves. Very Euro-intelligentsia. It is the best of its kind.

After our bad start things improve, she realizes I'm talking about a different T.V. appearance (she seems sensitive about the one in which she and Jonathan Miller talked Culture and got sent up). She's interested in England, but not very, I suspect.

It's bumpy until we talk about *The Texas Chainsaw Massacre*. Then we know, we absolutely know, that we're talking about the same things. It's struck us both that this brilliantly made, hideous film enthused about by people like Paul Morrissey, praised by the *Time Out* crowd, a key motif of arty punk, has really breached some pyschic barrier. To treat stuff like this from an 'Art' standpoint is quite insane. Think instead of a generation of American kids watching schlock horror at drive-ins. Think of the teenage girl who shot two people because she was bored. This, it turns out, is Susan Sontag's preoccupation now; the relationship between the aesthetic and the ethical. She has been taking notes on it for years, the strength and weaknesses of 'the aesthetic way of looking at the world'.

From then on we compare notes, we get on, I forgive her the put-downs, her taste for the lugubrious Patti Smith. She lets me go round the following Sunday to waste her time, and this is generous, since she's sick and has things to do.

I show her my schedule of nasty cultural symptoms, from *Chainsaw Massacre* to Angel Dust – the drug that produces cheap instant maniacs; she gives me a precious copy of her piece on Leni Riefenstahl. We talk about the aesthetic legitimization of terrible things. I hope she writes her piece, it should be an important one, making, as always, new connections. She is solemn, irritating; she's one of the best arguments for the moral usefulness of intellectuals. She's worth reading.

Two-Lane Brownstone

Harpers & Queen, January 1976

This is the story of a gently raised Sussex girl who married a Yank and left her beloved England to become a housewife in Murray Hill, New York. Nicola Waymouth, for this was her name, having been married to a Mr Nigel Waymouth before, met Mr Kenneth J. Lane, a wry elegant bachelor who was rather big in the jewellery business, at – depending on whether you believe Mr or Mrs Lane – either Maxine de la Falaise McKendry's or John Richardson's place in New York about three years ago. They began to see one another more and more and, this time according to Mr Lane, decided that as they didn't get along they had better get married.

They were married on 17 February at Caxton Hall where, as Mr Lane notes, the fake flowers were replaced with real ones in their honour. After the ceremony, Lady Diana Cooper got up and said, 'The woman should keep the marriage licence.' However, Mr Lane demanded it as soon as they left the office. After that they went on to Mark's to be greeted by old friends like Manolo Blahnik and Paloma Picasso, and a good time was had by all. The flowers were extremely well arranged and three vicars in different churches across the land apparently prayed for them. Then they repaired to another small party with three hundred or so young friends. To round the day off they went on to Mortons. They spent the wedding night at Blake's Hotel.

Perhaps the most telling remark of the whole exciting day was made by Lord Goodman, Nicola's guardian, to Mr Lane when giving away his ward. 'You have a treasure in my ward,' he said. 'I hope you realize that and I hope you have the cost of the upkeep.'

Mr and Mrs Lane are now settled comfortably in a cosy

brownstone, hard by Lexington Avenue. The furnishing was mainly done by Mr Lane, who has a sharp eye for these things. As his wife says, 'He's a perfectionist, even down to the door hinges.' His tastes do not run to understatement or bland simplicity so it is just as well that 'Our tastes are practically the same in everything.'

The main rooms are rather dark and crammed full of exotica and oddities and rich textures. 'If you're a pack rat you're a pack rat,' says Mr Lane. Tables are covered in collections of elegantly arranged bibelots. Two blackamoor busts rest on either side of the chimneypiece and an oil of an African prince stretches between them. It's quite something. Even the walls have been finished so as to look like antiqued patent leather.

The house, they admit, like many other aspects of their sophisticated marriage, is much more New York than London. 'Would this house look right in London?' says Mrs Lane.

It has turned out to be a very lucky conjunction on the domestic front, since Mr Lane had a lot of objects that Mrs Lane wanted, and vice versa. They have only slight points of disagreement.

Mrs Lane is totally unsympathetic to contemporary art whereas Mr Lane does not mind it. Mrs Lane likes to move the skulls round the house rather than keep them in the drawing-room all the time. Mrs Lane will make her mark on the house, however, since she is currently decorating a new library and boudoir they are having built. For the boudoir she has the contrasting simplicity of Leningrad colours in mind. Mr Lane thinks it will turn out to be as simple as Leningrad.

Despite the comforts of home, this is not a homebound couple who sit up at nights with television and needlepoint. They go out almost every night. Since there is more activity on more different social fronts in one New York evening than in a week in London, and since the Lanes are just about the hottest couple in New York at the moment, this is not altogether surprising. If one were to credit Mr Bob Colacello, that stalwart recorder of the New York scene, in his 'Out' column in *Interview* magazine, not only do they go out every night but to several different places a night. New Yorkers like them for it, whereas in London people tended to be rather . . . snide about Nicola for being so glamorous and out-at-night. She is caustic about this sort of English reaction. 'The English don't try. Only one person in twenty tries – they could have more style, but they are frightened of showing front. The Americans do try, and all credit to them for it. That's why this city is the heartbeat of the Western world.'

It is a sophisticated marriage between sophisticated people. Mrs Lane is very young, in her early twenties, and Mr Lane is in his early forties. Mrs Lane has been married before. Mr Lane has not. However, Mrs Lane is grown-up before her time. Her father died rather early on so this may have speeded things up. They seem very well suited and to take great pleasure in one another. Mr Lane is obviously as pleased as Punch with his bride. He has reason; the first time I saw her I thought she was attractive, by the third time I realized she was a ravishing and unusual beauty whose gingery red hair set against very white skin are startling and quite aggressively feminine. She has a handspan waist, a ridiculously long neck and very good legs. Since extreme style tends to be rather asexual, it is nice to note that she is also sexy. She must be irritating to smart New York women, who tend to be rather . . . rugged. 'If you wear that dress,' says Mr Lane to his child bride, 'you'll make every woman in the room look twenty years older.' He prefers her to wear make-up, otherwise he fears people will think he's been cradle-snatching.

Since their marriage they have fused together to a remarkable degree so as to become rather more than the sum of the parts. New Yorkers, who tend to be sentimental – after a fashion – like this romantic story. All the new and disturbing movements – liberation for men and women – mean that the number of new and attractive married couples after the conventional pattern has shrunk rather drastically. In London Nicola used to table-hop between groups like the Country Weekend set, Earnest Conversationalists on Serious Matters (she collects late nineteenth- and early twentieth-century books, mainly for their bindings – Mr Lane mutters that she can't read), the Bianca Jagger set and her own Sussex folk.

Her own style, however, is fairly classical in most things. In clothes she prefers Saint Laurent – going for the more severe lines that suit her. She likes Kenzo: 'His clothes allow women to look like little girls – or little boys. They allow one to behave badly' – but she does not appear to wear them.

'Because Nicky is so pretty,' says Mr Lane, glowing, 'she has to wear very simple clothes. Somebody like Diana Vreeland, who has a face like a cigar-store Indian, wears the most marvellous clothes imaginable – absolute oriental splendour, and she never looks wrong.' Both Lanes come alive at the sound of Mrs Vreeland's name. Mrs Vreeland, who is head of the Department of Fashion at the Metropolitan Museum of Art, and formerly editor of American *Vogue*, is in their view the very soul of New York, the wittiest and the youngest New York girl of all.

They pose for us. This is something they are good at, intensely professional, accommodating, all the while saying a number of mysterious things to one another which I don't understand. They put their faces together. 'Oh, but we never touch,' says Mrs Lane. 'We will, for the photograph,' says Mr Lane.

They broke up the following year. I met Nicky Lane, wide-eyed and legless in Maunkberries and she muttered something about how I was perfectly right about the *not touching*. They were a *very* odd couple, and I wrote it very much as a tongue-in-cheek Insider's piece, as a kind of early go at the new Gossip World.

They were the mid-seventies new Glamourous Couple – *Interview/Ritz* society – and the interesting thing is to trace the linkages. Nicky Lane had originally had a hefty clip of money from her father, Harold Samuel, who died rather mysteriously when she was small. Her elder brother Nigel had been very big on the rich hippie scene in the late sixties/early seventies. I remember when we went up to see Michael X and his Black House commune for black kids in 1970, it turned out Nigel

Samuel had been bank-rolling them. Later he was *busted for drugs* in Eaton Square. It was very typical of the way style shifted from late sixties to mid-seventies that his sister was into this very coated-paper, new glamour, New York style.

Bowie Night

A party in Thea Porter's little shop in Greek Street, which is definitely one of those personal front room types of shop. The combination is Middle East, Haute Bo, Rich Hippie, which is still around in a big way though it's going disco. Very London/ Paris/New York. The lavatory's done up in one of the Osborne and Little foil-based papers. Very Fifth Avenue sixties psychedelic. The Andrew Logan mirror glass palm tree at the door must be about the latest update on this line of thinking.

I talk to this Oxbridge Young Socialist type who knows *everyone*, he's on about the S.W.P., and it sounds as if he knows all sorts in it, known Paul Foot for yonks, that kind of thing. He told me he's *on the left* of the Labour Party, whatever this means, and he's saying all sorts of sardonic insider things and smart analogies. He thinks Wedgie is an unoriginal thinker. I can't take very much of this and keep-it-light, besides which I've seen something interesting in the corner.

In the corner is the *biggest Bowie casualty I've ever seen,* and I've seen a few: at the gigs and that big dancer clone and my young friend, who's a really bad case. But this is the most, man. She's done up completely as late 72 Bowie i.e. the ginger Joe Brown crop, long at the sides and the back, a wasp-striped leotard, all in one job, in ochre and black and the little ballet shoes and the one chandelier earring which is actually a silver leaf hanging from a red star. But the main thing is, *she's got the full tilt mime face on*, red circles on the cheeks, red lips and red round the eyes on a white base – the full clown job. Her teeth, like Davids, are a bit . . . weaselish.

When we talk, it turns out she's very Artistic. She's done half a course at Ealing Tech. and then Vidal Sassoon. She's

241

been doing a piece on the Contemporary Dance Theatre in Paris for *De-Luxe* magazine which is just starting up then, as part of the post-*Ritz* boom. It's been nothing but a round of parties in Paris, she says, and that's where she met Thea.

David, whom she hasn't met, she thinks is a very creative person but she isn't sexually interested in him, *not without his make-up anyway*. When she thinks of him, she always thinks of the clown face. She thinks of him as a *mime*, there's a lot of Kabuki in him – do I know the Kabuki style? Her mime act, which she is working up, she says, is more in the style of Teriyana. Terry who? He's apparently the greatest living Japanese mime. David's been heavily influenced by the Kabuki. People don't seem to realize what a big influence Japan has been on David.

What does she do now? Art. 'Well, I done a sculpture here, I done a picture there.' It's half Cockney – she's not laying it on – and half Art School hippie. This must be what the Beckenham Arts Lab was like. She's not really a sculptor or a painter, she must be more an Artist. I suggest a *multi-media person*. She reckons this sounds about right. She knows a lot of the punk people but it's too *aggressive* for her and she's scared for her little boy, Milo, who's named after Miles Davis. He's five · and he's doing fantastic drawings already. There are some things about punk, she says, that are very creative but some of the people are horrible.

We go on round the corner to Louise's, the dyke club in Poland Street. Louise was at the party. She's a very chic French madame with grey waves and a black dress. Louise's is a nice cosy little club, a little red box, where the floating population of freaks who aren't gay but would get beaten up for looking like that, the oddities, the contingent without a name, are really starting to collect in a big way round 1975/6. The evolved Bowie freaks, and the original punks, feel at home in Louise's – and down the Sombrero and Rods and all the older type cosy, glitzy gay clubs. And this includes Malcolm and Vivienne.

Over the last year, the more *definable* punks have been going down Louise's which, of course, makes for tensions. The newer punks aren't so cosy and though Louise's prides itself on keeping an open door to the oddities, there are problems.

Down Louise's that night are Malcolm McLaren – with Sid and Nancy – and Steve Strange, who had a different name then and is done up just like a miniature Vivienne Westwood with black candy floss spikes and a camouflage bondage suit, plus the mixture of dykes and punks.

We have a little dance. Frankie's a very *expressive* dancer, lots of hand signals. Centre floor, Steve Strange is stretching the bondage strides with the new steps. Then we talk to the D.J. She's a jolly girl called Caroline with a toughie crop and an almost punk look. She's a friend of my new friend, Frankie. *Frankie Stein*. She's very worked up about the way punk is taking over the club and spoiling it. There's an atmosphere. She says people stop her in the street because of the way she's dressed – drainpipes, high heels, dyed crop – and ask her if she's a punk. She has two answers to this – 'no, I'm a lesbian' or 'no, I'm Jewish'. She says Malcolm's an evil influence. He's fascistic and there's something very fascist about the punk thing. I say, 'Oh, come off it . . . anyway, Malcolm's Jewish himself.' But she sticks to her line. When we sit down again, I'm sitting next to Malcolm who's edging away, talking in a very low urgent way – he's giving Sid a lecture . . . *you gotta do this and that for the sake of the group, and stop pissing around and so on*, and Sid's moaning like a little kid, *do I have to*. Malcolm's saying, yes, you've got to and Nancy's immobile on the other side saying nothing. What is it that Sid has to do? Afterwards, Frankie whispers that she's scared of Sid and I say, well, yes, he doesn't seem a very nice type of person. But he does seem totally cowed with Malcolm.

We go back to her little squat in Kensington Gardens Square, a stucco square behind Whiteleys. Up in the top room which is pretty tidy and comfortable, I meet her pals, which is to say a cross cut of sci-fi, alternative rock 'n' roll, art hippie life, right across from 1966/7. They're camping out at the top of this big empty Performance type house. There's John, a Scots hippie junkie. He doesn't look wasted, he looks in very good form. Then there's someone a bit intermediate, a long-haired, *Time Out* 1972 type, and Toby, an art student with silvered hair in the Bowie Wedge. Toby, it turns out, has read all my stuff and knows it better than I do. He wants to talk about Art and Punk. We see the morning in, listening to Diamond Dogs. Through the window you can see the twinkling sci-fi red light on the post office tower. We talk about apocalyptic nonsense and Bowie and the end of everything. The junkie shoots up (why can't he go in the other room), Toby tells me he might get into clothes designing and Frankie tells me about the mime act she's working up.

Louise's closed soon after. Just couldn't handle the punk invasion. Steve Strange went off to do the Moors Murderers. Caroline went to D.J. at Billy's, another little gay boite on Meard Street, off Wardour Street. Steve Strange was on the door, and a lot of the freaks went – not the pinheads; by then, things had divided back into the original people who were *into posing* and the pinheads. Most of these Billy's people were into Bowie. Caroline and Steve wanted to do something about Bowie, to show that he was special. In November 1978, a Tuesday, they got up a Bowie night. Frankie did her act, which was taking on some *secondary* Bowie characters a bit further, *developing them in mime*. Out of that, of course, came Neon Night at the Blitz, the ascent of Steve Strange, Studio 21 and the whole new old world.

A Day On The River

We're back at the pier early. The police want us off. They want everyone off the boat. I don't mind either way; I've had a nice day and it's the man's boat after all. But I stay on because I want to see fair play – see what happens. Branson's arguing with the top cop, he's in his Merry Prankster element, throwing the ginger locks around and grinning hugely. But there *are* people getting off here and there. Branson is mainly on about the fact that they've booked the boat *for the day* and the police are saying, well, the owner wants you off. There are Black Marias all round the Embankment and on the bridge and a tidy little crowd waiting – all to celebrate Virgin Records promotional Sex Pistols Jubilee up-river boat trip.

After some more in this vein and some megaphone work the police come on. They're going straight for whatever look like the trouble types. I stay on until the little whirling scrums around you mean you just have to move. This is no particular bother because they're not going at everyone – it's hardly the S.P.G., various people around are having their own little fights. I slip off with Jon Savage from *Sounds*, Stephen Lavers the Bionic Boy, and Zecca, who's the pianist for one of the more dreadful 'punk' bands in the world, ex-Warholites, Cherry Vanilla and her lot.

People say afterwards that the police have had it in for Malcolm ever since the business of the Lonesome Cowboys – he'd been had up for selling those cowboy T-shirts with the guys with the duelling dicks. But they don't seem to be doing anything very systematic. Back at Waterloo Pier we go up the stone steps and watch from the top. It's chaos, the police

245

are coming back dragging a few by the ears with them, including Vivienne Westwood who's gone dead-dog, still shouting. They're hauling her up the steps. I'm not really worried for her because it doesn't look as if she's getting hurt, and she dearly loves an argy-bargy (like with Judy Nylon who actually applauded at Ferry's Albert Hall concert. Anti-Ferry had been a *cause*.) So this little tableau of wildcat Vivienne Westwood and the coppers is coming up the steps towards us, when Zecca, who is basically a short-haired hippie and a gent, starts saying how they're being brutal with her and so on and we're saying 'Oh, come on, Zecca'. We can't stop him, he's off to her rescue. 'For Christ's sake, that's a woman you've got there.' So they take him in too (obstruction). Then, of course, we *have* to stay around because we're going to have to bail him out or do the necessary – he could be deported otherwise.

On the Embankment I feel very blank – all around there are kid's shouting 'They've got Malcolm' and 'They're doing Malcolm over in a corner' and so on, having a little gossip about it and having the time of their lives. What I feel mainly is that I'd heard this before – at Archway with the black kids outside the police station, and at the Carnival, and compared with that this is all play power gone sour. Savage drives up to the station where there is absolutely nothing to be done, we're far too early, they've barely got them in. They've got to do their stuff first.

On the steps outside is Roadent, this suitably rat-featured creature, the 1977 Face, who's a famous part of the Clash organization. He has a name for various bits of self-laceration – and unlikely parentage they say. And we do what one does – have another little outraged gossip about it all and go for a drink. By now we're four, which is Savage, Lavers and somone I've seen around before and certainly heard a lot about – that Tony Parsons from N.M.E. We've never exactly met, and we hardly exchange two words this time either. He's O.K. but I reckon he glowers too much.

The pub is real madness, a bigger jolt than anything we've seen today which included, one has to admit, one or two little fights on the boat – but absolutely nothing compared to what you see at gigs – and all the Fascist police shock horror and so on. The pub is the most absolute 1984/1948 Jubilee time warp possible, because in there they're all doing their high summer, 1977 colour supplement, street-party number. They've got an old girl in a boater at the mike, singing all the old songs to the old crowd in the old cracked voice. Where they get them from in trendy, up-market Covent Garden I can't think, all swaying about like a kind of cheerful cosy Jack Warner Cockney crowd scene who'd kill on sight. I know Savage, who is well into these paranoid montages – London's Outrage, tower blocks and fifties ads – will pick up on the 1984 number. I can *see* his copy for next week's *Sounds*.

We're not welcome; Parsons is looking like what the Average *Mirror* Reader would see as proto-typical punk, i.e. he has the God Save The Queen T-shirt on and a black leather jacket, and the others look fairly *defined*. (I look fairly *general* – white Lee drainies, white socks, brogues, white Arrow button-down.) We were served, there's no excuse not to, but since we're not joining in it's pretty much like draft dodging, and a certain amount of nudging's going on.

At our table the talk seems to centre on social control and repression. I can't go along with this. We break off in a desultory way. I take Savage to the Zanzibar and we have a drink while we wait to see what's to be done about Zecca. Zecca had been very talkative on the boat, very interesting about his background; hippie to punk. He was telling us about the Anvil in New York where the really grotesque stuff went on. He'd been saying at that point he started asking himself what he was doing – 'Is this decadence? . . . this *is* decadence . . .' *Idiot*, we can't leave him there.

In the Zanzibar, as ever, the L.A. sun shines at cocktail hour in the other time warp, the graphic design Café Society 10CC world. Nick, who runs it, had already told me how they had to have a *policy* about punks after a couple had sliced themselves in the lavatories and upset the patrons – that's really it, so far as he's concerned. I find this incontrovertible. So it's a Brandy Alexander and a Pina Colada.

In his account in next week's *Sounds*, Savage says we go into 'the sickening cutesy-poo decadence of the Zanzibar'. That's the last time I'm taking him there.

Private Eye

Olga's Kurt Geiger heels, her tree-trunk legs, are pounding the gravel along the Mall in a big way. She looks about six foot as she goes smashing forward, that telegraph pole walk. She looks more than usually odd. She's got a new white confirmation three-piece from Elle, with a waistcoat and a flower in her button hole – this is before her accident and her shaven head number. She's made up very brightly, oil colours, so she's really like a ship's figure head, *solid wood*. She's going on at the top of her voice about anyone and everything, mainly the famous people who ought to be there with us. She stops to talk to each policeman about how she should get into the stands at Horse Guards Parade. The crowds are getting really thick and there's a lot of bobbing and weaving to get in the ticket holder's queue for the seats – which aren't proper seats, they're stands, scaffolding built up in tiers with planks on them. In the queue, everyone's looking at her as usual because of the way she carries on in her odd accent, half rogue deb and half refugee gutteral, with the deep dropped 'r's. Our seats are really good ones towards the front. There's a big wait and the sun's right in my eyes. Olga's brought her couture binoculars.

I've never seen the Trooping, except for the two-minute clips on the second half of the *News at Ten* and I'm expecting to be bored rigid like in the theatre – I've come for the party after.

And this is where I couldn't have been more wrong, because once they get into it, the crimson ranks divvying up better than Busby Berkley, and the Queen coming along and *taking the salute from her men*, in that little hat, I'm into a set of unstoppable *involuntary reflexes*. I'm hoping nobody's noticed. I've got a lump in the throat, and this is *exactly* a lump in the throat, slightly panicky – I'm trying to swallow and I can't. The other

thing is that I'm crying, I simply can't stop it. All this un-
toward flood of motor failure is bad enough *but at the Trooping of
the Colour*; to have these atavistic feelings at the Trooping of the
Colour is enough to put you right off your stroke. What next,
Red Square, St Peters . . . .

The fact is that the Trooping is one of the most beautiful
pieces of formal design you could see. They don't miss a stroke.
Just like the jokey pictures in the populars, the guys faint from
time to time – somebody'll fall out of line, and they'll put him
away neatly and everything goes on as sharp as ever. The thin
red lines close ranks. It's better than a dozen Crimean war
films. The Trooping serves up everything I saw in my media
childhood, T.V., movies, the *Mirror* – total recall.

When she actually takes the salute, one has an intuition of
how the country works, so profound as to be . . . totally useless as
an acid trip, i.e. when I get home I haven't a clue what it
meant.

Olga is not similarly taken, she goes on nattering to people to
the side, in front, behind – she'll talk to anyone. Afterwards,
more gravel crunching, we go down and off across Horse
Guards Parade and into Downing Street for the party.

Twelve Downing Street is deeply weird. You don't realize
how big it is – it's just London town-house size outside – and
just how much it's *re-constructed* in this Civil Service Brewer's
Georgian. *The centre of power is repro.* It's got door cases in the
correct moulding shapes but *concrete*, and the same round the
fireplaces. Bolecton mouldings in concrete. The panelling has
the same look. It's all reconstructed . . . not exactly *fake*, more
Army Issue, Trad Anon., 'period', timeless. Even the leather
sofas in the big back room and the light fittings. It's all big,
good quality bijou.

The party is champagne and some very Civil Service snacks,
cucumber sandwiches. In the big back room which looks onto
the garden the T.V. is re-running the Trooping on video – it's
going on and on all the time we're there. In the next door
garden, Callaghan's out with what looks like, from the robes, a
load of Nigerians . . . oil talks?

Once we're actually there, Olga, of course, wants to call her

friends. She likes an impromptu party. Come and join us at
No. 12 – sometimes she says No. 10. She calls Anthony Schaeffer and asks him and Diane to come, and Mandy Pitt. We go in
the big side office with all the leather desks and so forth, and
more of this weirdo reconstructed panelling and the brass centre
lights with the banks of switches. Olga calls just about everyone
she can think of to say come on down to Freddy Warren's
Downing Street Trooping beano.

Anyway, Shaeffer says he's coming. We go back in the big
room for more of what seems to be the Buckingham Palace
Garden Party set, i.e. worthies, plus a few sleeker types moving round. I meet someone I think I know, and Olga certainly
does. As it happens I don't, it's simply that he's an ex-
newscaster from the first generation and I must have seen him
every night as a kid. He's called Huw Thomas. He now has a
consultancy that teaches one how to behave on T.V. – how to
come across well. It's for politicians and industrialists. I consider his quickie course very seriously.

I start looking out for Olga who will by now, I imagine, be
half-cut and need watching. She does; Anthony Schaeffer's
turned up alone and he and Olga are in red hot argument. As
far as I can make it out, it's about something that did or didn't
happen in one of his brother's plays. Although it should be on
the level of keep-it-light, Shaeffer looks really quite irritable.
Olga's carried away. I tell her, 'Come off it Olga, he should
know, it's his brother.' She's having none of it, she wants a
wager. Shaeffer says *'half a million'*. She may be half-cut but
she's not that daft. Anyway, they settle at a hundred thousand.
I'm saying this is loopy, but by this time I've had much more
than usual, I'm fairly silly too. I write it all down and witness
whatever it is, and I'm thinking, how long is it before she starts
double tracking on this.

I've also got half an eye on Sir Freddie Warren and his
secretary because they're *Mrs Wilson's Diary in miniature*. Freddie Warren anyway is somewhere between Wilson and George
Brown to look at *and* listen to. His secretary's a neat little person who looks like the Stork cake mix queen of Norwood 1955
and they're talking about helicopter outings and so on. 'That

was nice, Freddie.' Little exchanges like that. It all sounds like the Slagheap Conversions press outing. *Private Eye was right.* Because I'm quite far gone at this point, it strikes me that this *is* how the country works, i.e. there's no one *there* inside Downing Street at all except for this type of carry on. *Orton* was right, the Trooping, the repro doorcases, the cheese puffs. I don't mind in the least, not now anyway.

Freddie Warren's very engaging. Afterwards, about five, when most of the people have packed off, Shaeffer saying a bit sourly he'll be back to Olga about her wager, Sir Freddie Warren says why don't we join him for another little drink with a friend – it's like one of those teenage days when you go on this chain 'Why don't we go and annoy . . . ' Mrs Thing, the Cake Mix Queen – she may be Miss Thing for all I know – drives us over to a flat in one of those Edwardian blocks at the back of St James's Park. I've been in this block before – big companies keep guest flats and the diplomatic put up people round here too. But that isn't the set-up *at all*. It's a nice tidy lady who could be someone's granny in carpet slippers – I think she's some kind of retired Civil Servant of the middling senior kind. The whole thing's as neat as pie with cream gloss paint and the glass fronted bookcases with the Literary Guild and History Guild, and the Ercol dining set. She's doing her best to talk to Olga who is in full flow, talking to no one in particular about Jimmy and Vere and Jocelyn and Nigel, sprawling across her sofa, taking a whisky with her *'Why, thank you'* Baby Jane Royal Family smile. Our hostess is looking at Freddie Warren; a big WHO IS THIS WOMAN? look, this woman who's breaking up my little island of Croydon in Westminster, lying around like this, talking away like this. I'm getting clear again by now. I keep to a Cinzano Bianco. Olga's straight on to the Bells.

We stay with poor Miss Assistant Principal till about seven. I reckon she'll need a fortnight's Wincarnis to put her straight, and I'm quite glad for her sake when we go. On the way back, as we turn the Ritz corner from St. James's into Piccadilly, Olga's getting back on course. 'You know,' she says, 'you may be right about Equus – d'you think he'll be back about it?'

After Olga went, on New Year's Eve 1979, there was a little piece in the *Standard* Londoner's Diary about Schaeffer as one person who was sorry to see her go because, so he said, she owed him £100,000. These writer types can be like that, can't take a joke.